POSTMORTEM

ESTABLISHING THE CAUSE OF DEATH

POSTMORTEM

ESTABLISHING THE CAUSE OF DEATH

Dr. Steven A. Koehler, MPH, PhD
and Dr. Cyril H. Wecht, MD, JD

Reader's Digest

A Reader's Digest Book

This edition published by The Reader's Digest Association
by arrangement with Elwin Street Limited

Conceived and produced by
Elwin Street Limited
79 St John Street
London EC1M 4NR
www.elwinstreet.com

A CIP catalogue record for this book is available from the British Library.

ISBN: 978-0-276-44230-8

Printed in China

Designed by Jon Wainwright, Alchemedia
Illustrations by Richard Burgess

Front cover images: Science Photo Library
Back cover images: Science Photo Library (top and bottom),
Allegheny County Coroner's Office (middle)

1 3 5 7 9 10 8 6 4 2

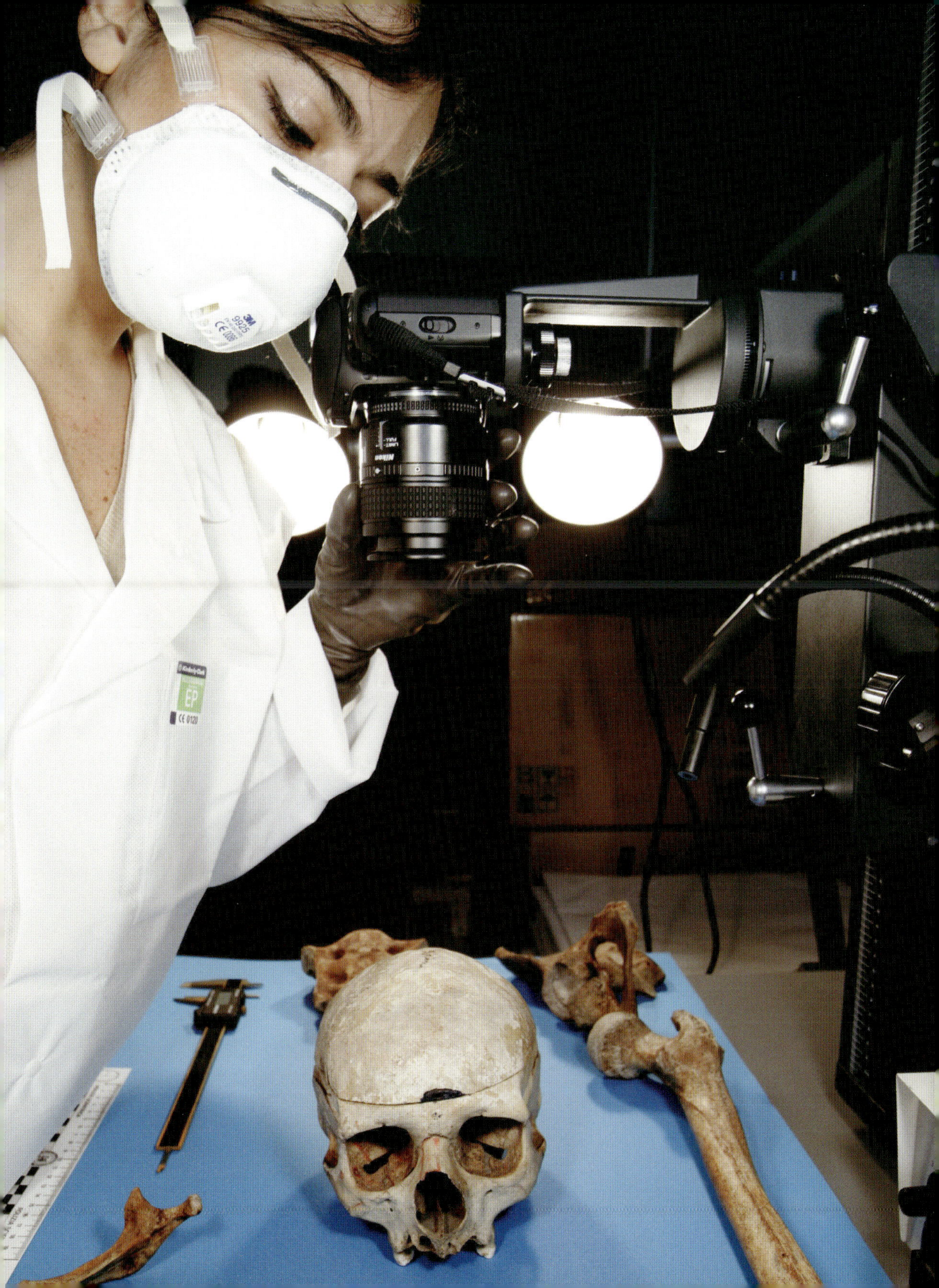

Contents

Introduction

Cyril H. Wecht, MD, JD

Former Coroner, Allegheny County
Professor of Forensic Medicine, University of Pittsburgh

The majority of people die relatively peacefully, either in hospital or at home, having received recent attendance from a doctor. Though these deaths are sad or even tragic for the deceased's next of kin, they are readily explained by naturally occurring medical conditions and bodily processes. However, not every death is so straightforward. Sometimes life ends surrounded by mystery, open to suggestion and inference or even in circumstances that lead to outright suspicion. It is in these cases that forensic specialists will take authority over the body of the deceased for the purposes of a postmortem examination.

The postmortem examination, also known as an autopsy, is a detailed medical and legal examination of a deceased person. Postmortems of one sort or another have been conducted for thousands of years, but it is only in the last century or so that scientific and medical knowledge has been applied to the process.

The coroner is the legal figure who has authority over postmortem examinations. The position of coroner (from the Latin *corona* meaning "crown") originated in medieval England, where it was first set forth in Article 20 of the Articles of the Eyre in September 1194. At that time the coroner was a representative of the king or queen, who conducted inquests over dead bodies, inspection of an individual's wounds, heard appeals for justice, recorded accusations and, where it seemed that a serious crime had been committed, had the power to arrest a suspect. The coroner was also authorized to arrest witnesses for further questioning and to appraise and safeguard any lands or goods that might later be forfeited by reason of guilt of the accused.

The first formal use of physicians in connection with the workings of the coroner's office occurred in Maryland in 1860. Since that time, there has been a gradual movement in the system of death inquests toward greater medical professionalization. One aspect of this is that many jurisdictions now have a medical examiner or chief medical examiner,

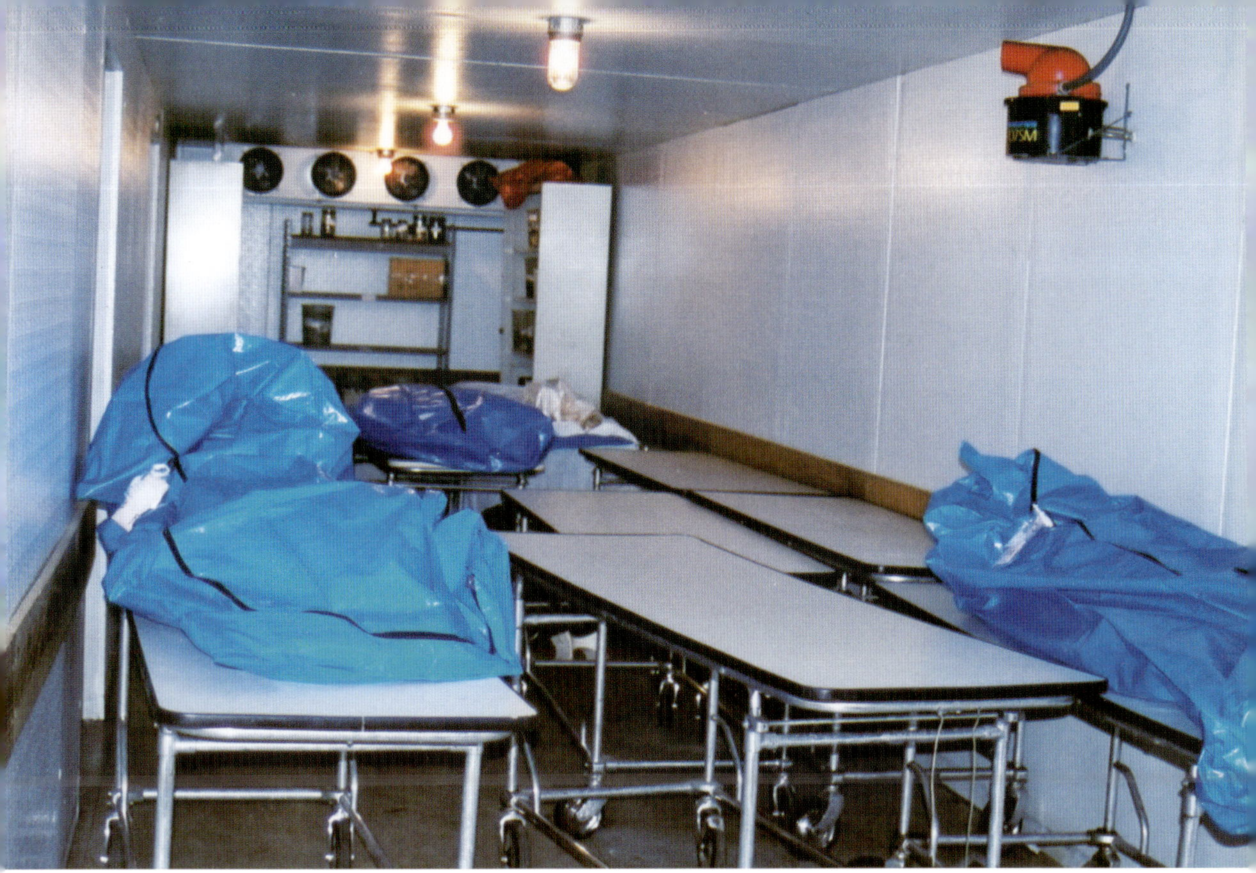

Above "The cooler," a large walk-in fridge at the morgue, where bodies are stored awaiting postmortem examination.

who must be a qualified doctor, holding authority over the investigation of suspicious or violent deaths.

In general, approximately 20 percent of deaths now undergo a postmortem examination. The coroner is responsible to make rulings on the cause and manner of death in those cases that come under his jurisdiction, including violent, sudden, unexpected or suspicious deaths; deaths involving drugs and toxic substances; deaths during medical treatment; deaths during employment; deaths during interaction with law enforcement agencies; and those cases in which a physician is not present during the time of death.

When there is an apparent victim of foul play, death investigations will be initiated. Many homicide victims are discovered by members of the public taking a walk in the woods, or the mail carrier noticing the mail and newspapers piling up, or a neighbor noting a foul odor from the apartment next door. Once a body is discovered, a large number of

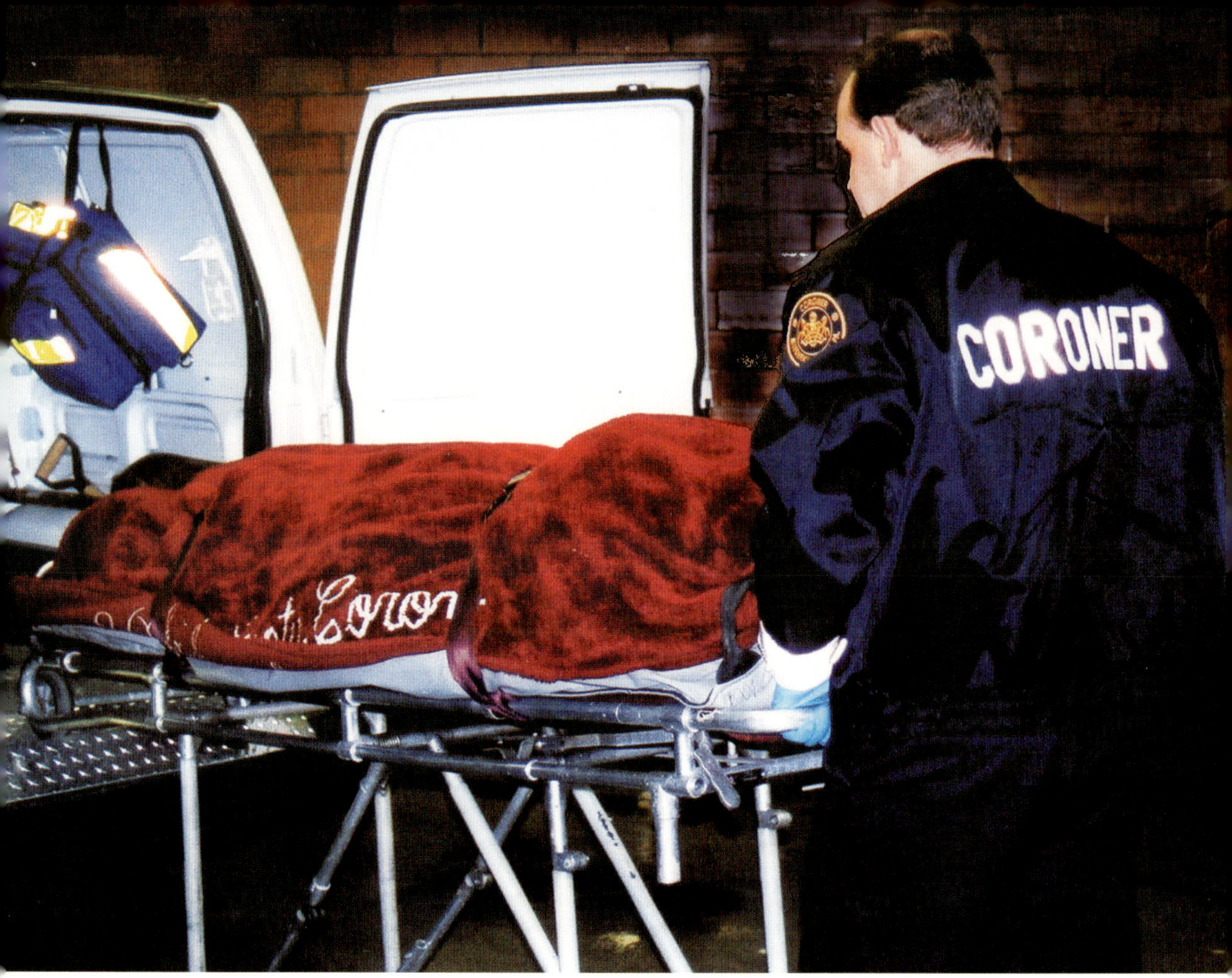

Above At the scene of a homicide, a death investigator loads the body of the victim into the van, ready for transport to the morgue. The body will be examined almost immediately, to make sure that evidence is not lost to the processes of decomposition.

individuals, each with special functions and duties, become involved in the investigation. The coroner's office will be contacted to initiate the steps toward a postmortem examination of the corpse.

About this Book

This book will take the reader to crime scenes and detail the role of the death investigators as they collect information and evidence, and prepare reports of the circumstances surrounding the death. The roles of other forensic specialists will also be described, including forensic pathologists, photographers, toxicologists, serologists, dental examiners, anthropologists, entomologists and epidemiologists.

Leading the forensic team is the coroner or medical examiner, and this role has two main parts: to make a positive identification of the victim and to determine the cause and manner of death. The methods of positive identification range from simple photo identification to sophisticated, computer-enhanced, three-dimensional facial reconstruction. The condition of the body determines the methods of determination used. The simplest method is comparing the body on the examination table to a picture on a driver's license. However, in cases of a plane crash or where only fragments of the body remain (for example, this was largely the case after the September 11 terrorist attack), identification can only be made through DNA matching. This book explains the different methods that pathologists have available to determine the positive identification of an unknown body.

The second role of the coroner is the determination of the cause and manner of death. This determination is made by first conducting an external examination of the body and then, if necessary, conducting an organ-by-organ internal examination. Occasionally, even the most meticulous examination may not reveal the cause of death. In such cases, the forensic pathologist relies on the experience of other forensic scientists. These include the forensic toxicologist who analyses body fluids for drugs, the serologist who analyses physical evidence and the firearms expert who analyses projectiles.

The culmination of the postmortem examination is the death certificate, which is a brief document, but one of great legal significance. The death certificate is an official declaration by the coroner regarding the cause and manner of death, and may play a crucial role in any criminal or civil proceedings that eventuate. Where the most gruesome crimes have been committed, the determination of homicide on the death certificate will be a key legal foundation for bringing about a conviction for murder.

In a court-room setting, forensic pathologists and other specialized forensic experts will often be called up on give testimony as expert witnesses, presenting their scientific findings in a readily understandable form before the judge and jury to help ascertain guilt or innocence.

Without the methods of the modern postmortem, we would have no means of achieving legal justice for the dead, no way of establishing the facts of violent crime and, ultimately, no way of establishing the truth about how some lives end.

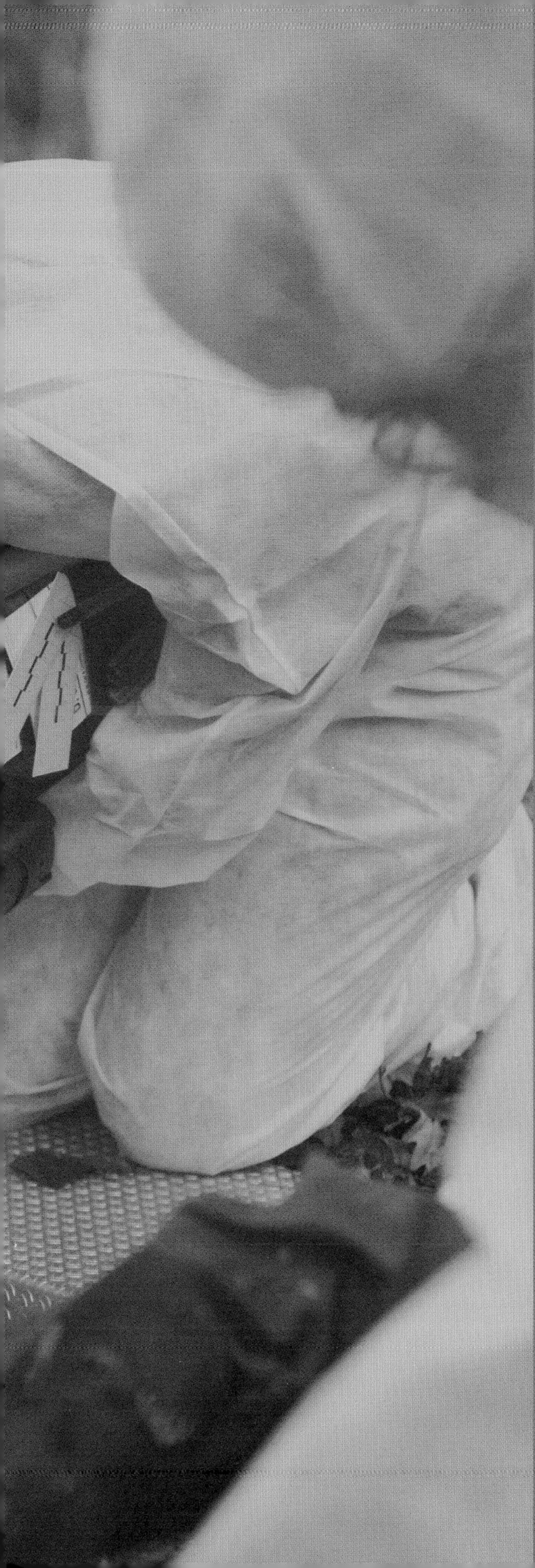

Chapter 1

When a Body Is Found

The discovery of a body at home, at work or in an uninhabited area initiates a rapid response by police, fire and emergency medical personnel. If the victim is dead on arrival, this is followed by the arrival of members of the coroner's (or medical examiner's) office and homicide detectives.

Crime Scene Investigation

Solving a crime always begins right at the scene, and successful investigation of the crime scene requires the specialized scientific methodologies of forensics personnel. Accurate reconstruction and evaluation of the events in question can be accomplished only through the correct interpretation of physical facts; but because much physical evidence is fragile, fleeting and easily destroyed, it is essential that those who respond to a crime scene know the importance of this evidence and can make the right decisions about how it should be identified, handled and preserved. In many cases, death investigators, homicide detectives and forensic scientists are able to theorize from this evidence the most likely explanation of what happened.

The investigation of any death scene starts much like a jigsaw puzzle: As information is collected and evaluated, the pieces come together and begin to form a picture of events.

Dead or Alive?

The idea of a crime scene brings to mind horrific events: a young man violently gunned down in a dark alley; a depressed middle-aged man discovered hanging next to a suicide note in a hotel room; a family out for a Sunday-afternoon drive, suddenly killed in a head-on collision with a drunk driver. These are all circumstances that will indeed require a thorough death investigation. Often multiple locations can be considered part of a crime scene, and each needs to be carefully investigated.

There are times when a victim is found injured but still alive, and therefore will be transported by ambulance or helicopter to the nearest medical facility. The victim may be stabilized and then transported to other medical facilities, remaining in care for days, weeks or even years before succumbing to his or her injuries. These complicated types of cases also require investigation by the coroner's office, and once the person is declared dead, the case comes under the coroner's jurisdiction. If the victim is at a medical facility, all intravenous lines and fluids, endotracheal tubes and other invasive medical paraphernalia must be left in place. Medical records will be requested from the facility for review by the forensic pathologist responsible for the case. In many instances a subpoena will be required in order to obtain those confidential medical documents.

This chapter, however, focuses on cases where the victim is beyond medical treatment and has not been moved from the crime scene. In these cases, the death investigator arrives at the scene and takes charge. Even though the death investigator has authority over the

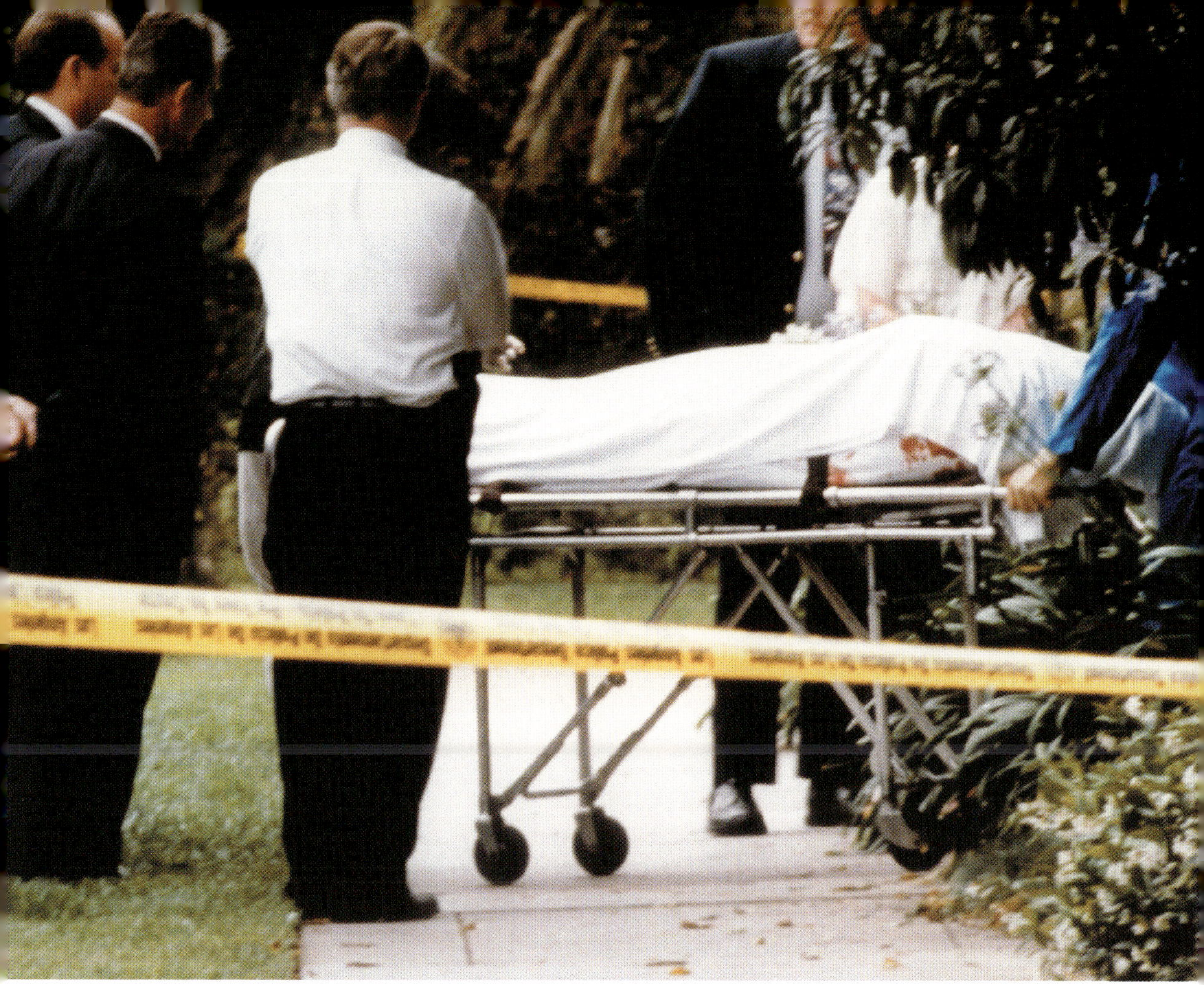

Above The body of murder victim Nicole Brown Simpson being removed from the crime scene in Los Angeles, California, with police and forensic personnel observing matters closely.

remains and their surroundings, the investigation must be conducted by a team of forensic and police experts who bring their own special experience to the case. It is essential that all death investigations be handled with a team approach, accepting that everyone involved brings some specific expertise that may ultimately uncover a crucial aspect of the case. To ignore this fact can easily result in a flawed investigation.

First on the Scene

"First responders" include emergency medical technicians, paramedics, fire department personnel and police officers. These are the people who will arrive first at a crime scene and, where the body shows no signs of life, will declare it dead on arrival (DOA). This terminology is also used in hospital emergency rooms when a patient is brought in for treatment but has already succumbed to illness or injury.

ORDER OF INVESTIGATION

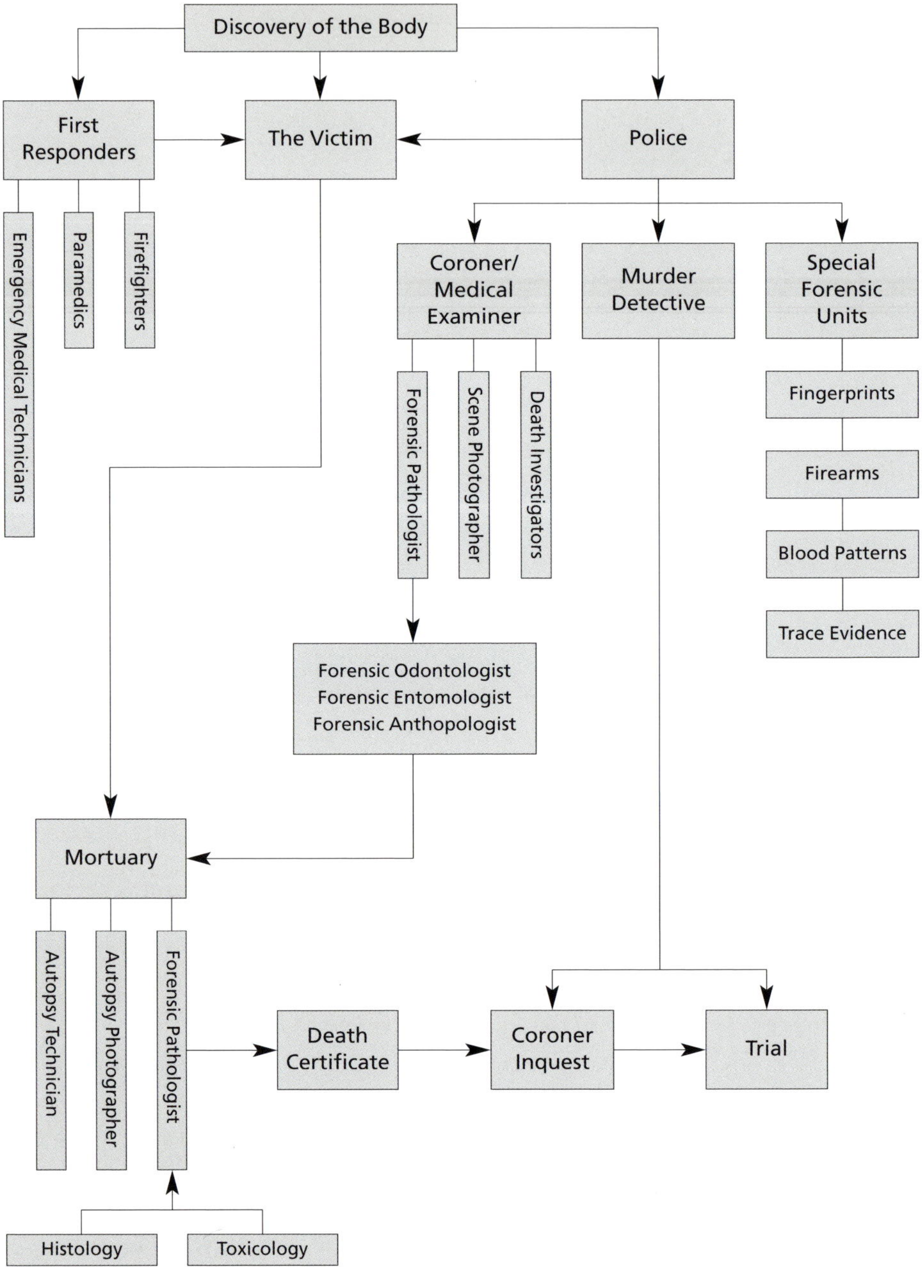

The dead-on-arrival diagnosis is an irreversible one that should be made cautiously. The decision to pronounce a patient dead in the field has not only medical significance but legal consequences as well. In most instances the emergency response team's first action is to feel for a carotid pulse on the side of the neck; it is the carotid arteries that carry blood from the heart to the brain, and so are a key factor in sustaining life. While this is being done, the clothing is usually cut or removed, providing access to the chest. This allows ECG (electrocardiogram) patches to be applied in order to determine if there is any electrical activity of the heart. If there is no activity of the heart, the monitor will show a flat line. If the patient lacks cardiac activity, the emergency response team personnel will check for rigor mortis (stiffening of the body) and livor mortis (purple discoloration of the body in the parts closest to the ground, due to pooling of blood). If the heart shows no activity and rigor or livor mortis are in evidence, the individual can be declared dead.

In some instances the determination is less complicated. For example, individuals who have suffered severe injuries ("trauma"), such as decapitation or evisceration (loss of internal organs), or bodies that are in an advanced state of decomposition may be pronounced dead without going through the usual protocols. Before leaving the scene, the emergency personnel should ensure proper coverage and protection of the deceased. They should also generate an incident report containing the names, addresses, phone numbers and other identification information available for any individuals involved in the incident.

Upon declaration of death by the paramedics, jurisdiction switches from the emergency medical team to the patrol officer at the scene, albeit only briefly, and then to the coroner's office. At this point the role of the patrol officer is to secure the scene.

In most cases the police arrive with or shortly after the emergency response team. The officer should note the position of the victim or victims, any injuries and the actions of the emergency personnel. It is the officer's job to seal a residence and encircle the death scene with a double perimeter of crime scene tape, preventing morbid curiosity seekers from entering the area under investigation. The outer perimeter is for various personnel not actively processing the scene, while the inner perimeter is reserved for the active investigative personnel, such as the coroner or medical examiner and the crime scene photographer. Preserving the scene is so important because failure to do so may compromise future prosecution.

Failing to Preserve the Crime Scene

If a criminal case gets to court, the defense will try to get every piece of incriminating evidence thrown out. They will question the legality of the search, how well the evidence has been preserved and how

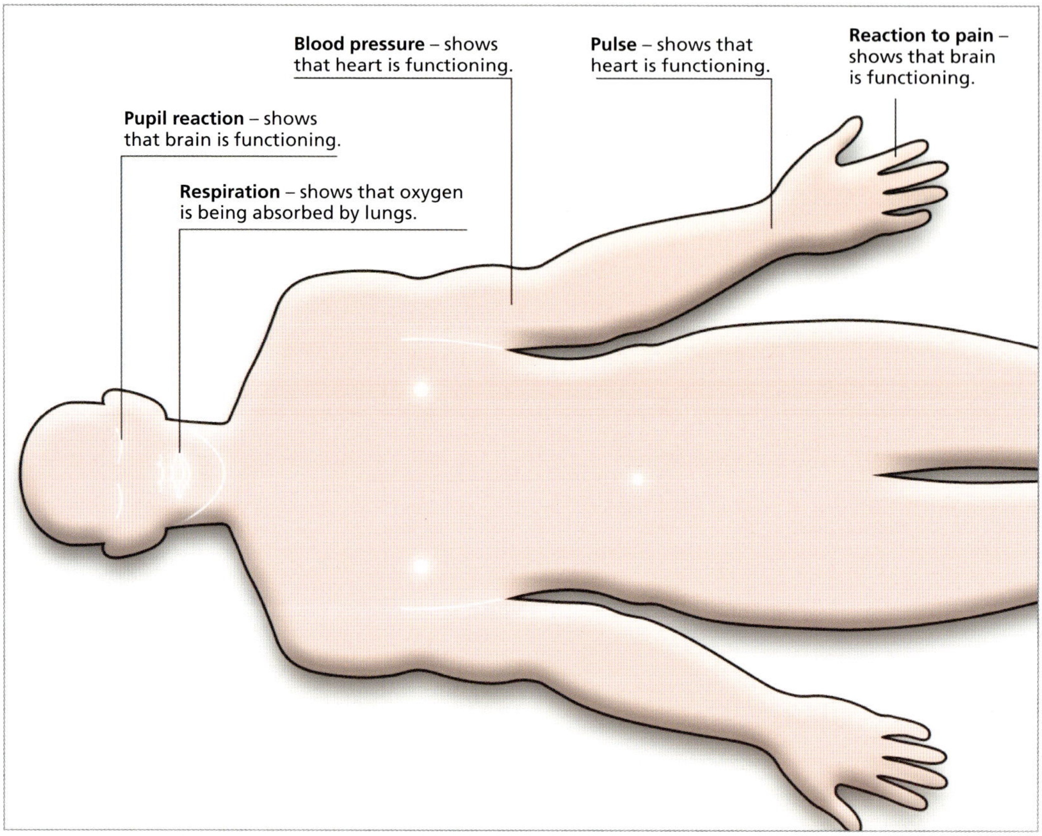

Above Diagram showing the "signs of life" that can be checked for when determining if an individial at the scene of a crime or accident is dead or alive.

accurately the crime scene has been documented and analyzed.

If the crime scene has not been fully preserved, the defense will call all evidence from the scene into question. If, for example, evidence is moved, the defense could question whether the evidence can be included in the prosecution. A knife by the body is now just a knife in the room.

Similarly, any moving of the body — unless for immediate medical assistance — should be avoided. Vital evidence can be gleaned from the position of the body in relation to the scene. Sometimes this position may even reveal evidence of "staging," where a homicide victim has been moved so that the death appears to be a case of suicide or an accident.

Contamination of many kinds can occur if a scene is not preseved. Footprints or fingerprints may be lost, while the value of trace materials such as DNA or fibers can be undermined. The more people attending a crime scene, the greater the chances that more footprints, fingerprints, DNA and trace materials could be transferred to the scene. Even if this doesn't destroy crucial evidence, it may make the identification of a criminal culprit more difficult.

Outdoor Crime Scenes

Outdoor scenes present additional problems for preserving evidence. Although animals can cause problems in an indoor scene — pets moving from room to room or moving the victim — it is the outdoor scenes, particularly after time has passed, that have greater animal activity. The activities of flies and maggots can help the forensic entomologist to establish a time line for the body, but larger animals can remove or damage both trace evidence and physical evidence.

Weather can cause serious problems, with rain and winds ruining evidence and changes in temperature throwing off time lines. Snow and ice may capture forensic clues such as footprints or blood spatters, but they also melt quickly when the sun comes out, thus destroying the evidence.

At all outdoor crime scenes, traffic, emergency and news vehicles, relatives of the victim and especially the general public must be kept from contaminating the scene.

Patrol Officers

While patrol officers are not typically part of the formal death investigation, they must take note of any physical evidence that may be destroyed, disappear or change in some way before other investigators arrive. This includes such things as a cold can of soda on a counter in a warm room, or a dry parking space on a rainy day. If such evidence is not recorded, crucial omissions may occur in the death investigators' report.

Other responsibilities of the first officer at the scene might include recording the times of notification, arrival at the scene and pronouncement of death, and who may have been at the scene. If witnesses are identified, they may need to be separated from one another to allow for more accurate interviews by investigators — all scenes should be considered potential homicides until the death has been thoroughly investigated. Patrol officers face particular challenges attending the scene of a violent crime, where the assailant is still present, and possibly in an agitated or dangerous emotional state.

Calling in the Forensics Team

When the crime scene has been secured, the next step for the officer is to call in the coroner's office. The death call is usually fielded by the investigative division, which is made up of death investigators and deputy coroners, and is staffed around the clock, seven days a week. This call initiates an inquiry into the facts and circumstances surrounding the death, including medical history, condition of the body and other information that helps to determine whether or not the case is within the coroner's jurisdiction.

IS THE DEATH A CASE FOR THE CORONER?

Not every death constitutes a coroner's case. In most jurisdictions, the death investigator is interested only in cases that involve sudden, unexpected, unexplained, traumatic or medically unattended death. The coroner investigates:

- all sudden deaths not caused by readily recognizable disease, or where the cause of death cannot be properly certified by a physician on the basis of recent medical attendance;
- all deaths occurring under suspicious circumstances, including those in which alcohol, drugs or other toxic substances may have had a direct bearing on the outcome;
- all deaths occurring as a result of violence or trauma, whether apparently homicidal, suicidal or accidental;
- any stillbirth or infant death occurring within 24 hours of birth where the mother has not been under the care of a physician or where the mother has suffered trauma at the hand of another person;
- all criminal abortions, regardless of the gestational age of the fetus;
- all hospital deaths that occur as a result of accidental injury during diagnostic or therapeutic procedures; all deaths following the accidental administration of excessive amounts of a drug; all operative and postoperative deaths in which the death is not clearly explainable on the basis of prior disease;
- deaths of all persons in legal detention, jails or police custody, including any prisoner who is a patient in a hospital;
- deaths due to disease, injury or toxic agent that occurs during active employment;
- any death wherein the body is unidentified or unclaimed;
- any death in which there is uncertainty as to whether it should be reported.

The Role of Death Investigators

When it has been determined that a death falls under the coroner's jurisdiction, death investigators respond at the scene and begin to collect information and evidence. The team arriving at the scene usually consists of two death investigators or deputy coroners, a scene forensic photographer and, depending on the circumstances and initial findings, criminalists such as ballistics, fingerprint, trace evidence and blood-spatter experts. Death investigators document all information at the scene in an initial report entitled "Circumstances of Death," which will be filed at the coroner's office for future reference.

Often the death investigators have to contact the family of the deceased to establish a more detailed medical, psychological or social history, as well as obtain additional descriptions of the circumstances surrounding the death. In cases where test results from the autopsy reveal information relevant to the health of other family members (most often, genetic disorders that may affect other members of the family), the forensic pathologist will make contact with them at a later stage.

In instances where communicable diseases appear to be present and may therefore cause a threat to the wider community, the death investigators will contact the local health department to warn them of the danger. But in cases that appear to involve homicide, the coroner's staff's main contact will be with members of the police and the prosecution.

Coroners and Medical Examiners

The role of a medical examiner and that of a coroner are essentially the same. They both have the function of determining the identity of a deceased individual and the cause and manner of death. The main difference between these two offices is administrative and political.

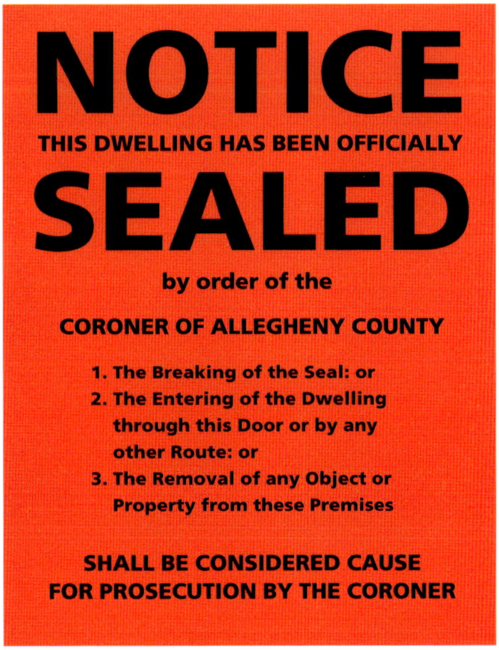

Above Example of the official notice posted by the coroner's office to seal a site for investigation.

A medical examiner must be a physician with special training in forensic pathology. By contrast, the coroner is an appointed or elected position and typically is held by an individual with no or limited medical training. Both medical examiner's and coroner's offices hire forensic pathologists to conduct the postmortem and determine the cause and manner of death.

Throughout this book we will refer only to the coroner — although in some jurisdictions this role actually falls to a medical examiner.

The Homicide Detectives

Another important group of investigators on scene is the homicide investigation team, usually consisting of two or more homicide detectives. The homicide investigators have five basic questions to answer:

1. Did the death take place where the body was discovered, or was it moved?
2. Was there any attempt to alter the scene?
3. Does the scene suggest a particular type of illegal activity (e.g., robbery, drug-related crime)?
4. Is a cause of death clearly apparent?
5. Are there sufficient clues to suggest how the crime occurred?

The Criminalists

Depending on the type of crime scene, the skills of specialized personnel called criminalists may be required. Criminalists are individuals trained in special disciplines within forensic science. They are concerned with physical evidence such as hair, fibers, glass, fingerprints, body fluids, blood spatter and firearms. At the scene they may help identify, locate and collect evidence that will provide additional information relevant to solving the case and ensuring that the actor or actors are properly prosecuted. If deemed necessary, a forensic pathologist, forensic anthropologist or forensic entomologist may be called to utilize their expertise in the case. The roles of these forensic scientists are described in Chapter 5.

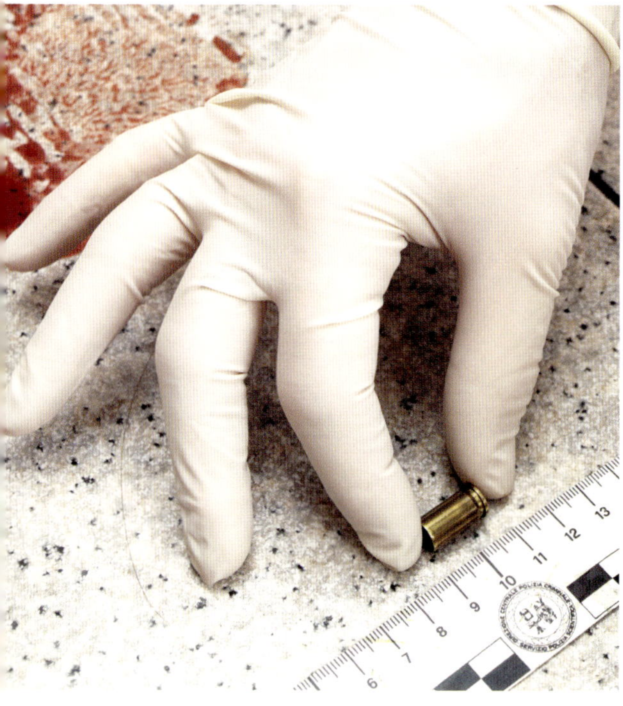

Left Forensic officer collecting a spent cartridge shell as part of evidence found at a crime scene.

CRIME-SCENE SPECIALISTS

- **Forensic serologist**
  Examines blood and other body fluids for clues about the person these fluids came from.
- **Forensic anthropologist**
  Applies the study of human bones to glean clues from skeletonized remains.
- **Latent fingerprint examiner**
  Locates, develops, preserves, compares and identifies latent fingerprints discovered during criminal investigations.
- **Blood-spatter examiner**
  Analyzes blood stains and patterns discovered during criminal investigations.
- **Firearm examiner**
  Identifies weapons and ammunition, analyzes the ballistic properties of bullets and determines the distance and trajectory of the shot. Also correlates the weapon with the bullet.
- **Forensic photographer**
  Photographically records details of crime scenes, autopsies and technical procedures during criminal investigations.
- **Trace evidence examiner**
  Analyzes microscopic and macroscopic traces of physical evidence such as hairs, fibers, paint, soil, polymers, glass and impressions.
- **Documents examiner**
  Analyzes irregularities in any legal documents such as wills, contracts and insurance policies.
- **Impression examiner**
  Analyzes physical impressions such as shoe prints, tire tracks, tool marks and fabric impressions. Creates casts and determines the type of object that produced them.

Crime Scene Photographer

The role of the crime scene photographer is to make a permanent photographic record of the physical situation in which a crime has occurred. These forensic photographs serve as crucial evidence in a court of law, so every death investigation must be photographed as if it was a homicide.

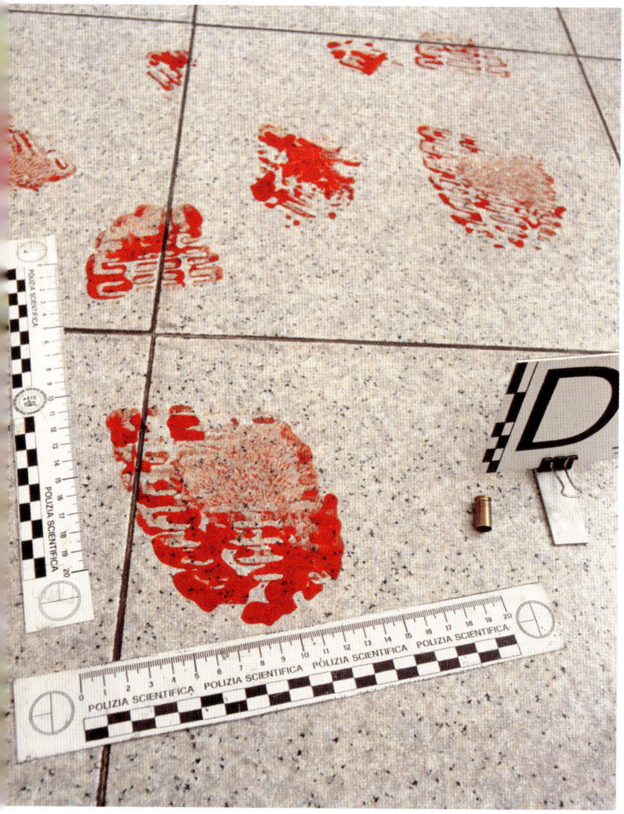

Above Measurement and labeling of crime scene evidence. Rulers provide a scale for photographs of the bloody footprints.

Photographing an Indoor Death Scene

An indoor death scene is photographed by what is known as the "four corners" method. This series of photographs starts in the doorway of the room in which the victim is located to capture a view as seen by someone who has just entered the room. Then the photographer takes images from the four corners of the room, thus producing a panoramic view of the scene.

The body is photographed next. The photographer starts by taking a full-length view, then left-side and right-side views of the body. If a weapon is present, then the photographs should show its relationship to the body. Next, close-up images are taken, especially documenting any piece of evidence that may be altered when the body is moved, such as blood trails, debris, hair and fibers. Material located under the victim or trapped within the hands, feet or mouth is also photographed.

Other forensic specialists such as blood-spatter examiners, fingerprint examiners and trace evidence collectors now conduct their duties. They are careful not to move the body while they detect and collect every scrap of potential forensic evidence. Once these specialists have completed their work, the body can be moved. If the body was originally

resting on its side, it is turned to allow full-face images to be taken.

With the body well documented in situ, other aspects of the scene such as the weapon, spilled drinks, piles of papers and furniture become the focus of attention. Adjoining rooms may also be photographed — perhaps even the whole house. Doors and windows are examined for signs of forced entry; broken window panes or torn screens are investigated and photographed. Outside the residence, impressions in the snow, mud or dirt must also be recorded.

Photographing a Motor Vehicle Accident

When scene photographers arrive at the site of a fatal motor vehicle accident, they may have to document a number of victims, including drivers, passengers and pedestrians. First images are taken at a distance, showing the relationship between the body, vehicle and landmarks such as utility poles, signs, traffic lights and natural terrain. Views should be taken from each of the directions of travel. Patterned marks on the victims must be documented, such as those caused by tires, grill, license plate and headlights. Victims within the vehicle are first photographed in situ, as are the seat belts and airbag (if present). If the victim has been removed by

Above Photographing a crime scene. A second and third investigator are inspecting the victim and the shallow grave from different angles.

emergency rescue personnel, the inside and outside of the vehicle are documented to illustrate the extraction process. Particular attention is given in the interior of the vehicle to the brake and accelerator pedals, the dashboard and the position of the keys in the ignition.

Brake and accelerator pedals These are compared against the driver's footwear. If a pedal has left an impression on the driver's shoe, this may indicate which pedal was engaged at the moment of impact.

Dashboard It is photographed to record the gear the vehicle was in, the position of turn indicators, if the windshield wipers were on, the amount of gas left in the tank and the reading on the odometer.

Ignition The position of the keys indicates whether the vehicle's engine was running at the time of the crash.

Next, skid marks and other marks in relationship to the vehicle are photographed. The vehicles involved in the death must be photographed from all sides and close-ups taken of any damage, old or new. The vehicles may also bear crucial evidence of the death, such as bits of clothing, blood smears, hair or human tissue.

Cameras and Film

The scene photographer uses both standard 35 mm cameras and various digital cameras. If a film camera is used, photographs may be taken on black-and-white, color print or slide film. Each type has advantages and limitations: Black-and-white negatives last the longest while retaining the fine details of the image. Color negatives have a shorter life span because over time the dyes in the negatives change and fade, but of course they capture the color aspects of the scene. Color slide film is more stable than color negatives and therefore lasts longer, and slides can be stored in wooden boxes without special environmental requirements.

Digital photography is easily stored as electronic data (pixels). These images can be stored in large numbers on CDs or DVDs, which survive an extremely long period of time — some estimate that they will maintain the integrity of their data for over 200 years.

Technical Forensic Photographer

Another type of scene photographer is the technical forensic photographer. The technical photographer uses special films and cameras to document bloodstains, blood spatters, fingerprints and other impressions found at the scene or on the body. These are highly detailed images that are planned to accurately record the scale of physical dimensions. Technical photographers spend most of the time working with high-magnification photomacrography, photomicrography, non-visible wavelength imaging (i.e., ultraviolet or infrared photography) and the digital image manipulation of photographic documents.

Death Scene Procedures

Before entering the actual scene, the death investigation team will interview police officers, medical professionals and witnesses in order to establish possible scenarios or preliminary theories. A high priority is placed on obtaining a tentative name, address, next of kin, age, date of birth and social security number of the deceased. The death investigators also record the name, title, phone number and affiliation of everyone at the scene, and put together a time line of known events leading up to the death.

Once the scene photographer has taken overall photographs, the investigation moves to the actual scene itself. The death investigator will initially examine the scene from a distance, and then move in closer until he arrives at the victim, all the while recording observations. When the investigator finally arrives at the body (or bodies), an overview of its status will

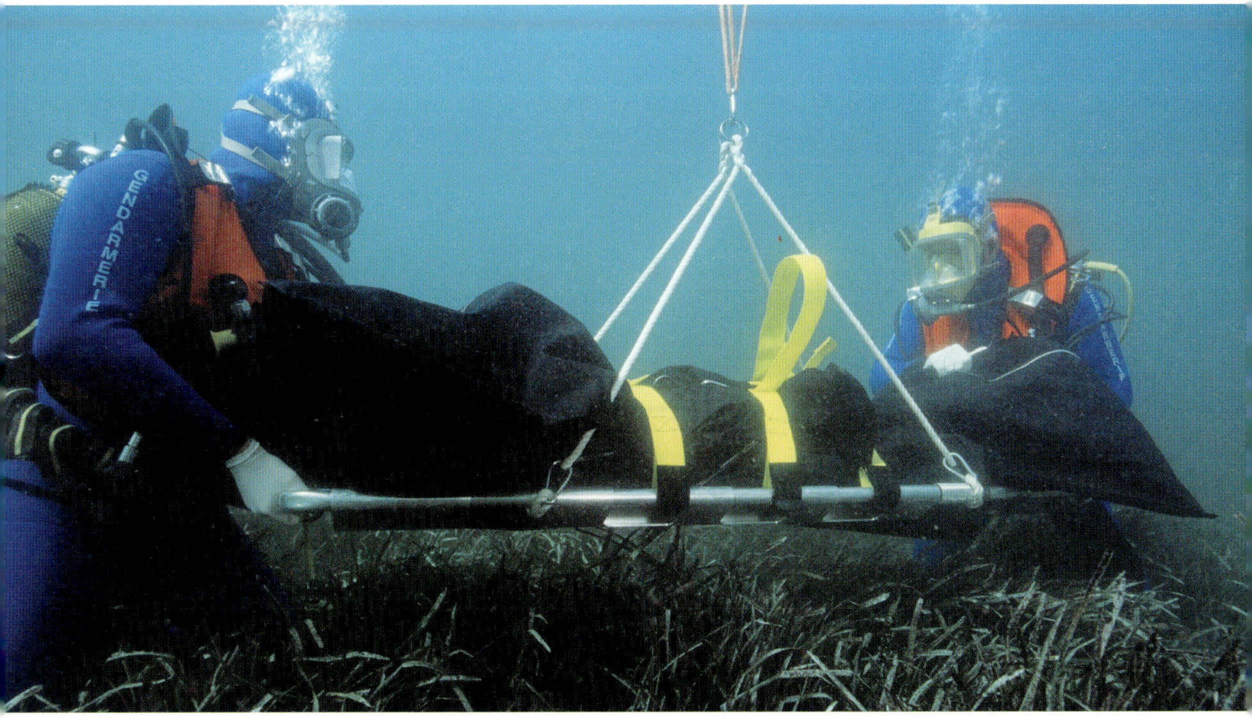

Above Recovery of a dead body from the seabed. As with any potential crime scene, great care must be taken to preserve, record and collect the evidence.

be recorded, noting any obvious injuries and thoroughly checking its position and condition. Important factors to be noted and photographed include whether the body is in a supine (on its back), prone (on its front) or lateral (on its side) position, and whether rigor mortis has set in. Rigor and livor mortis can be used by the investigator to calculate an approximate time of death and whether the body's position has been altered.

Handling Evidence

In collecting evidence from a crime scene, the investigators must bear several goals in mind. They must reconstruct the crime, identify the person who did it, preserve the evidence for analysis and collect it in a way that will not contaminate it. An investigator may use combs, tweezers, containers and a filtered vacuum device to collect any hair or fibers at the scene and then seal them in separate containers for the lab.

Personal Items

Focus will next be directed towards the clothing and other items of significance on or around the victim. The remains will be thoroughly searched by the death investigator in the presence of police officers. Any item discovered at this time will be inventoried, recorded and, if deemed necessary, photographed. Some of the items discovered at the scene or on the person may provide particularly valuable information: the cell phone is examined for the last number called, the last incoming call and the calling history. It is not unusual for a pager or phone worn by the victim to receive a call during the examination of the body. The incoming number is noted and the device is turned over to the homicide detectives. Personal items such as address books, PDAs and computer files often help the investigators to establish with whom, where and what the victim may have been doing prior to death. A search of these items may also provide the next of kin and relevant medical information. The search of the victim may reveal medical alert bracelets, providing immediate health information. The evidence and effects will be secured by the death investigator for submission to the forensic science laboratory as evidence, or for return to the next of kin.

Contraband

Another important factor to check for on the scene is the presence of drugs, drug paraphernalia and possible injection sites. In many instances these items may be quite obvious, but sometimes they may have been tampered with. Extreme caution must be used when coming in contact with needles, razor blades and the like, because of the danger of infection. Any contraband must be packaged in a biohazard sharps container labeled accordingly and transported as evidence to the crime laboratory. Legal medications must also be located and inventoried; without these drugs, toxicology testing can become quite difficult, time-consuming and expensive to perform. In complex cases, the death

Above Forensic scientists preparing articles for blood sampling during criminal investigation. A pair of jeans, a T-shirt and a shoe have all been collected from the victim, while a small axe has been found at the crime scene. All are spattered with blood samples that may be crucial to the investigation.

investigator may call in a pathologist to conduct a preliminary medical examination at the scene.

While all these items of physical evidence are being collected, appropriate photographs of the body will be taken by the scene photographer. An exact replication of the scene can never be created, so this is the only opportunity for accurate photographic documentation.

Time of Death

One of the key questions that need to be addressed is the time of death. As mentioned above, the death investigators calculate this based on rigor mortis and livor mortis (which also help to establish whether the victim has been moved), as well as a further factor known as "algor mortis." Algor mortis refers to the temperature changes that occur in the body after death. The human body usually has a slight increase in temperature immediately after death, followed by a steady decrease until the body temperature equalizes with the environmental temperature. An internal or core body temperature is taken at this

Body Temperature (Algor Mortis)

Normal human body temperature is between 96.7°F (35.7°C) and 99.0°F (37.2°C). After death the body processes stop and the tissues begin to break down. This breakdown is initially caused by a buildup of bacteria that also cause the core body temperature to increases for the first few hours. Typically, the body loses temperature at a rate of 1.5°F (0.8°C) during the first eight hours, then 1°F (0.6°C) an hour until the temperature of the body is at equilibrium with the surrounding environment. Many factors affect these rates, including layers and types of clothing, the surface the body is on and whether the body is in the sun or shade or submerged in water. The mass of the body and the air temperature are the key factors.

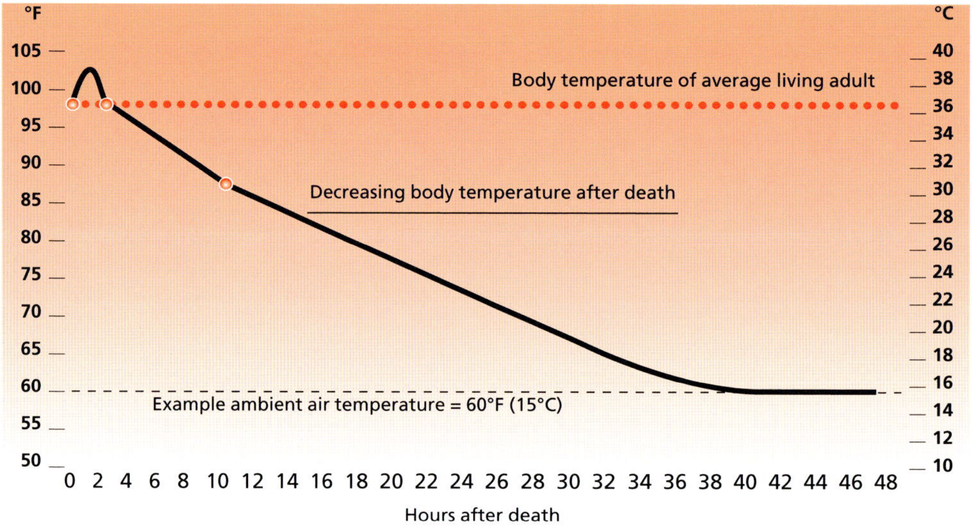

time by inserting a specially designed thermometer into the victim's liver. The ambient air temperature or room temperature at the scene is also established and recorded.

The victim is also examined for any type of insect or animal activity, known as anthropophagy. As unpalatable as it may be for the inexperienced layperson, maggot and/or blowfly presence is an extremely important factor for the investigator and certainly helps to establish some idea of the time of death. If there are maggots or other insects near or under the body, they must be collected and brought back to the morgue.

Further Tasks

Before taking the body back to the morgue for an autopsy, a few more tasks need to be completed at the scene. Even though a tentative identification may have been made prior to the investigator's arrival, a positive ID should be attempted at the scene. A photo identification form such as a driver's license would be the first choice or, less frequently, someone at the scene who personally knows the deceased might make a visual identification. If no positive identification can be made, then the remains must be listed as unknown until a more accurate method of identification, such as fingerprints or dental records, can be utilized.

In the event that death was due to a physical altercation or involved a weapon, the hands of the deceased must be placed in fresh, clean paper bags and secured with tape at the wrists. The bags are used to contain and preserve any evidence that may be on the victim's hands. Examples of this evidence include gunshot powder residue, blood or trace evidence located under the fingernails. It is also essential that paper bags be used as opposed to plastic, because paper allows the hands to "breathe," thus avoiding condensation that may otherwise destroy the evidence.

Weapons located at the scene are normally collected by the homicide detectives and submitted to the forensic science lab for latent fingerprints and ballistics analyses such as distance and caliber studies. The investigators should never remove bullets or clothing from the body or otherwise change any relationship between the body and its environment while at the scene. To do so at this time would risk destruction or loss of important evidence. Instead, these items are recovered during the autopsy, where the environment can be controlled.

Rigor Mortis

Rigor mortis is a condition wherein the muscles of the body harden or stiffen after death. This is caused by chemical changes within the muscle fibers when lactic acid is produced and accumulates. The accumulated acid causes protoplasm in the muscle cells to gel and makes them rigid. This process typically begins during the first 4 hours after death and is complete within 12 hours. This rigidity may last for another 12–18 hours, after which it dissipates and the muscles become flexible again.

Once the victim has been removed from the scene, the police and crime lab personnel will continue to process the vicinity for additional evidence that might be recovered.

Death Investigation Gone Wrong

The actions taken or not taken at the beginning of an investigation can have major implications for the way a case will be processed. For example, if the police are called to a residence and fail to conduct a detailed room-by-room search, victims or critical evidence can be missed. A death investigation can be jeopardized if the scene is not properly secured, because family, neighbors, curious passers-by and even the media may enter. This could lead to the contamination of evidence and the removal or addition of material, and greatly reduce the admissibility of the evidence recovered from the scene.

Livor Mortis

Livor mortis appears as purple discoloration of the skin in the "dependent" parts of the body (those parts that are the lowest points according to the position of the body). This discoloration is caused by blood settling out of the capillaries and draining into the lowest gravitational regions of the body; the color is purplish because it is a deoxygenated blood pigment.

Livor mortis begins immediately after death but normally takes 2 hours before it becomes visible. Between 4 and 8 hours after death, the livor pattern is "unfixed" and can shift if the body is moved, for example, from faceup to facedown. Between 8 and 12 hours after death the lividity becomes "fixed" and will not shift even if the body is moved.

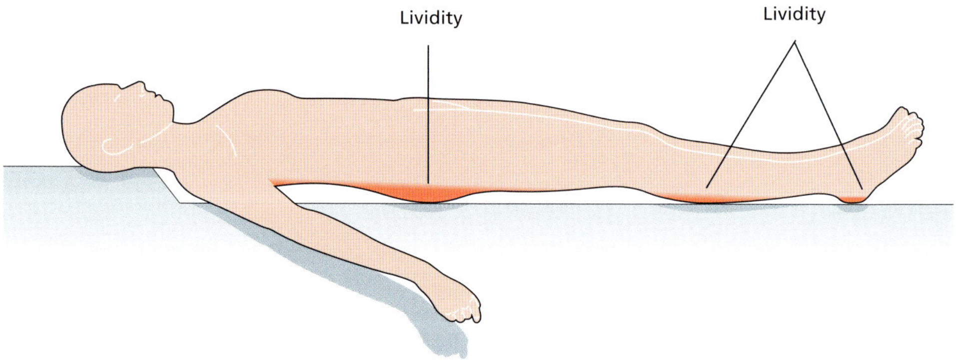

By examining the livor mortis, or postmortem blood pooling, experts can determine how long the body has been in a particular position, as well as the time of death.

Transport to the Morgue

After the death investigators have completed their processing of the body (photographing the body, bagging the hands, taking core temperature, etc.), it is then prepared for transport to the local morgue, where it will undergo further examination by a forensic pathologist. The body is kept in its original position as much as possible to protect physical evidence, placed onto a fresh white sheet or shroud, and then placed into a disaster- or bodybag. The bag is labeled with the appropriate identification information and locked to guarantee that no tampering takes place on the way to the morgue. The packaged body is then placed on a stretcher and wheeled to the coroner's vehicle and taken to the office.

The death investigation now shifts from the crime scene to the examining team, namely the forensic pathologist and the various specialized criminalists. If the death investigators have done their job meticulously, there will be plenty of evidence to uncover.

Case Study TRACE EVIDENCE AT THE SCENE

The mail carrier noticed that the mailbox had not been emptied for two days. He became concerned because the young lady residing at the apartment always used to collect her mail, so he called the police. The police entered the apartment, which was leased to a 26-year-old female. In the bathroom was located a female, dead on arrival. The police sealed the apartment and called the coroner's office and homicide detectives.

THE INVESTIGATION

Death investigators arrived on the scene and entered the residence, noting the condition of the apartment. The front door did not appear to be forced open, while inside the apartment several small tables were overturned, and the victim was laying facedown in the bathroom. The victim was wearing white shorts and a black jogging top, and there was an electrical cord wrapped around her neck. The investigators determined that the death was suspicious and requested that a scene photographer and a trace evidence criminalist come to the scene.

Meanwhile, the homicide detectives were interviewing neighbors, co-workers and the family of the young woman. The landlord made a positive identification of her body. The detectives were informed that the woman had recently been through a nasty divorce; there was also a restraining order against the ex-husband, stating that he must remain at least 1,500 feet (450 m) from his ex-wife. The detectives went to the place of employment of the ex-husband and informed him of the death, questioning him about his movements for the past few days. He stated that he had had no contact with his ex for over two months.

CRUCIAL TRACE EVIDENCE

Back at the apartment, the photographer was documenting the scene and then the victim. The body was carefully rolled over. One of the death investigators noticed some white fibers or hairs on her black top, and asked the trace evidence criminalist to collect them. This was done at the scene because this type of trace evidence might have been lost during the transport of the body.

The examination of the body revealed that the woman had died from ligature strangulation, and the manner of death was homicide. The white material discovered on her top was studied by the trace examiner, first to determine if it was hair (human or animal) or fibers (natural or manufactured). Under microscopic examination it was determined that the white material was fur from a white cat. The victim did not own a cat, nor did any of her friends or family. The detectives obtained a search warrant of the ex-husband's home, and discovered that he did own a white cat. A sample of fur was collected and later compared to the one found on the victim. The hair had been on the ex-husband's clothing, and during the struggle with the ex-wife the fur had been transferred from the man to the women. This placed him at the scene of the crime.

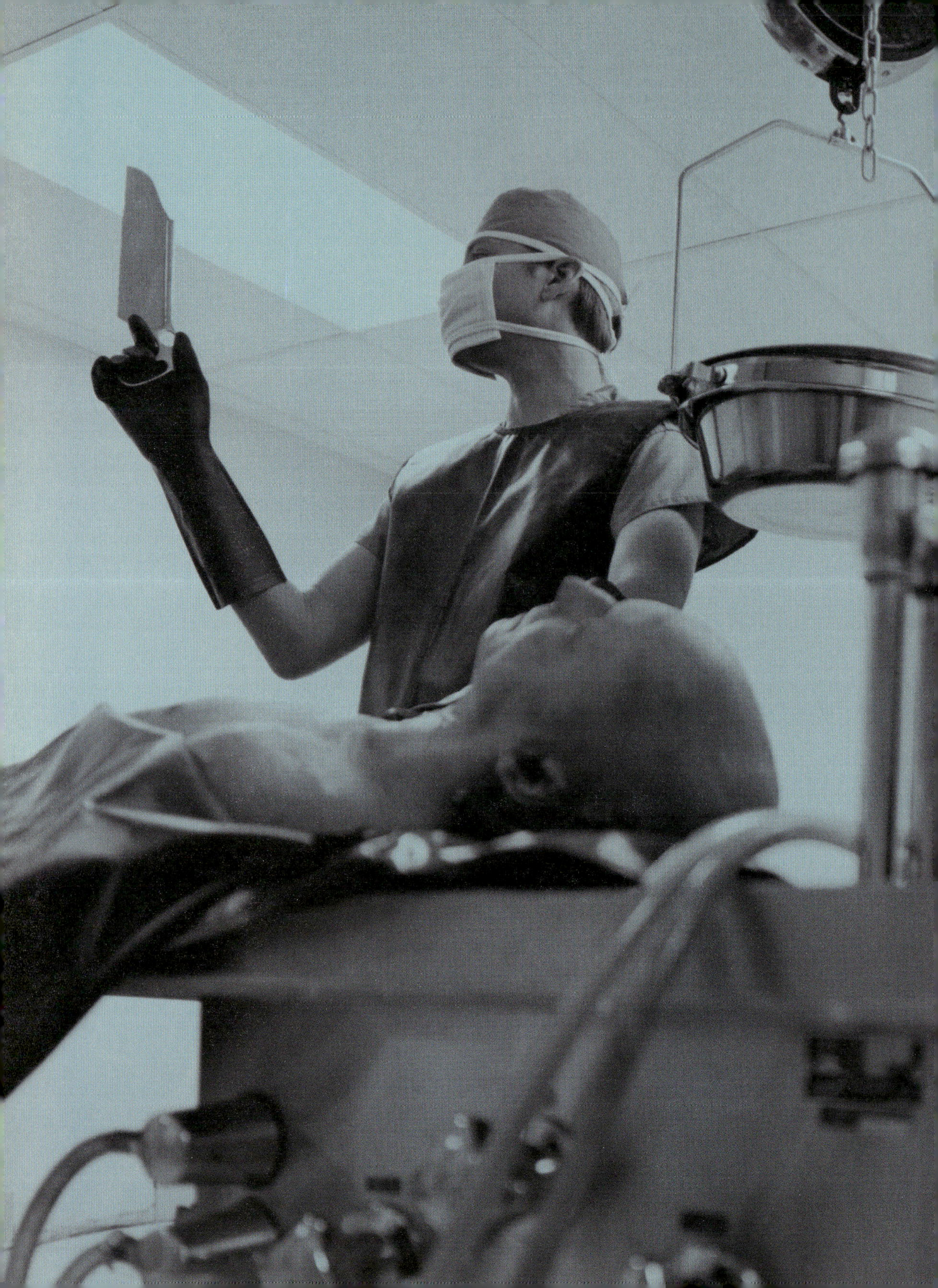

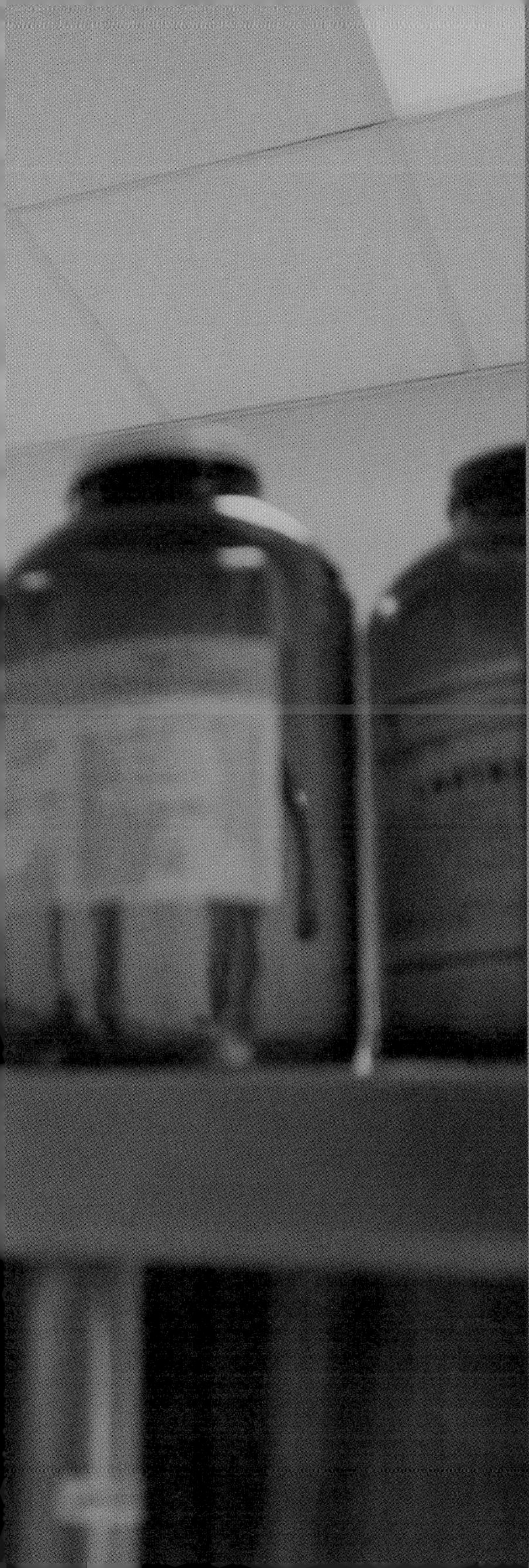

Chapter 2

The Autopsy Room Protocol

Just as living patients tell their physicians where it hurts, the dead talk to the forensic pathologist through the autopsy. The forensic autopsy is the final examination of a body prior to burial or cremation, and involves scientific external and internal examination in order to determine the cause and manner of death. As well as determining the circumstances of death, the autopsy aims to make a positive identification of the individual.

Examining the Dead

The practice of examining the dead is not new. In the 17th century BCE the Egyptians had a thorough knowledge of poisons, differentiated stab wounds and made determinations regarding the cause and manner of death. Even earlier, the Chinese published information on poisons in 3000 BCE. The physician Antistius examined the assassinated Julius Caesar in 44 BCE, and determined that only one of his 23 stab wounds was fatal.

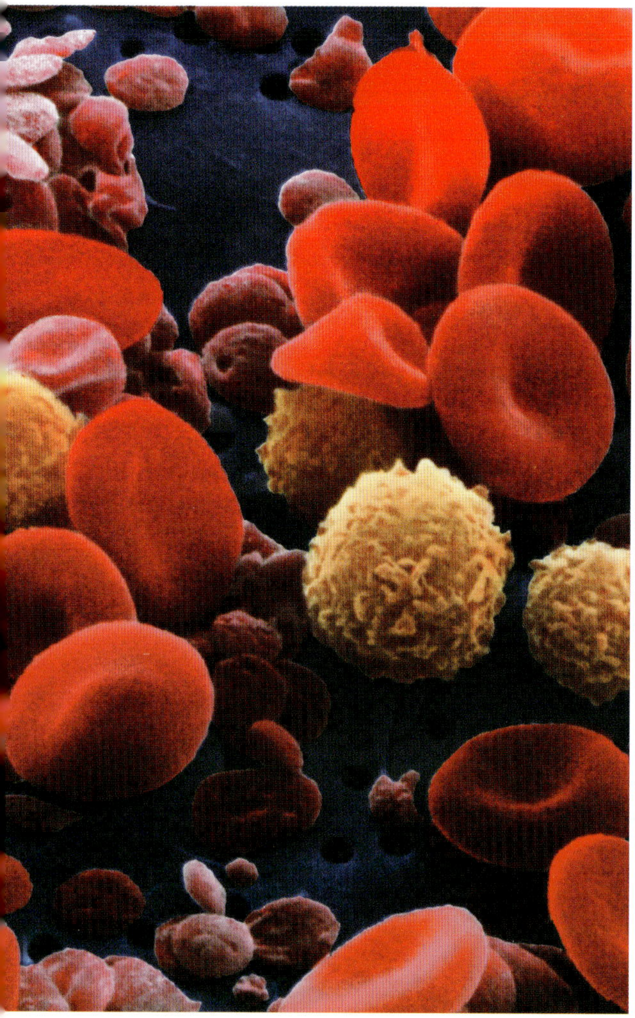

By 1236 CE the Chinese had collated a manual, the *Hsi Yuan Lu*, outlining the proper procedures for investigating death. The book suggested that the medical examiner should conduct a thorough and systematic examination of every corpse found in suspicous circumstances, and also described some key means of interpreting the body, such as how to distinguish between a drowned body and a body thrown into the water after death, and how to tell whether burning had occurred before or after death.

Emergence of the Modern Autopsy

The forensic methods we use now are not too different in principle from those practiced by the ancient Chinese, Romans and Egyptians. However, we are now assisted by the superior scientific technologies that have been developed over the last few centuries, allowing us to

Left Image of blood cells as seen through a scanning electron microscope. Such images are created by bouncing electrons off an object in a vacuum, creating a gray-scale three-dimensional image, which can later be colored for visual effect.

THE TECHNOLOGICAL BUILDING BLOCKS OF FORENSIC SCIENCE

1591	Hans Janssen and his son Zacharias invented the first practical microscope.
1826	The first permanent photographic image was developed by Joseph Nicéphore Niépce.
1813	Mathieu Orfila, "the father of toxicology," published his work on the classification of poisons, *Traité de toxicologie générale*.
1836	James Marsh developed a test for detecting small traces of arsenic in human tissues.
1858	Sir William Herschel introduced the concept of fingerprints.
1895	Wilhelm Conrad Röntgen identifies X rays and begins to explore their special properties.
1882	Alphonse Bertillon developed "anthropometry," a system for identifying criminals based on body measurements.
1893	Hans Gross published his influential *Handbook for Examining Magistrates* — the first modern guide to forensic science.
1901	The ABO blood-group system was established.
1901	Serology testing became able to distinguish human blood from animal blood.
1912	Comparisons between bullets located at a scene and those fired from a specific gun were conducted by photographic enlargements.
1925	The comparison microscope revolutionized the analysis of trace evidence by allowing simultaneous comparison of two objects.
1932	A method was developed to measure alcohol in the blood.
1965	The scanning electron microscope was developed, allowing magnification 150,000 times.
1984	The first DNA "fingerprint" for an individual human being was created.

The Real Sherlock Holmes

Dr. Joseph Bell was a professor at the University of Edinburgh Medical School who inspired Arthur Conan Doyle to create the character Sherlock Holmes. Doyle was taught by Dr. Bell as he studied to become a doctor, and in the second year of study he was selected to serve as Dr. Bell's assistant in his hospital ward.

Bell had a remarkable ability to deduce a great deal about his patient, emphasizing the importance of close observation in making a diagnosis. He was renowned for being able to determine the occupation of the patients by studying their hands. These skills, celebrated through the Holmes character, who used them to fight crime, earned Dr. Bell the reputation as a pioneer of forensic science, in a time when science was not often used in the investigation of crimes. Bell's focus on minute traces of evidence was an early forerunner of forensic techniques developed in the 20th century.

Right Dr. Joseph Bell, "the real Sherlock Holmes."

examine physical evidence with incredible precision. Some of the earliest crucial scientific developments were the technologies that enhanced our power to see the world around us. The use of lenses in microscopes and magnifying glasses gave the examiner of dead bodies a new tool for detecting the tiniest pieces of evidence. As light-refracting microscopes have improved, and scientists have gone on to develop the electron microscope, our visual reach has become tinier still. Photographic technologies have also been crucial in allowing us to capture visual images and store them as permanent forensic records.

Another field of scientific endeavor that has played a key role in modernizing the postmortem examination has been the development on our anatomic understanding. The Scientific Revolution in Europe in the 17th and 18th centuries led to new understandings of how the human body works. The vital organs, and the circulatory, respiratory, excretory and nervous systems that they form, were studied as independent but connected physical units, helping us to understand physical life, and indeed death.

In the late 19th century, modern medicine began to be applied to the examination of dead bodies on a regular basis. Legal and procedural protocols were established to ensure that reliable and expert opinions could be formed regarding the identity of a deceased person, as well as the cause and manner of their death.

A Body Arrives at the Morgue

When a body arrives at the morgue, it is unloaded from the coroner's van, wheeled onto a floor-mounted scale and weighed for recording in the autopsy report. The body is then logged in by taking a video ID photograph and adding a new entry to the log-in book. The log-in entry includes the coroner's ID number, the age, sex, race and name (if known) of the victim, and the date and time that the body was brought in. The body is then transferred from the van stretcher and placed on a morgue gurney. An ID tag is placed on the toe of the body and a matching one is affixed to the body bag. Once the body is on the gurney, a block is placed under the head, allowing the blood to drain away from the head region. The body is then wheeled into a 40°F (4°C) cooler.

Death Investigation Report

The death investigator must now return to the coroner's office to write the death investigation report. This report documents and summarizes the information collected from the scene, interviews and data from external sources such as paramedic's trip reports, police reports and medical records. All reports contain four basic sections: demographic information (age, gender, ethnicity — e.g., "25-year-old white female"); next-of-kin information (who is closest to the person by blood relation, marriage or legal guardianship and should be first to know of the death); past medical history (looking out especially for any previous medical condition that may have been the cause of death or a contributing factor to the death); and the circumstances that led to the death.

The "circumstances of death" section is the most variable part of the death investigation report, as the type of death will dictate the information collected. For example, the information collected on a fatal motor vehicle accident includes the type of vehicle or vehicles involved, location of the occupants, their use of restraints, road conditions and the path, any known use of intoxicants, speed and behavior of the vehicles. On the other hand, the information reported on a death by violent assault will detail weapons found at the scene and signs of a struggle. For every type of death there will be detailed, relevant information that must be reported.

Why the Toe?

The ID tag is tied to the toe for two reasons:

1. The site normally does not bear forensic evidence.
2. The site is easily accessible when the body is inside a body bag.

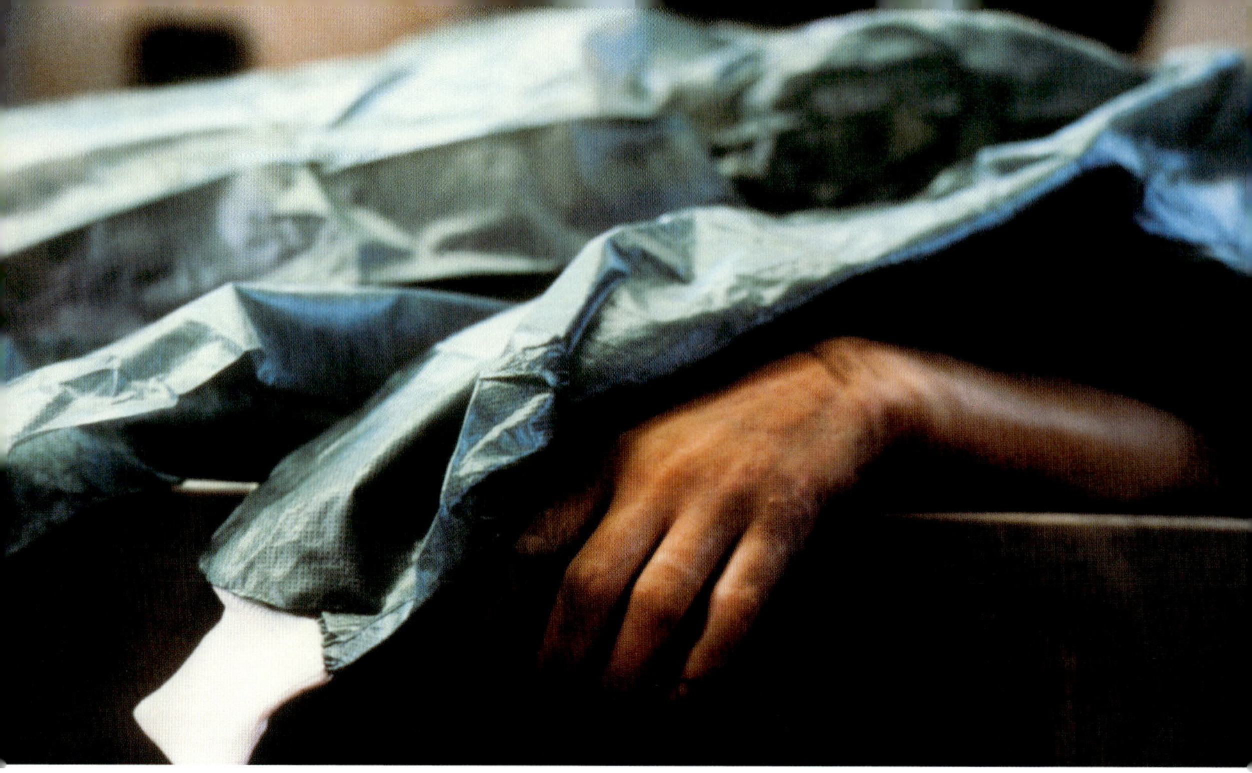

Above Body of a 20-year-old white female who has been dead for two days. In this case, the postmortem examination found that she had died from a cardiac virus.

Case Study THE NEED TO ESTABLISH IDENTITY

A city work crew was cleaning a storm drain when they discovered a body in an advanced state of decomposition. The remains were taken to the morgue and examined by a forensic anthropologist, who determined that they belonged to an adult black male between the ages of 25 and 30. The coroner's office contacted the police missing persons department and was informed that more than 100 individuals matched that description, and it was considered impractical and expensive to use DNA comparison to establish the identity. More information was needed to narrow the search.

The vital clue came when a clothing examination revealed words on the T-shirt associating the victim with a regional softball team. Tracking down members of the team revealed when the shirts had been available for sale, and this date narrowed the field of possible missing persons to fewer than 20. The police contacted the relevant families, and one mentioned that their uncle was a softball fan who had gone missing three days after a game. Dental records were used to make a positive identification of the individual.

The Cooler

After initial processing and registration of the body, it must be stored in a cold chamber to prevent decomposition while awaiting identification or postmortem examination. There are two basic types of cooling chamber:

Short-term chambers are about 40°F (4°C) and can be used to store a body for a few days or weeks. In such a chamber the body will still decompose slightly, but at a very reduced rate.

Long-term chambers are much colder, at about 0°F (–18°C) or as low as –10°F (–25°C). In these chambers the body will freeze completely, halting all decomposition processes. Long-term chambers are generally used for storage of bodies that have not been postitively identified.

The types of coolers vary from the large walk-in type to wall units with pull-out drawers. The walk-in types typically have a capacity of 40–50 bodies; as well as bodies on autopsy carts, more bodies can be stored on three or four rows of shelves lining the walls. These shelves will be used for bodies that are in for longer-term storage, such as bodies for which no positive identification has been made.

In addition to the main cooler, large coroner's facilities often have a smaller cooler, located in the basement, that is used to store bodies that are in advanced stages of decomposition, or bodies that may be contaminated by insects or infestations.

In case of power loss to the facility, coolers have a backup power supply to maintain the internal temperature and therefore keep the bodies preserved at all

Cryogenic Preservation

Modern cryonic technology now allows us to store human bodies in a stable state for extremely long periods of time, by lowering their temperature to well below freezing point. In the United States a number of humans, as well as favorite cats and dogs, are now being kept in long-term cold storage in hope that one day they will be "reawakened" when science discovers a way to reverse the process.

Cryonic storage works by reducing the body's temperature very quickly immediately after death, before any form of cellular breakdown can occur. The body is first reduced to –40°F (–40°C) for temporary storage, then later cooled to –32°F (–35°C) for long-term stability, using liquid nitrogen. The freezing process must be conducted with great precision, making sure that ice crystals do not form, as these damage the vital organs.

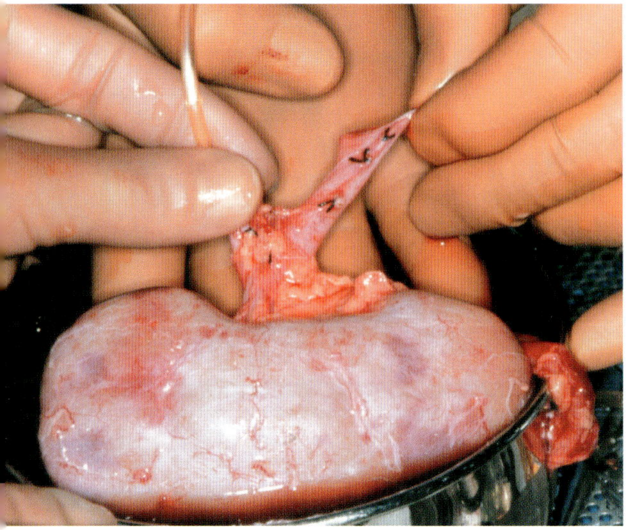

Above Donor kidney being prepared for transplant. A saline solution is passed into the kidney to maintain the functioning of its filtration system.

times. If a power outage is expected to be extensive, the coroner will call for refrigerated cargo trailers to be brought to the site, and the bodies will be transferred from the cooler to the trailers.

Unidentified Bodies

Not all bodies that arrive at the morgue are identified. Victims of fires, bodies in an advanced stage of decomposition or skeletonized remains may be labeled as "Fire Victim #1," "Fire Victim #2," or by where the body was located — for example, "Brown Street #1." The first role of the coroner's office is to establish the identity of all the victims.

Unidentified bodies may be stored indefinitely in the cooler, as there is no way of contacting next of kin, and this may present legal barriers to disposal of the remains. Many coroner's offices have one or two unidentified bodies in storage at any given time. The different methods of making a positive identification are described in detail in Chapter 6.

Organ Transplants

Sometimes, before a body arrives at the morgue, organs will already have been removed for transplants. When an individual is pronounced dead at a death scene or in hospital, or declared brain dead, modern medicine now views this as an opportunity for organ donation. Whenever it appears that the deceased may have organs suitable for transplantation because the death was recent and the body in good condition, the coroner's office contacts the organ recovery authorities and notifies them of the death. The organ recovery authorities must have permission before making a transplant, either as specified on the deceased's driving license or by contacting the next of kin and gaining their permission.

If permission is granted for an organ transplant or transplants, the organ recovery authority contacts the coroner's office to gain their approval to recover organs, and to check on any limitations due to the condition of the body or the coroner's requirements. For example, if the deceased had been shot in the chest region, the transplant team would be instructed not to touch the chest organs, but could still transplant abdominal

Transplanting Organs from the Living and the Dead		
Organ	**Sources (Donor)**	**First Successful Transplant**
Cornea	Deceased only	1905
Skin	Deceased and living	1937
Heart	Deceased only	1954
Kidney	Deceased and living	1954
Pancreas	Deceased and living (rare)	1966
Bone marrow	Deceased and living	1967
Liver	Deceased and living	1967
Heart and lung	Deceased only	1981 (partial lung)
Lung	Deceased and living	1987 (whole lung)
Hand	Deceased only	1998

organs such as liver and kidneys, or could still transplant the corneas from the eyes.

Once all the necessary permissions have been obtained the transplant team collects the body and takes it to an operating room, where the removal of organs is conducted under the same conditions as an operation on a living person. During the procedure, step-by-step photographs of the process are taken and delivered to the coroner's office, to make sure that they have everything documented for future reference.

The Most Common Transplant

The most common and most successful organ transplant is the kidney, which doctors have been able to transfer from one human to another since 1954. Kidneys can be kept alive for several days outside the body, if cool and sterile conditions are maintained. There is also the added advantage that the human body can survive with only one of its two kidneys, so a living person can become a kidney donor where necessary.

Even with kidneys, however, there remains the danger that the organ will be rejected by the immune system of the new host, because the body will recognize it as being "foreign" to itself. To counteract this effect, all donation recipients of kidneys and other organs have to take drugs that suppress the activity of the immune system ("immunosuppressants") for the remainder of their lives.

The Autopsy Room Personnel

The autopsy suite is staffed by three main groups of personnel: autopsy technicians, autopsy photographers and forensic pathologists. These three types of personnel each have specific roles and duties that come together during the examination.

Autopsy Technician

In the early hours of the morning the autopsy suite comes alive, and the autopsy technicians are the first in. The autopsy suite is headed by the chief autopsy technician and is staffed by a varying number of subordinate autopsy technicians, depending on the size of the office. They obtain the death investigation reports, prepare the paperwork for the pathologist and specifically set up the autopsy table for each death. Each case folder contains a copy of the investigation report, an examination sheet and a draft

Below Layout of the examining area in the autopsy suite.

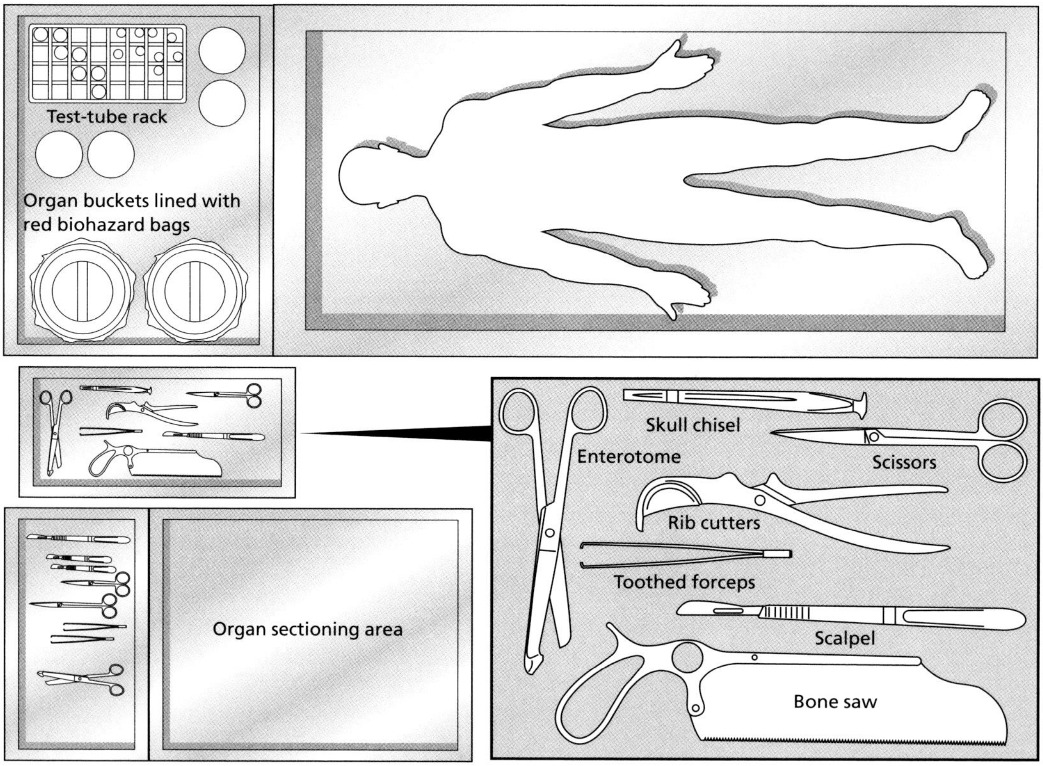

death certificate. Each examining table is set up with an organ bucket lined with a red biohazard bag, two jars filled with formaldehyde, a stock jar, a histology jar and a test-tube rack containing glass tubes of various sizes for collecting blood, bile, urine and eye fluid. At the head of the table are arranged two scalpels, scissors, forceps, a ruler and a cranial saw.

To the side of the main table is a smaller examination area where the pathologist examines the organs and cuts small sections to be placed in the jars of formaldehyde. The technician places several long knives, scalpels, scissors, a ruler and forceps in this area. Once the tables are set up, the technicians wait for the pathologist to determine which bodies will be examined and the types of examinations to be performed.

When they arrive for a shift, the autopsy technicians change from their street clothes into layers of protective clothing. They put on blue or green scrubs, a disposable apron, two layers of latex gloves, covers for their shoes, a mask and a face shield. At the start of an examination the technician takes the body from the 40°F (4°C) cooler and with the help of another technician removes it from the body bag and places it on the stainless steel examination table. Once photographs, descriptions of the clothing, and forensic evidence have been collected they then remove the clothing, placing it on large white sheets of paper. These sheets are later folded in a manner that prevents trace evidence from being lost, before being taken to a forensic lab for analysis. After a second set of photographs is taken, the technician washes the body.

Performing Dissections

Under the supervision of the pathologist, the autopsy technician cuts open the body, collects body fluids and then removes and weighs each of the internal organs. The technician also operates the X-ray machine. Once the examination has been completed by the pathologist, the technician adds a small amount of formaldehyde to the red biohazard bag containing the organs, ties the bag and places it in the chest cavity. The chest plate is put back in position and the body is sewn up. The body is then washed with cold water, toweled dry, placed back in the body bag and returned to the cooler.

After an autopsy is completed, technicians must record some basic

How to Become an Autopsy Technician

Unlike pathologists and autopsy photographers, who are formally trained prior to practicing their skills, in many jurisdictions no special training is required to become an autopsy technician. Only recently have technical schools begun to train people for this task. Most autopsy technicians enter the profession first as a summer or part-time volunteer, though some come to the coroner's office with medical or anatomical experience as former emergency medical technicians, paramedics or nurses.

Autopsy Photos in the Digital Age

Most coroner's offices have now switched completely to digital photography. The images are downloaded to the computer system's main server so that the pathologist's office computer can retrieve any image on the system to review, enlarge and print.

information, such as the weight of the organs and the amount of fluids collected, into the computer database. They pass on various items of collected evidence to the forensics lab and wash the tables, floors and walls with disinfectant. At the end of the day the aprons, gloves, mask and shoe covers are placed in a biohazard container, while the scrubs are sent off for laundering.

Autopsy Photographer

All bodies brought into the coroner's office are photographed by the autopsy photographers. Their responsibility is to document photographically the condition of the body, sites of trauma and the internal organs. Autopsy photographers are specifically trained in anatomy, physiology, ways to orient images to the anatomical body and the use of manual and digital cameras.

The autopsy photographer first takes images that document the body when it arrives at the morgue. Full-length images of the body are taken, front and back, which may be required later if identity comes into question. If the victim has ECG patches or intravenous (IV) lines, or has been given an endotracheal tube (ETT) to help airflow to the lungs, these are documented. Full-length front and back views of the body are taken again after the clothing has been removed. The body is then washed with cold water, wiped dry and photographed again. Close-up views are taken of wounds, bullet holes, fractures, surgical scars and other identifiable marks such as tattoos. The documentation of scars and tattoos is important in helping to identify the body, and is done at the same time as all the factors that might be involved in the cause of death are recorded.

During the autopsy the organs of the body are photographed twice: first in situ to document the location and severity of disease, and second after they have been removed and cleaned.

The photographer is frequently guided by the pathologist in taking the images. Over a period of time injuries, especially bruises, might disappear or change in appearance, while human memory fades. Pathologists may conduct over 300 autopsies a year, and it is impossible to remember the details of each case. For this reason the autopsy photographer's work is crucial.

The images taken during the scene investigation and the autopsy may also

Opposite A cadaver laid out on the slab with formaldehyde-filled stock jars, and scales for weighing organs in the background.

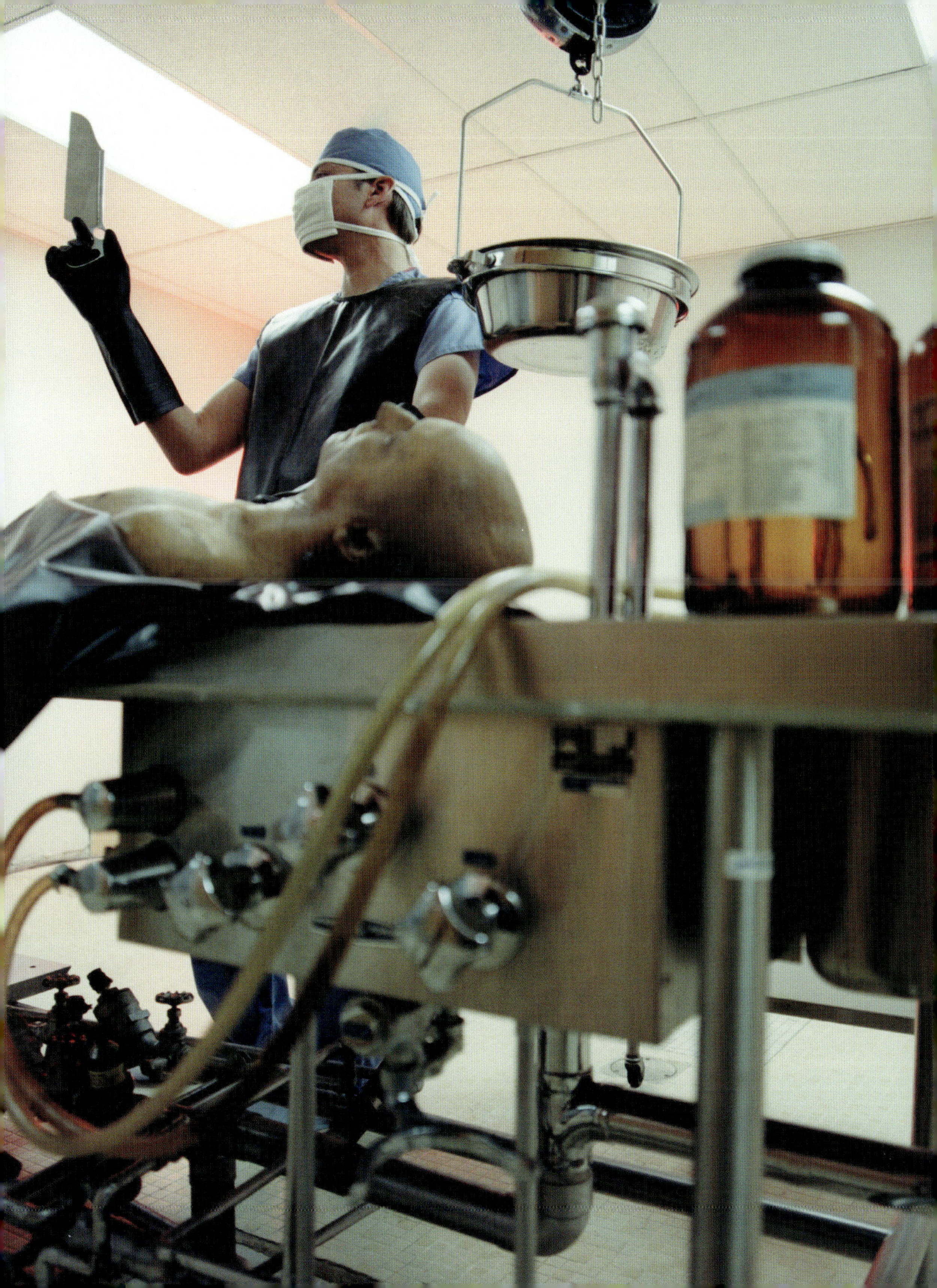

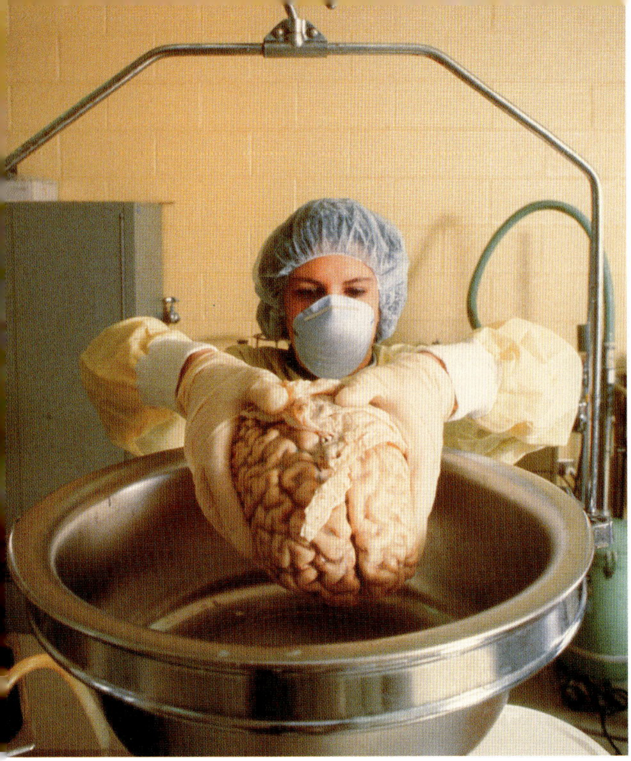

Above The autopsy technician weighs the brain as part of the postmortem procedure.

serve as evidence in criminal or civil trials. When forensic pathologists are called to testify as to the cause and manner of death, they often employ images to help illustrate the way the individual died. The photographic department helps the pathologist select the best images to use, highlights the images with arrows and prints the images to the size requested.

Photographs can readily display information too small to be seen by the unaided eye, such as the cancerous cells of a tumor, or objects too distant or out of sight from normal view, such as aerial photographs of a crime scene. They can even be used to show things that would otherwise be totally invisible because the human eye is not sensitive to the wavelengths involved, such as infrared or ultraviolet images.

Forensic Pathologist

The central figure in the autopsy suite is the forensic pathologist. It is the pathologist's responsibility to decide whether a complete autopsy is required (both external and internal) or just an external examination, and then to carry out this process to determine the cause and manner of death. *Cause of death* refers to the physical fact that caused the body to cease functioning and refers to the way in which this occurred, such as repeated blows from a blunt instrument. *Cause of death* refers to the classification of mechanisms that ultimately resulted in the individual's demise, for example, "severe cranial trauma." *Manner of death* refers to a classification of how those mechanisms occurred — by means natural, suicidal, accidental, homicidal or undetermined.

A forensic pathologist is a physician with specialized training in anatomic and clinical pathology. Anatomic pathology is concerned with the diagnosis of disease based on gross and microscopic examination of cells and tissues. Clinical pathology is the microscopic study of blood, urine and other body fluids to determine the levels of chemicals in the body. Clinical pathology also looks at the body's biochemical processes, such as hormone and enzyme production. To become a forensic pathologist, the physician must take an additional year of forensics training conducted in a large coroner's office, then pass a national examination in order to become a board-certified forensic pathologist. There are currently about 700 certified forensic pathologists in the United States.

Types of Pathologists

There are basically three types of pathologists: hospital, clinical and forensic. A hospital pathologist practices *anatomic pathology*, looking at the anatomy of cells, tissues and organs for evidence of disease (*pathology*). Thus, the hospital pathologist looks at cells (*cytology*) — in slide preparations such as Pap smears and in fine-needle samples — and at surgically removed specimens and tissue biopsies (*histology*). They might also occasionally perform non-coroner hospital autopsies. The primary instrument of the hospital pathologist is the microscope; however, a pathologist can tell much about a specimen by simple visual inspection — in fact, all examinations begin with this *gross pathology* inspection.

A clinical pathologist investigates cells, tissues and body fluids through laboratory testing. Thus, clinical pathologists typically take a leading role in the hospital clinical chemistry laboratory, microbiology laboratory, hematology laboratory, blood bank and genetic laboratory.

Finally, forensic pathology is the application of pathology to medico-legal questions. The primary tool of the forensic pathologist is the autopsy. As hospital pathologists have significantly decreased their performance of routine autopsies, the main expertise for autopsy examinations now resides within the forensic pathology community. Typically, forensic pathologists practice their profession as medical examiners, but they may also practice as independent consultants to prosecutors and criminal defense attorneys, or as hospital pathologists performing some forensic autopsies as an occasional adjunct to their regular practice.

FORENSIC PATHOLOGIST VS. CORONER

- The forensic pathologist is specially trained to examine a body to determine the cause and manner of death.
- A forensic pathologist can also be hired to perform private autopsies and to testify in court.
- The coroner is typically a lay individual appointed or elected to oversee the operation of the coroner's office.
- Coroners hire forensic pathologists to conduct examinations.

Preparing for the Autopsy

Before beginning an autopsy the forensic pathologist is provided by the autopsy technician with copies of all the necessary reports and records. The actual examination will also require an autopsy cover sheet (containing basic information about the deceased), a working copy of the final autopsy report to be used by the pathologist while conducting the examination, and a draft copy of the death certificate.

The pathologist may also go to the crime scene, before or after the autopsy, to help create a scientific reconstruction of the events leading to death. Visiting the scene may be critical in identifying inconsistencies discovered later during the investigation and autopsy.

External or Complete Examination?

When a body is brought to the morgue it will undergo one of two types of autopsy: either an external examination only, or a complete examination that covers both external and internal aspects (each of these will be described in detail in Chapters 3 and 4 respectively).

The pathologist has various factors to consider in deciding which type of examination should be performed:

1. The type of case is the most critical factor. The forensic pathologist reviews information contained in the death investigation report, police reports and medical records. Office protocol usually requires that certain types of cases, such as homicide, motor vehicle accident, overdose, industrial accident and medical misadventure, automatically receive a complete postmortem examination. However, the pathologist must choose which type of examination to apply when the case is a suicide or natural death. Suicide by either hanging or gunshot through-and-through is typically only given external examination. Deaths that appear to be from natural causes of illness and have a well-documented medical history are also likely to receive external examinations only.

2. The family may express strong opposition to a complete autopsy. The next of kin may know that the deceased had expressed feelings against an autopsy, or they may themselves be opposed to the examination. However, the pathologist must weigh the family's wishes against the legal ramifications of not conducting an autopsy.

3. The postmortem examination may be opposed for religious reasons. For example, if the victim is an Orthodox Jew, a rabbi may need to be present during the examination. Muslims

☐ CITY ☐ COUNTY
DATE ____________
TIME ______ HRS.
☐ A.M. ☐ P.M.

EXTERNAL EXAMINATION

OFFICE OF THE CORONER

☐ NATURAL ☐ ACCIDENT
☐ SUICIDE ☐ PENDING
COMMENT ____________
☐ DICTATED

NAME: ______________________________ AGE ________
LAST FIRST M.I.

HEIGHT ____________ in.
WEIGHT ________ pounds

☐ WHITE ☐ BLACK ☐ INDIAN ☐ OTHER ☐ CLOTHED ☐ PARTLY CLOTHED ☐ NAKED
☐ SCARS ☐ TATTOO ☐ OTHER IDENTIFYING MARKS ____________

PROBABLE CAUSE OF DEATH ______________________________ ☐

PRESERVATION
☐ good
☐ early decomposition
☐ putrid
☐ skeletonized

TEMPERATURE
☐ warm ☐ cool
☐ cold ☐ frozen

RIGOR
☐ absent ☐ moderate
☐ marked ☐ lysed

LIVOR
☐ absent
☐ purple ☐ pink
☐ ventral ☐ dorsal
☐ fixed ☐ non-fixed

NUTRITION
☐ adequate ☐ obese
☐ cachetic ☐ jaundice
☐ ascites ☐ edema
☐ cyanosis

EYES
☐ brown ☐ blue
☐ hazel ☐ other
☐ arcus senilis
☐ cataract ☐ OD ☐ OS

PUPILS
LEFT ______ cm
RIGHT ______ cm

HAIR
☐ black ☐ brown
☐ red ☐ blond
☐ bald ☐ dyed
☐ gray ☐ other
☐ moustache
☐ beard
☐ upper teeth
☐ lower teeth

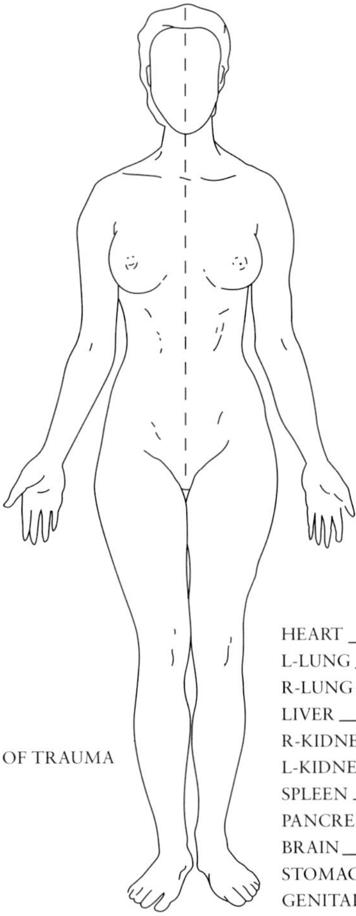

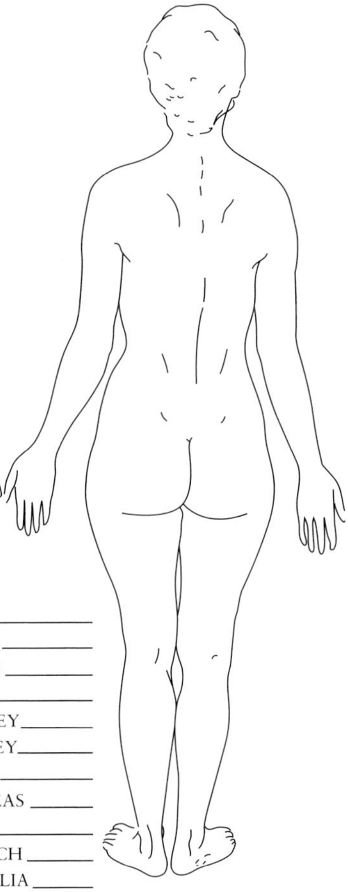

HEART ________
L-LUNG ________
R-LUNG ________
LIVER ________
R-KIDNEY ________
L-KIDNEY ________
SPLEEN ________
PANCREAS ________
BRAIN ________
STOMACH ________
GENITALIA ________

☐ EXTERNAL SIGNS OF TRAUMA
☐ contusions (C)
☐ abrasions (A)
☐ lacerations (L)
☐ punctures (P)
☐ incisions (I)
☐ amputations (---)
☐ fractures (xx)
☐ gunshot wounds

TOXICOLOGY
☐ heart blood urine ☐ CSF ☐ other ________
OTHER TRACE EVIDENCE ____________
PROSECUTOR ____________

Above Sample external examination sheet used by the forensic pathologist for female cadavers.

are generally opposed to autopsy altogether. While forensic pathologists are respectful of these religious beliefs, they must once again consider their legal obligation to determine the cause and manner of death.

Post-autopsy Procedures

After completion of the autopsy the pathologist has to fill in the autopsy cover sheet, the draft death certificate and the autopsy protocol. The working copy of the death certificate is then given to the senior death investigator, who fills in the official state certificate of death. Most states require that the death certificate, even if it reports cause of death as "pending," must be completed within 72 hours of the discovery of a body.

The forensic pathologist also completes a final autopsy report, which is a detailed document containing descriptions of all aspects of the body examined, right down to specific organs, organ systems and other body parts. The last pages of the report describe the results gleaned from microscopic and chemical lab analyses.

The information detailed in the final autopsy report yields the cause and manner of death to be assigned on the death certificate. This is a legal conclusion by the forensic pathologist, and may determine whether an individual is charged with a crime, is sued for civil negligence or receives insurance benefits.

QUESTIONS TO BE ANSWERED IN THE AUTOPSY

- WHO is the deceased?
- WHERE did the injuries and ensuing death occur?
- WHEN did the death occur?
- WHAT injuries are present (type, distribution, pattern, cause and direction)?
- WHICH injuries are significant (major vs. minor injuries, true vs. postmortem injuries)?
- WHY and HOW were the injuries produced? What were the mechanisms causing the injuries and the actual manner of causation?
- WHAT actually caused the death?

The Pathologist in Court

The forensic pathologist's job is not necessarily over once the death certificate and autopsy report are signed and finalized. Where criminal charges are involved, a few months or years later the case will go to trial. The forensic pathologist, considered to be an expert witness, will be required to testify regarding the facts of the case, especially the cause and manner of death. He or she is also allowed to give opinions in response to hypothetical questions.

☐ CITY ☐ COUNTY
DATE ________
TIME ______ HRS.
☐ A.M. ☐ P.M.

EXTERNAL EXAMINATION

OFFICE OF THE CORONER

☐ NATURAL ☐ ACCIDENT
☐ SUICIDE ☐ PENDING
COMMENT ________
☐ DICTATED

NAME: ______________________ (LAST FIRST M.I.) AGE ______

☐ WHITE ☐ BLACK ☐ INDIAN ☐ OTHER ☐ CLOTHED ☐ PARTLY CLOTHED ☐ NAKED
☐ SCARS ☐ TATTOO ☐ OTHER IDENTIFYING MARKS ________

PROBABLE CAUSE OF DEATH ______________________ ☐

HEIGHT ________ in.
WEIGHT ________ pounds

PRESERVATION
☐ good
☐ early decomposition
☐ putrid
☐ skeletonized

TEMPERATURE
☐ warm ☐ cool
☐ cold ☐ frozen

RIGOR
☐ absent ☐ moderate
☐ marked ☐ lysed

LIVOR
☐ absent
☐ purple ☐ pink
☐ ventral ☐ dorsal
☐ fixed ☐ non-fixed

NUTRITION
☐ adequate ☐ obese
☐ cachetic ☐ jaundice
☐ ascites ☐ edema
☐ cyanosis

EYES
☐ brown ☐ blue
☐ hazel ☐ other
☐ arcus senilis
☐ cataract ☐ OD ☐ OS

PUPILS
LEFT ______ cm
RIGHT ______ cm

HAIR
☐ black ☐ brown
☐ red ☐ blond
☐ bald ☐ dyed
☐ gray ☐ other
☐ moustache
☐ beard
☐ upper teeth
☐ lower teeth

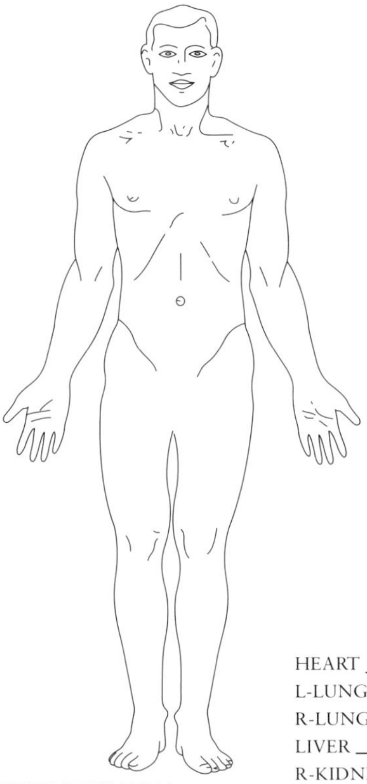

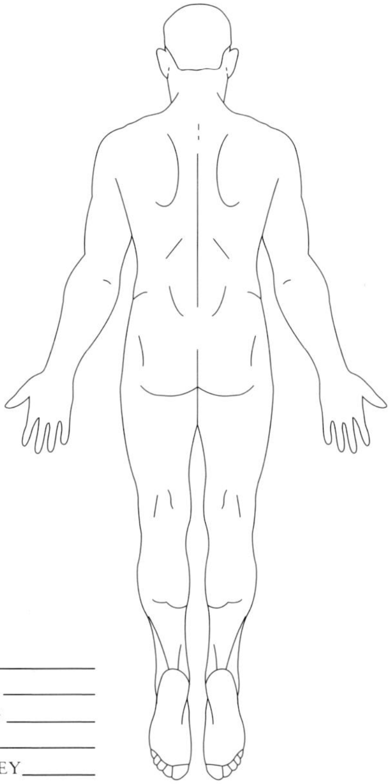

HEART ________
L-LUNG ________
R-LUNG ________
LIVER ________
R-KIDNEY ________
L-KIDNEY ________
SPLEEN ________
PANCREAS ________
BRAIN ________
STOMACH ________
GENITALIA ________

☐ EXTERNAL SIGNS OF TRAUMA
☐ contusions (C)
☐ abrasions (A)
☐ lacerations (L)
☐ punctures (P)
☐ incisions (I)
☐ amputations (---)
☐ fractures (xx)
☐ gunshot wounds

TOXICOLOGY
☐ heart blood urine ☐ CSF ☐ other ________
OTHER TRACE EVIDENCE ________
PROSECUTOR

Above Sample external examination sheet used by the forensic pathologist for male cadavers.

Real-Life Forensics: Cases Gone Wrong

Unfortunately, there are times when suspicious or unexplained deaths have not been properly investigated. There are cases when an autopsy is not performed, but should have been, or when the autopsy is performed in an incomplete or inaccurate manner — or even by a person who does not possess the appropriate skills and training. The following pages describe examples of such cases and the consequences of failure to scientifically determine cause and manner of death.

Above Warren Commission investigators went to the room in the Texas Schoolbook Depository from which Lee Harvey Oswald was alleged to have fired the fatal shots. Tests with a rifle scope showed how he could have targeted the president in his open car.

ASSASSINATION OF PRESIDENT JOHN F. KENNEDY 1963

> The Death

On November 22, 1963, President John F. Kennedy was assassinated in Dallas, Texas. He was pronounced dead at Parkland Memorial Hospital. The Warren Commission Report concluded that the president was killed by a lone gunman, shooting from behind and striking the president twice. Even after 43 years, however, there is still strong disagreement about the exact anatomic locations of the gunshot wounds.

> The Cause of Dispute or Controversy

The first controversy occurred when the dead president's body was removed from the county where the death occurred. In contravention of Texas law, the body was flown to Bethesda Naval Hospital in Maryland, near Washington, DC. The autopsy was then performed by hospital pathologists with no training or experience in forensic pathology.

The number of shots fired and the position of the shooter or shooters remained in doubt. Based on eyewitness statements there appeared to be a shooter located in front and to the right of the motorcade, but these doubts were never resolved because the locations and pathways of the wounds were not precisely recorded. The brain was not sectioned and examined according to coroner's practices, nor were adequate and appropriate photographs and X rays taken of the wounds. Slides and photographs that were taken — of Kennedy's chest and skin wounds — later went missing. Finally, the government refused to release the investigative reports, photographs, X rays and microscopic slides related to the assassination. The findings of the Warren Commission Report in 1964, stating that Lee Harvey Oswald had acted along in killing the president, did not succeed in dissipating the ongoing sense of subterfuge.

> The Consequences

- Continuing controversy regarding the assassination after more than 40 years, with rejection of the official governmental report by three-fourths of the U.S. public.
- Mistrust and lack of confidence in the federal government.

1969 MARY JO KOPECHNE

> The Death

On July 18, 1969, Senator Ted Kennedy, Mary Jo Kopechne, friends of Kennedy and members of Robert Kennedy's campaign staff were attending a party in Chappaquiddick, at Martha's Vineyard, Massachusetts. That evening, around 11:15 p.m., Ted Kennedy offered to drive Mary Jo Kopechne to the ferry. He later claimed that he was unfamiliar with the road, and that this resulted in his vehicle going off the side of a small, single-lane wooden bridge and into the water. The vehicle landed on its roof. Kennedy was able to escape, but his passenger did not.

> The Cause of Dispute or Controversy

Kennedy did not report the accident immediately, but instead summoned friends to help in attempts to retrieve Kopechne from the car. He then returned to his hotel, and did not report the accident until the next morning, by which time the police had already found the body in his car. For this Kennedy would later receive a suspended two-month jail term for leaving the scene of an accident.

The state deputy medical examiner examined Kopechne's body at the scene after she was removed from the car, and noted no evidence of trauma. He therefore ruled that the death was due to drowning, and no autopsy was performed. During the embalming process, however, the lack of water in the lungs suggested the possibility of death by suffocation, not drowning. Nonetheless, the body was transported to another jurisdiction and buried, since Kopechne's parents had by this time filed an injunction against any further postmortem examination. Formal legal actions to have the body exhumed and autopsied were repeatedly rejected.

> The Consequences

- Exact cause of death was never scientifically established.
- Personal and professional harm to Senator Kennedy.
- Significant emotional trauma for the deceased's family.
- Loss of public confidence in the criminal justice system.

VINCENT FOSTER JR. 1993

> The Death

Vincent Foster Jr. was White House deputy counsel and a close friend of both President Bill Clinton and Hillary Clinton. On July 20, 1993, his body was found in Fort Marcy Park, just outside Washington, DC, with an apparent gunshot wound to the head. According to Park Police a .38 Colt revolver was found in his right hand. The death was ruled a suicide. The autopsy report concluded that Foster died of a single gunshot entering the roof of the mouth and exiting the back of the skull. A suicide note was discovered 36 hours after the discovery of the body.

> The Cause of Dispute or Controversy

A thorough, diligent, and immediate scene investigation by trained criminalists and experienced homicide detectives was not undertaken. The U.S. Park Police who examined the body were not equipped for or trained in homicide investigation. There were disputes over the location of the weapon, and an early witness claimed that there was no weapon at the scene. The position of the body was inconsistent with a suicide. The bullet was never found, and there was a lack of blood or brain matter at the scene. No metallic fragments were recovered from the head, and carpet fibers discovered on the body were never examined. FBI analysis of the weapon failed to find any trace of blood, and this was never explained.

The autopsy was performed using defective X ray equipment, and the crime scene photographs appear to have been lost. One more crucial omission was not to have the body examined immediately at the scene in order to determine the most likely time of death and confirm the place of death.

> The Consequences

- Considerable speculation, conjecture, rumors and outright allegations of cover-up directed at President Clinton.
- Severe emotional trauma for the deceased's wife and children.
- Damaged reputations for numerous government and professional individuals.
- Perceived subversion of the criminal justice system.

1996 RON BROWN

> The Death

On April 3, 1996, Ron Brown, the U.S. secretary of commerce, a prominent African-American political figure and close friend of the Clintons, died during the crash of an airplane carrying more than 30 people on an official tour of Bosnia-Herzegovina. The body was brought to Dover Air Force Base, Delaware, for examination by forensic pathologists at the Armed Forces Institute of Pathology. They declared that Brown died from trauma due to the crash and, ignoring a suspicious hole in the skull, ruled the death to be an accident. No autopsy was conducted on the body.

Above Ron Brown at the podium, representing the United States Department of Commerce.

> The Cause of Dispute or Controversy

Despite the gross observation by an experienced military forensic pathologist that a defect at the top of Ron Brown's head bore all the external characteristics of a gunshot entrance wound, an official decision was made not to perform a complete postmortem examination. In fact, that pathologist was subsequently disciplined when he publicly expressed the basis for his concern and his disagreement with the decision not to perform an autopsy. No exit wound was located, and a bullet may have been lodged in the abdominal region. Some forensic pathologists felt that Brown's injuries were not serious enough to cause death, and that he might have survived the actual crash.

> The Consequences

- Controversy to this day as to whether Ron Brown's death was a government conspiracy.
- Serious blight on the professional reputation of various armed forces forensic personnel.
- Great suspicion within the African-American community throughout the United States, and loss of confidence in the U.S. government.
- Subversion of the medico-legal investigative system.

ANTHONY PROVIANO

1997

> The Death

On December 28, 1997, Anthony Proviano, a medical student traveling from Cincinnati to his family home in Pittsburgh for Christmas holidays, was found dead on a hillside behind the hotel where he had checked in the evening before. During his stay at the hotel he had befriended a female prostitute who was also a self-confessed heroin user. Proviano was discovered on an abandoned road near the motel with an apparent gunshot wound to his chest and a .25 caliber pistol approximately 100 feet from his body.

Above A police sketch of the man last seen with Proviano, Doug Main. Main would later be implicated in Proviano's murder.

> The Cause of Dispute or Controversy

The local Ohio County coroner ruled the death a suicide and refused to order an autopsy. The family arranged for a private autopsy, and the forensic pathologist concluded that the manner of death was most probably homicide. Examination of the hands, not conducted during the initial investigation, revealed gunshot powder residue. After years of investigative pressuring, the manner of death was officially changed from suicide to "undetermined." A newly elected coroner later changed this to homicide, and murder charges were eventually filed against the prostitute and her husband. She was convicted in a trial by jury, though the charges against her husband were dismissed.

> The Consequences

- Prolonged suffering for the victim's family.
- Great financial expense to the family and various government agencies.
- Loss of confidence in the legal system.

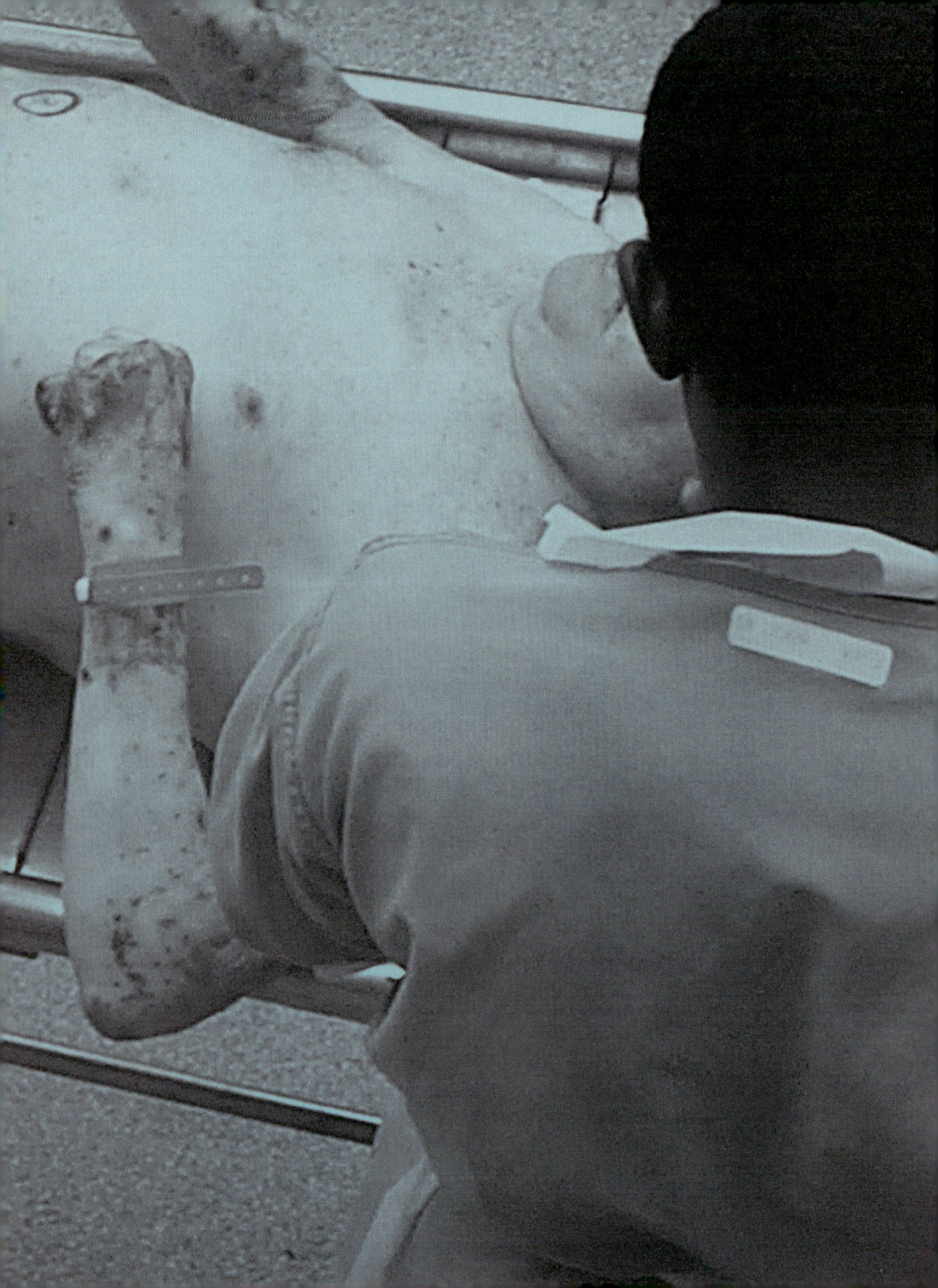

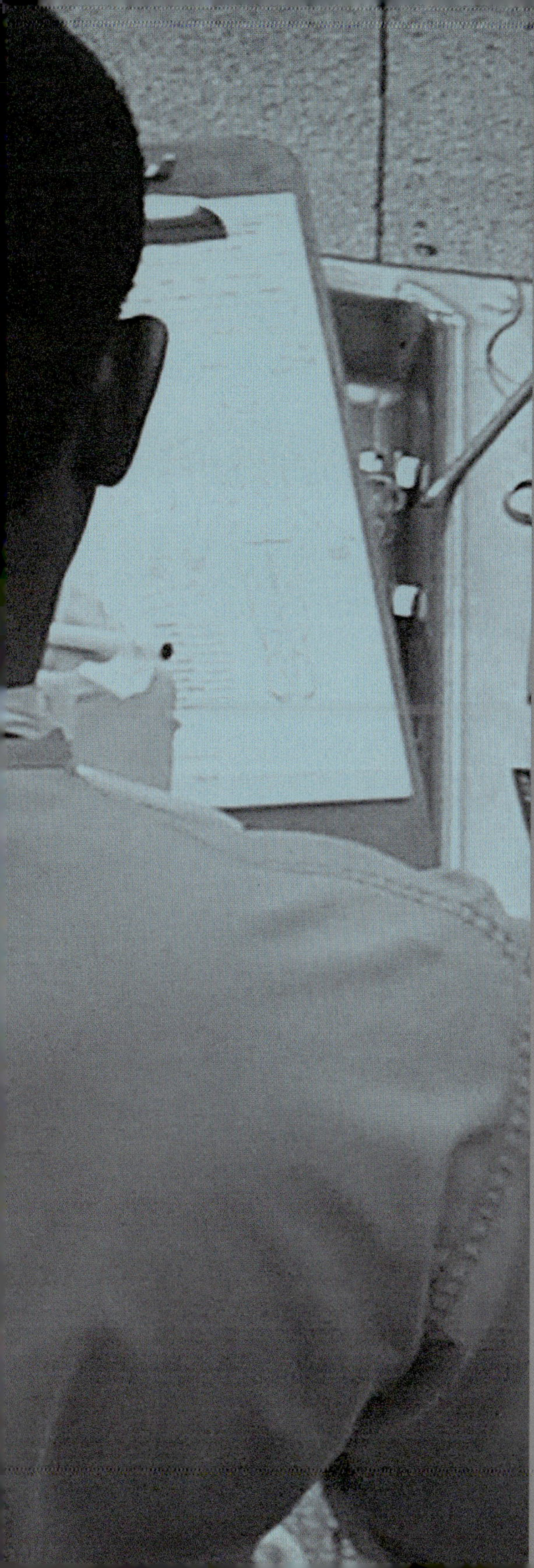

Chapter 3

The External Examination

The external examination is a detailed process of visual detective work, reading the symptoms of the body's surface to draw conclusions about the victim's fate. In many cases, the external examination will be enough to make a reasonable decision about cause and manner of death, though in some cases it will reveal suspicious signs that suggest the need for a full internal autopsy.

The External Examination Process

The goal of the external examination is to create a complete descriptive record of how a body appears at the time of the autopsy. Before actually examining the body, the forensic team follows a detailed process for photographing the body and documenting the clothing. There then follows the full head-to-toe physical description of the body and, finally, any other special forensic processes that are required according to the case. All bodies receive an external examination regardless of the type of autopsy ultimately decided upon.

Pre-autopsy Photographs and Clothing Description

The examination begins by removing the body from the cooler and placing it on the examination table. The body is then photographed according to a strict protocol, as mentioned in Chapter 2.

Death Rejoices

Following a medical tradition, postmortem examination rooms in Western countries often have a sign on the door reading "*Hic locus est ubi mors gaudet succurrere vitae.*" This Latin inscription translates as: "This place is where death rejoices to teach the living," a reference to the vast amount of medical knowledge that we have obtained from examining dead bodies.

The body is first photographed head to toe as it arrived from the scene. The following images are also taken: an overall image of the body faceup and facedown, and a close-up of the head. The body is then rolled onto its side and the back and buttock areas are examined and photographed.

If there is forensic evidence on the body or the clothing, that evidence is collected prior to removal of the clothing. The examination and description of the clothing includes noting its condition, such as wet, dry or dirty, the presence of any odors, and tears or holes. The clothing is removed layer by layer, and each layer is described in terms of the type of clothing, color and condition. The pants and shirt pockets are searched for evidence by the autopsy technicians. In cases of homicide the clothing is wrapped up in white paper sheets and taken to a forensic science lab for processing. If the death is non-suspicious, the clothing is placed in a brown paper bag and given to the funeral director when the body is taken away for last rites.

After all the clothing has been removed and documented, the body is then photographed again.

Opposite The autopsy photographer uses a step-ladder to get a good view of the whole body from above.

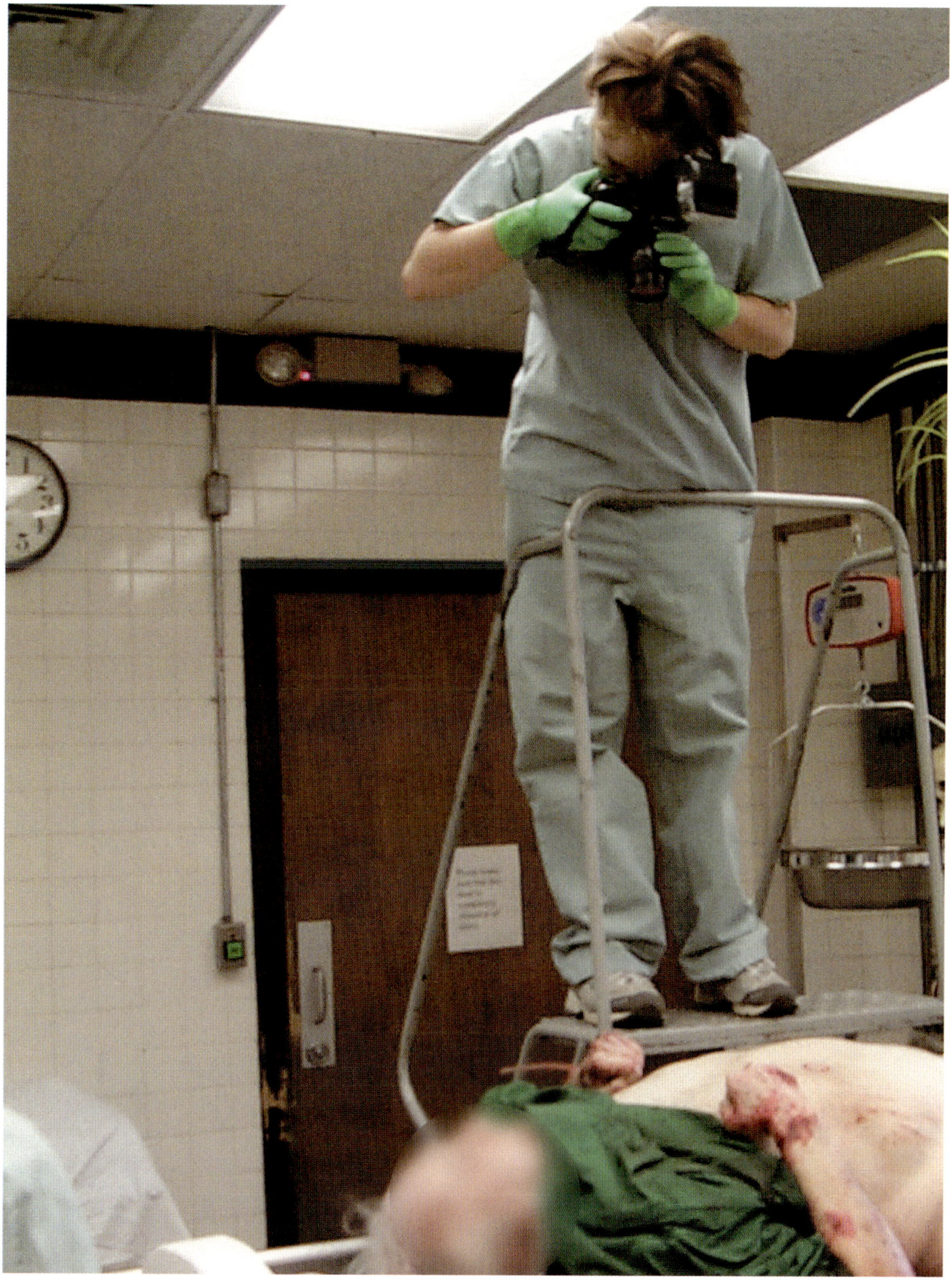

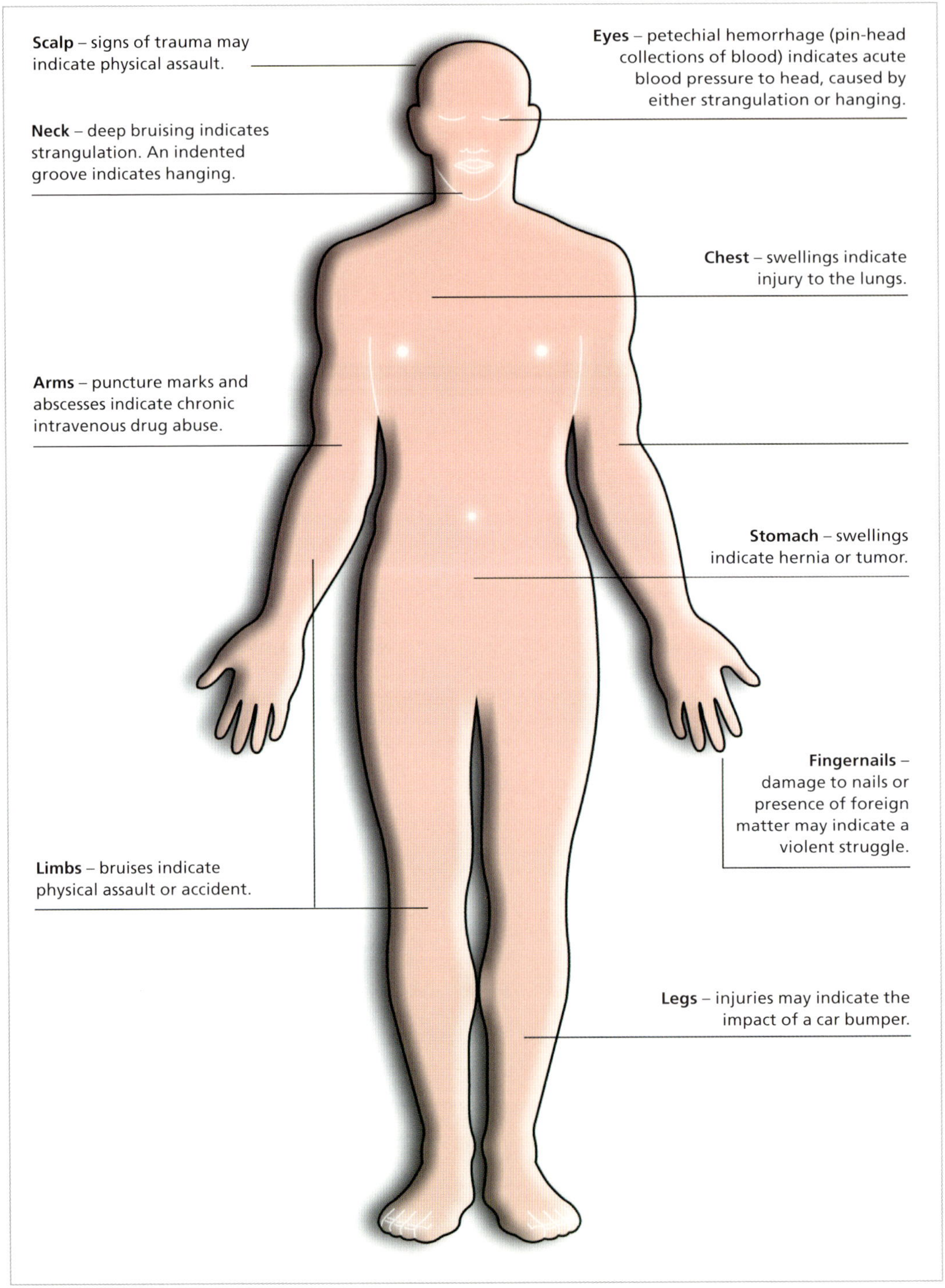
Scalp – signs of trauma may indicate physical assault.
Neck – deep bruising indicates strangulation. An indented groove indicates hanging.
Arms – puncture marks and abscesses indicate chronic intravenous drug abuse.
Limbs – bruises indicate physical assault or accident.
Eyes – petechial hemorrhage (pin-head collections of blood) indicates acute blood pressure to head, caused by either strangulation or hanging.
Chest – swellings indicate injury to the lungs.
Stomach – swellings indicate hernia or tumor.
Fingernails – damage to nails or presence of foreign matter may indicate a violent struggle.
Legs – injuries may indicate the impact of a car bumper.

The Body Examination

The now naked body is given an overall desciption by the forensic pathologist in terms of body development, state of preservation, body temperature and level of nutrition.

Body development

This refers to the physical development of the body, using descriptive terms such as *skinny*, *muscular* and *overweight*.

State of preservation

Preservation of the body is described as *good*, *early decomposition*, *putrid* or *skeletonized*, and any areas of skin slippage are noted.

Body temperature

Temperature is noted in general terms such as *warm*, *cool*, *frozen* or *cold*.

Nutrition

The level of nutrition is described as *undernourished* or *emaciated*, *adequate*, *well-nourished*, *obese* or *morbidly obese*.

The pathologist also notes rigor, livor and algor mortis displayed by the body (see Chapter 1). The full external examination then begins, starting at the head, working down the neck and torso to the groin area, then examining each of the limbs, from shoulders and hips right down to the fingers and toes.

Head

Starting at the head, the hair is described by color, length and grooming. If a moustache or beard is present, its color and length are noted and described. The pathologist opens the eyelids and documents the color and pupil size of the eyes. Signs of petechial hemorrhage will also be checked for on and around the eyes and face. Petechial hemorrhages are small pinhead-sized collections of blood caused by an acute increase in venous pressure that in turn causes rupture of the thin-walled venules. The presence of petechial hemorrhages is a classic sign of death from asphyxiation, compression of the neck or strangulation — any of which would result in extreme blood pressure in the head. But these signs may also be found in some natural deaths, so the forensic pathologist must be careful not to overinterpret this finding.

Next the pathologist examines the nose for fractures and foreign bodies, then the lips are checked for signs of recent trauma and pulled back to expose and examine the teeth. The upper and lower dentures are described in terms of whether teeth are natural or artificial, overall condition and any particular dental work. The oral cavity is examined for foreign material and the presence of trauma to the tongue. Finally, the pathologist carefully feels the head for

Vitreous Humor Potassium Level

The eyeball contains a clear fluid called vitreous humor. Normally in a living person this fluid contains a low level of potassium. After death the potassium level increases, so forensic testing of this factor can help determine time of death.

The vitreous humor has testing advantages over the other body fluids because it is isolated from other systems of the body, and hence less susceptible to rapid chemical changes and contamination.

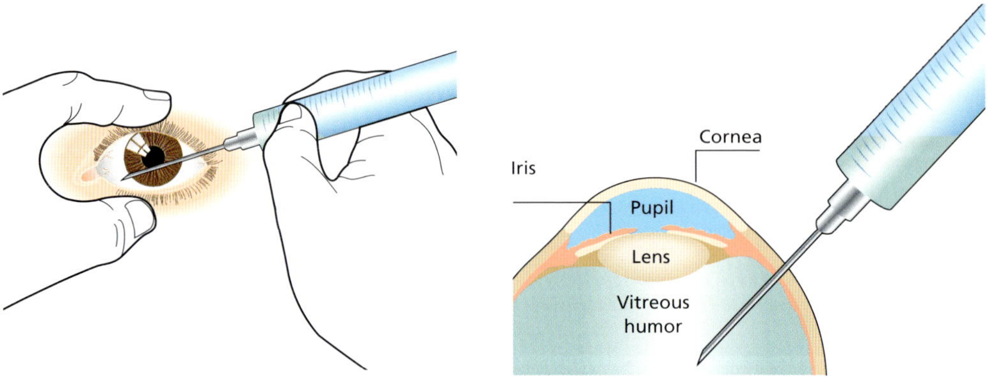

Above Samples of the vitreous humor are removed from the eyeball using a fine-bore syringe.

any lumps, deformity or trauma that may be visually obscured by the hair. To miss such a detail could undermine the findings of the autopsy altogether.

Neck and Torso

When the head has been completely examined, the neck region is checked for symmetry, deformity, fractures or other signs of trauma. Moving down, the pathologist examines the chest region for anything unusual. Sometimes one side of the chest will be swollen; this may be a sign of a tension pneumothorax, an injury to the lungs that allows air to enter the chest cavity with each breath but does not allow air to escape. In the abdominal examination the pathologist will once again look for swelling or bulges, and also check for solid masses by manually kneading the region. Abdominal swelling can be a sign of gas production, whereas a mass could be a possible tumor or a hernia. The pelvic region and external genitals are examined next, and any trauma is noted and described in detail. Bruises discovered during the examination may have a major impact on the course and type of further examination, as they usually suggest the infliction of blunt-force trauma on the victim.

Opposite The forensic pathologist records the entire external examination it progresses.

Signs of Strangulation

The key external features of manual strangulation are deep bruising to the neck region. Internally, the key feature is fracture of the hyoid bone. The hyoid bone is a U-shaped bone above the thyroid cartilage in the neck. Severe pressure to the neck typically fractures this bone, most frequently in cases of manual strangulation.

Diagnosing Carbon Monoxide Poisoning

Individuals who commit suicide by carbon monoxide poisoning display a classic bright cherry-red discoloration of the skin. Carbon monoxide binds to hemoglobin molecules in the blood, and does so far more powerfully than oxygen molecules. Therefore, oxygen is prevented from binding to the hemoglobin, resulting in death from lack of oxygen.

Signs of Hanging

A detailed external examination of individuals who die by hanging (usually a case of suicide) can reveal several key findings. The groove in the neck will have an imprint or impression of the type of rope used, while the angle of this groove can aid in determining the position of the body. The presence and location of petechial hemorrhages could differentiate a partially suspended victim from an individual who was completely suspended. In cases where the body is completely suspended, blood flow is totally obstructed to the brain so that there is neither swelling

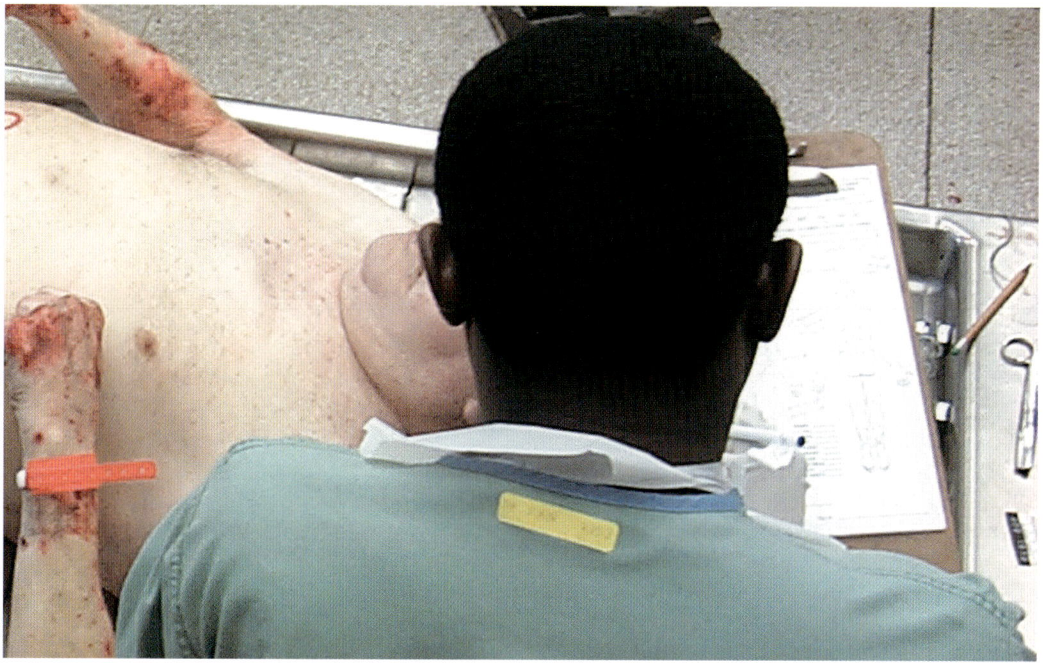

STATES OF PRESERVATION

- **Immediately after death**
  Life is expired, but the muscles are still warm and flexible; blood is still evenly distributed around the body and chemical breakdown has not noticeably commenced.
- **Cool and rigid**
  Limbs become rigid; body temperature begins to decrease toward the ambient temperature but is still well preserved.
- **Early decomposition**
  Skin shrinks, making it seem as if the hair and nails are still growing.
- **Infestation**
  Rigidity dissipated; insects begin to gather and lay eggs.
- **Advanced decomposition**
  Internal tissues decaying; maggots hatch and grow.
- **Bloating**
  Stomach swells due to accumulation of gas; this can also cause a dark liquid to be discharged from the nose and mouth of the corpse; body exudes an intense and unpleasant odor.
- **Extreme decay**
  Body shape becomes grossly distorted; face dark purple or green and tongue protruding.
- **Disintegration**
  All soft tissue loses its form, converting into liquids and gases.
- **Skeleton**
  All soft tissues have disappeared; insect and animal life has moved away; only bones and teeth remain.

nor petechial hemorrhage above the noose. When the hanging is partially suspended (i.e., feet still touching the ground), the pressure does not totally close the arteries, so the face typically displays congestion, edema and bulging eyes, with petechial hemorrhages on the face.

Limbs

The extremities are examined next, starting with the shoulders and working down to the fingers. The fingernails are specifically examined and described in terms of length, presence of debris and presence of polish. Presence of debris under the fingernails may suggest some sort of struggle before death, and where the debris is biological material resulting from a struggle with an assailant, it may provide crucial DNA evidence. In addition, broken or missing fingernails are noted. Next, the legs and toenails are examined in the same manner as the arms and fingernails.

Very occasionally the poisonous bite of a snake or spider may have played a part in the cause of death. As well as showing up later in toxicological analysis and microscopic examination of organs, these bites can also be discovered in the external examination of the limbs, where they will appear as tiny puncture marks. Similarly, intravenous drug abuse, as well as showing up in toxicological analysis, will typically reveal injection marks in the arms or legs. Chronic intravenous drug abuse will typically show up in abscesses and other deformations of the skin.

Skin Slippage

Skin slippage is when the outer layer of skin comes off the body when pulled. This effect is often seen on bodies that are in an advanced stage of decomposition, usually 2–3 weeks after death. However, skin slippage cannot be taken as a direct indicator of time of death, as the time taken for it to occur depends greatly on ambient heat and humidity.

In cases of homicide and assault, the external examination of the limbs may also occasionally reveal the most horrific symptoms of all: signs of torture. Cigarette burns, scalding from hot water and electrical burns are among the symptoms of torture that the pathologist may encounter.

Medical Treatment

The next item noted is evidence of recent medical treatment, such as surgical scars. This might also include endotracheal tubes helping air reach the lungs, electrocardiogram electrodes and intravenous catheters. In some cases the forensic pathologist might have allowed the removal of organs or other tissues for the purpose of transplant prior to arrival at the morgue. The transplant team must record the condition of any organs (e.g., eyes, heart valves) or tissues (e.g., long bones or skin) that they remove, and pass these records on to the forensic pathologist.

Gun-Related Examination

In cases involving gun violence, special processing will be required to reveal the details of these events. For example, if the victim suffered a self-inflicted gunshot wound, the region may be X-rayed. The reason for this would be to document how the projectile (bullet) went through the body, to show the location of fractures and the bones involved and the presence and location of any residual foreign materials.

If a firearm was discharged at the scene, gunshot residue testing is conducted on the victim. When an individual discharges a firearm, the burned and unburned powder deposits on the firing hand, the clothing and possibly on the victim if close enough. The test for the presence of these fine particles is carried out with an atomic absorption analysis kit, which detects elements from the bullet primer such as barium and antimony on the hand that fired a weapon. This residue is removed by swabbing the back and palm of both hands using a small cotton swab saturated with 5 percent nitric acid. These cotton tips are then analyzed for the presence or absence of the elements in question.

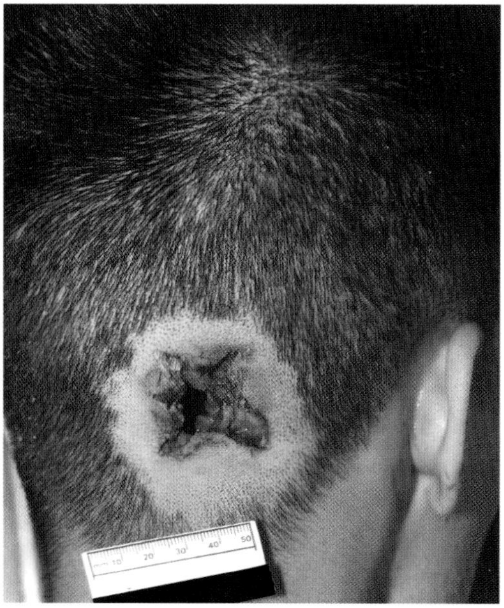

Above A star-shaped contact entrance wound.

Entrance and Exit Wounds

Entrance Wounds

Entrance wounds are classified by the distance the muzzle of the firearm was from the body when it was fired. There are three basic types: contact wound, close contact wound and distant wound.

Contact Wound

This is when the end of the barrel is pressed against the skin as the weapon is fired. The surrounding skin typically does not display soot or tattooing, but it may bear an abrasion imprint from the muzzle of the gun. The size of the wound depends on the underlying structure: If the barrel is placed against a bone, say the skull, the wound will be large and star-shaped. The same weapon placed against the stomach would produce a small, circular wound.

Close Contact Wound

This is when the end of the barrel is not touching the skin, but is very close to it or anything up to 2 feet (60 cm) away when it

Case Study ACCIDENT OR SUICIDE?

A young part-time refrigeration repairman did not report to work and his boss became concerned. He drove to the employee's residence and discovered that the door was locked and called the local police for assistance. Inside the garage at the young man's residence, police discovered a truck with a white male lying across the bench seat. The body was examined for signs of life, but there were none. He was pronounced dead at 5:45 p.m.

THE INVESTIGATION

The police officer took several photographs of the scene and the body, while death investigators were called in. They examined the scene and noted that the body was very cold to the touch. A driver's license provided positive identification of the victim, while drug paraphernalia consisting of a spoon, a small piece of aluminum and a bag of white powder, all on the dashboard, suggested a possible cause of death. There were also two Freon canisters, which were used by the victim to store Freon removed from older refrigerator units.

The body and other evidence were transported to the coroner's office. The pathologist's immediate impression was that the death had been a drug overdose, so he decided to conduct an external examination only. This autopsy revealed no sign of trauma or foul play.

Several weeks later, everything changed when toxicology screening results turned out to be negative for legal or illegal drugs. At this point the pathologist had a problem: a case of a young victim with no significant past medical history or disease, no signs of trauma and no toxic levels of drugs in his system. But the body had already been released and buried.

The pathologist reviewed the death scene images taken by the police officer to see if there was anything else that could possibly have caused the death. He noticed the driver's side window had small droplets of condensed water on it. The death investigators' report noted that the body was cold to the touch and that there were two open Freon tanks inside the vehicle. A forensic epidemiologist then conducted research to determine if Freon could be linked to death, and found that it had been recorded as a cause of death when humans were exposed to it in an enclosed space. The toxicologist retested the blood sample, this time for the presence of Freon — it turned out that the blood did indeed contain a high level of the toxic substance.

THE FINDINGS

The pathologist could now identify the cause of death as asphyxiation due to Freon exposure. As for the manner of death, there were two possibilities: accidental or suicide. If the canister's leak was accidental and the victim had fallen asleep in the cab, the manner could be accidental death. But there was evidence to support suicide, including the facts that the victim was found in an isolated location and that the tanks were in the cab, as well as the victim's knowledge of the chemical features of Freon. However, there was no suicide note located at the scene. The pathologist ruled the death accidental.

Case Study DEATH OF A RETIRED FIREMAN

At around 9:00 p.m. on a Sunday evening in July police were called upon to investigate a loud sound that had come from the house of an elderly man. The police knocked on the front door several times, but got no answer. They kicked in the front door and began a search of the two-story house, soon locating an elderly white male with what appeared to be a gunshot wound to the right temporal region. After a quick physical assessment of the victim, he was pronounced dead at 9:22 p.m. The police contacted the coroner's office, exited, secured the house and waited for the death investigators to arrive.

THE INVESTIGATION

At 9:50 p.m. two death investigators arrived on the scene and began photographing the residence and interviewing the neighbor. The neighbor informed the investigators that the deceased was a 79-year-old retired firefighter who lived alone. He had complained of severe back pain that had been increasing over the past two years.

Inside the dead man's home the investigators located his body in the bedroom, seated in a chair. The dead man was wearing a white T-shirt and blue pajama pants. On the nightstand was a prescription bottle labeled "oxycodone," a powerful painkiller. On the floor were a 9 mm automatic handgun and one spent shell. Examination of the victim revealed what appeared to be a gunshot wound to the right temporal region of the head. The investigator then took several photos of the victim and the weapon. His hands were then enclosed in paper bags for gunshot residue analysis. The body was wrapped in a white sheet, placed in a body bag and transported to the morgue.

THE EXAMINATION

A microscopic examination of the head wound revealed small blackish materials around its perimeter. X rays showed multiple small fragments of metal in the head and multiple skull fractures. From the arrangement of these it was deduced that the bullet had entered the right temporal area, traversed the brain and then exited the left temporal area. A death investigator returned to the residence to see if there was a bullet lodged in the walls or furniture.

THE FINDINGS

Later that day the forensic pathologist received a call from the death investigator at the scene. He had located a bullet lodged in the wall to the left of the victim. Several weeks later the toxicological analysis of the blood showed oxycodone within the therapeutic range.

Based on the external examination, past medical history and X rays, the forensic pathologist had little doubt in completing the death certificate with the cause recorded as gunshot wound to the head, and the manner of death as suicide. In this death, an external examination was all that was needed to resolve the case.

is fired. The skin surrounding a close contact wound typically displays burning (blackened skin), soot (powder) or tattooing. Burns are produced by ignited powder exiting the gun along with the bullet, while soot is also projected from the barrel, though it is distinguished because it can easily be wiped off the skin. Tattooing is caused by particles of unburnt and partly burnt powder being driven into the skin, so that they cannot be wiped off. The size of a close contact wound is typically small and circular.

Distant Contact Wound

When the end of the barrel is a more than 2 feet (60 cm) from the skin there will be no evidence of burning, soot or tattooing. The size of the wound is typically small and circular.

Putting Suspects on the Spot

One of the latest technologies to aid the field of law enforcement is a new gunshot residue test kit that can check a person's hands for gunshot residue "on the spot" in five minutes, even at the scene of a crime. The test involves swabbing the suspect's hands, saturating the swab with several reagents, then waiting five minutes. The swab is then examined for a blue or brown color, which indicates the presence of gunshot residues.

Exit Wounds

Exit wounds are free from burning, soot or tattooing. They are usually irregular in shape and larger then the entrance wound because of the way that the projectile force of the bullet has dispersed as it passes through the body.

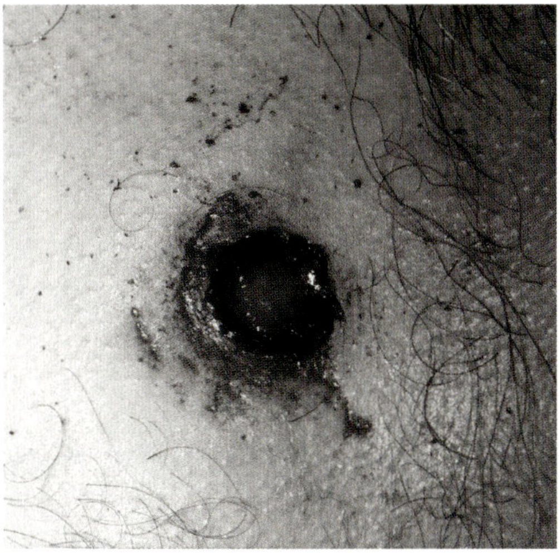

Above A close-contact entrance wound, showing tattooing from unburnt or partially burnt powder that has entered the skin.

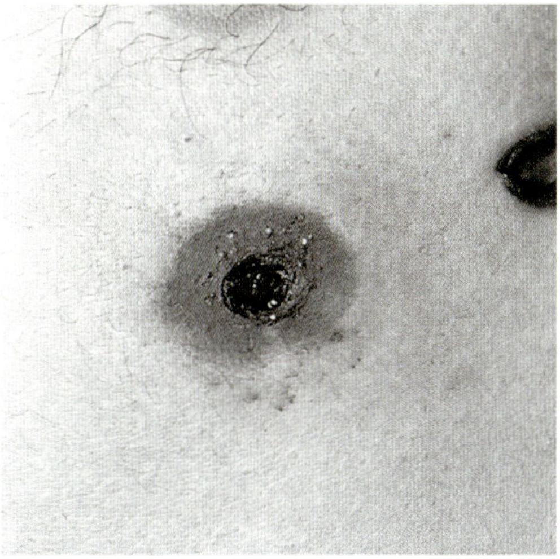

Above A more distant entrance wound, but still close enough that there is some soot on the skin around the wound.

Bruising

A bruise, or contusion, is an area of hemorrhage (bleeding) located under unbroken skin, which is revealed externally through colored, clearly visible patterns. This most often results from blunt-force trauma. These areas of injury can be inflicted unintentionally during a motor vehicle accident or fall, or even from routine placement of an intravenous tube. However, they can also be intentionally inflicted during physical altercations, child abuse, elder abuse, sexual abuse or self-abuse. Often forensic experts can learn a great deal about the events surrounding this violence by thoroughly examining the bruises.

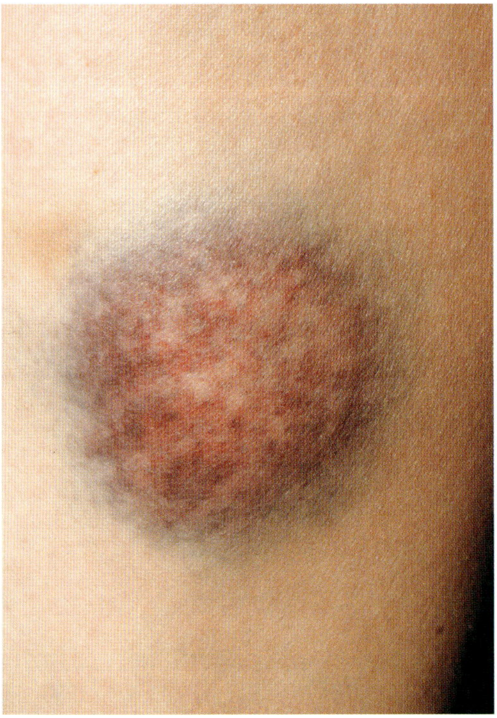

Above A major thigh bruise sustained from blunt-force trauma to a living patient. The mixture of red and purple coloring suggests that this bruise is about two days old.

The two key questions that forensic pathologists should be asking upon seeing a contusion are "How old is each of the contusions?" and "Is the appearance of the contusions consistent with the events that allegedly caused the contusions?"

If a contusion is documented on a dead body, then usually this will stimulate a police investigation into events and a coroner's investigation into the death. These investigations can uncover a great deal of information surrounding the time interval between the infliction of the contusion and death.

For example, in a case where parents arrive at a hospital emergency room with a deceased young child, they might state that their child had fallen from a bunk bed and was discovered unresponsive four hours later. But if the examination of the child by the pathologist revealed several bruises of different colors, this would indicate that they were of different ages. This finding could raise enough suspicion to trigger a homicide investigation into possible child abuse.

The current method of dating a contusion is to examine the color of the bruise, describing it as red, purple, magenta, orange or chartreuse. The observed color is compared to a table citing the sequence of color changes by time intervals to determine the approximate age of the contusions.

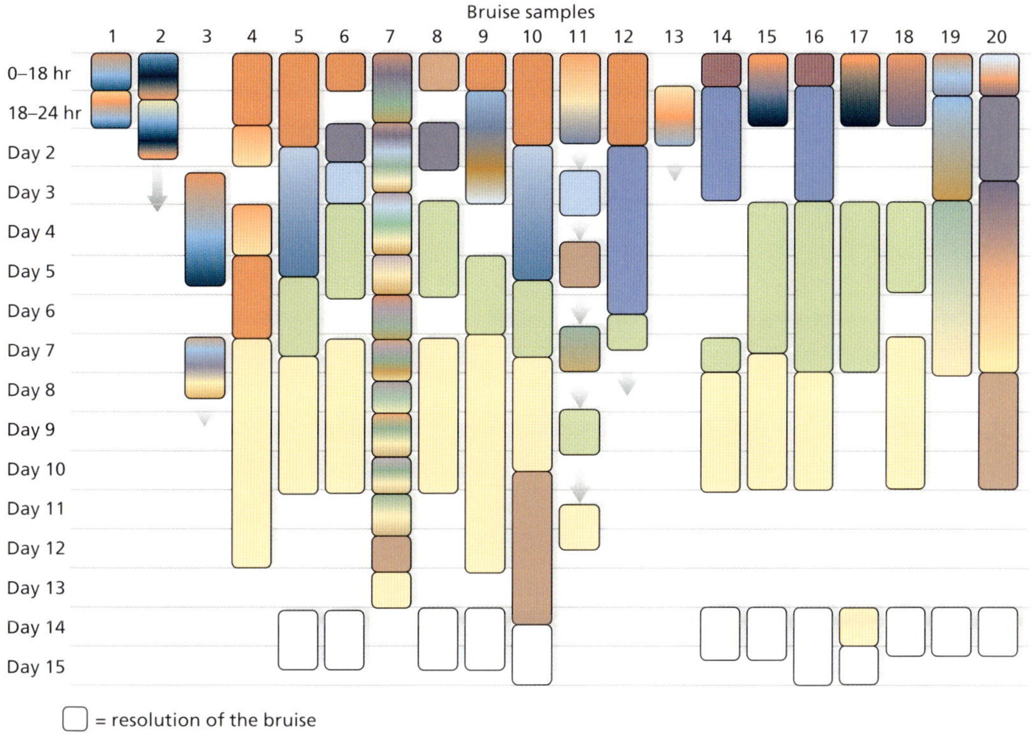

Above Chart shows the color progression of twenty different bruises as monitored by medical researchers. Color changes are due to hemoglobin degradation in the blood.

Burns

Burns are one of the major forms of potentially fatal injury that will be revealed in the external examation of the body. There are a number of quite separate types of burns arising from a range of traumatic circumstances: thermal, electrical, chemical and from overexposure to ultraviolet light (in sunshine) or to X rays (during misjudged medical procedures).

Thermal Burns

Thermal burns are soft-tissue injuries caused when the skin comes into contact with heat. The source of heat can be dry or wet, with wet heat causing scalding. Flames produce radiant heat that initially causes whitening of the skin, then blisters, and if kept in contact for a length of time will produce roasting and charring of the site. Burns produced by scalding appear as bleached areas of the skin. Liquids above 130°F (55°C) are capable of causing injury to the skin.

Electrical Burns

When a person touches a live electrical wire or a high-voltage power line, or is struck by lighting, electricity passes through the body. This can cause severe tissue damage and may cause death if the voltage crosses the heart, where it will disrupt the pulsing of the heart muscle. Low voltages require several seconds of exposure before causing a burn, but high voltages cause burns within a fraction of a second.

The nature of electrical burns may also give clues as to whether the damage was caused by an alternating current (AC) or direct current (DC). AC exposure causes a sustained muscular contraction called tetany, which may cause a hand gripping a live electrical cable to become locked in position, exacerbating the injury. DC exposure, by contrast, usually causes a single muscular contraction that tends to throw the body back. High-voltage AC exposure can also cause tetany of the heart muscle, meaning that the heart becomes stuck in a sustained state of contraction, thus failing to pump the blood that provides oxygen to the cells of the body.

A major difference between electrical burns and other types of burns is the presence of entrance and exit wounds. The entrance, or contact, wound appears grayish or white and ulcer-like, with the soft tissue torn open and surrounded by corrugated margins and dead tissue. At the exit site, the tissues are split in a laceration that resembles a puncture wound. Exit wounds are often found on the bottom of the feet, where the electricity "escapes" the body by being drawn into the electrical current of the earth beneath.

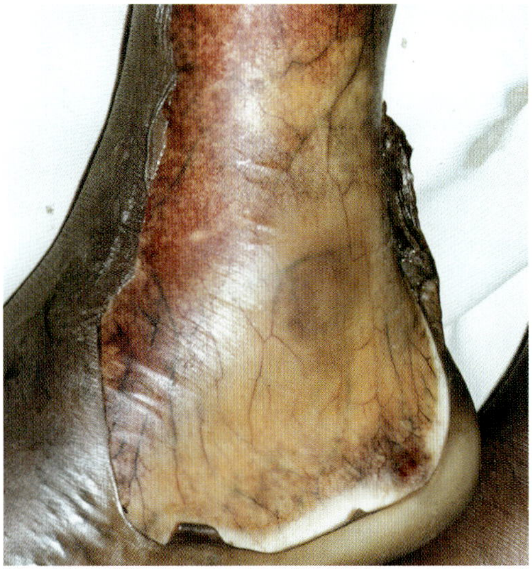

Above Extensive third-degree burns on the leg of a victim.

Chemical and X-ray Burns

Chemical burns are characterized by inflammation of the skin, ulcerated patches and discoloration and staining of

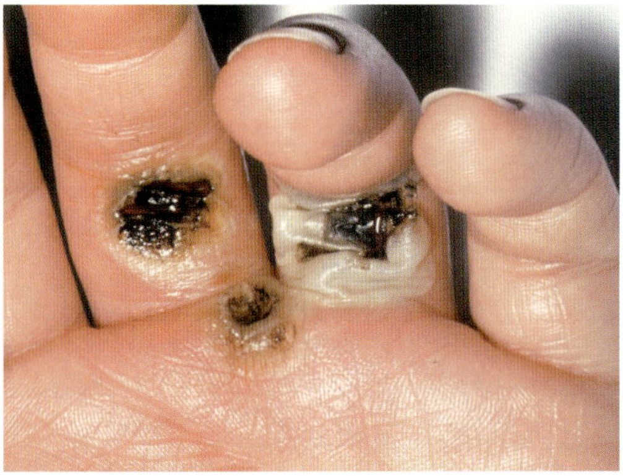

Above Mild electrical burns on the hand of a living person.

the skin. Burns caused by extremely alkaline chemicals (such as bleach) cause the skin to turn white and soggy, with a soapy feel to the touch. Burns caused by extremely acidic chemicals eat away at the soft tissue, causing a rapid process of disintegration.

Burns caused by X rays depend greatly on the intensity and period of exposure. The skin may become inflamed and red, but after some time the inflammation subsides, leaving a bronzing of the skin. In higher exposures there may be atrophy (death) of the superficial tissues, obliteration of the blood vessels and shedding of hair.

DEGREES OF BURNING

- First degree — superficial, with damage confined to the outer layer of the skin. The area initially appears red and swollen, and over time the skin peels away.
- Second degree — destroys the upper layers of the skin. The affected area displays blisters.
- Third degree — destroys the epidermis and dermis layers of the skin. Scarring is caused and this typically requires skin graft to repair.
- Fourth degree — complete charring or destruction of the skin and underlying tissues.

Motor Vehicle Accident Injuries

There are certain signature injuries that the pathologist will come across when examining victims of motor vehicle accidents, though the type and location of injury is affected by the victim's position within the vehicle, the use of restraints and the actions of the vehicle during the accident.

If the driver was not wearing a seat belt, external trauma from impact with the steering wheel is typically seen in the chest region. The internal examination would further reveal multiple fractures of the ribs, tears and contusions of the lungs, and often tears in the aorta — the major artery through which blood is pumped from the heart. Examination of the driver's face will reveal multiple lacerations caused by impact with the windshield. If the driver was restrained with a seat belt these injuries would be reduced, but the seat belt may produce bruising to the chest, rib fractures and lacerations of the liver. Unrestrained front-seat passengers typically display external knee injuries, as they are flung forward, striking the dashboard. Front-seat passengers also often have head injuries caused by windshield impact.

Back-seat passengers are less likely to die in a motor vehicle accident, though if they are unrestrained they may receive potentially fatal head injuries from the

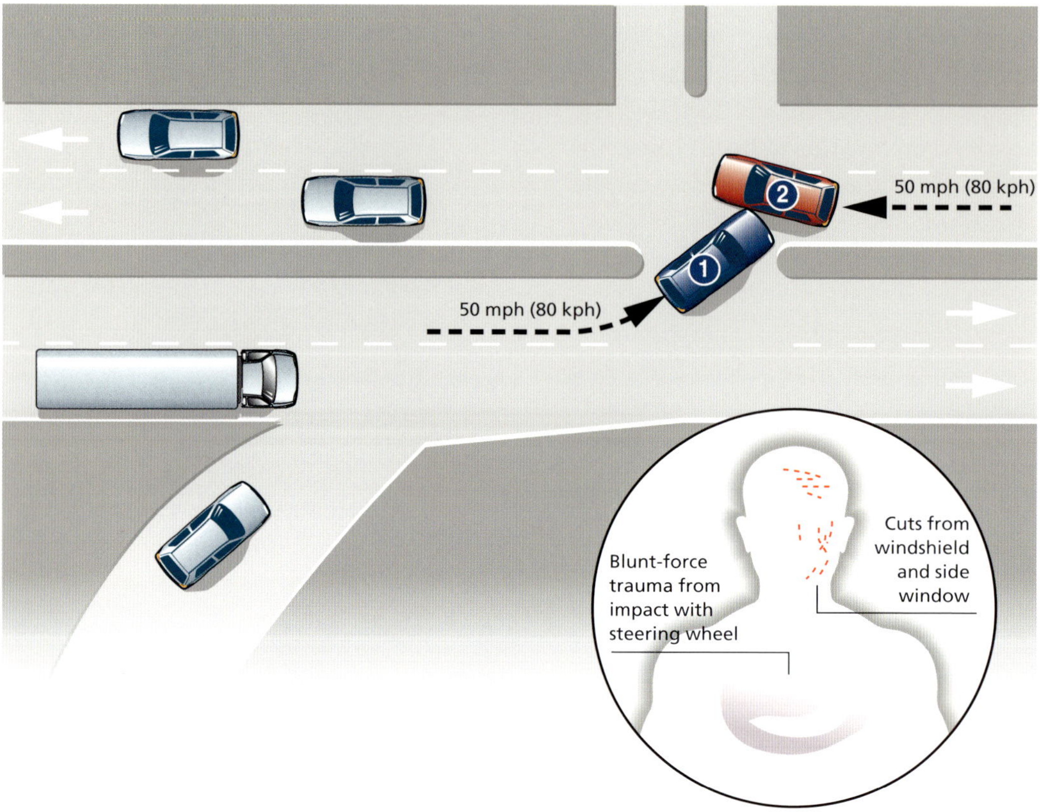

Above An example of a motor vehicle accident and resulting injuries. The driver of car 1 will suffer blunt-force trauma to the chest; the driver of car 2 will suffer blunt-force trauma to the chest and arms and cuts to the head.

seat in front. However, an unrestrained passenger sitting in the middle back seat, between the two front seats, risks being thrown right through the windshield and out of the car, sustaining head injuries that may well be fatal.

Driver or Passenger?

It is critical to the investigation to distinguish the driver from the passengers. Making this determination may be crucial when legal questions of culpability arise, as it is the driver who has control of the vehicle and therefore may be held responsible for a crash. However, making this determination is more complicated when the vehicle occupants are not wearing restraints, as they may be ejected from the vehicle at the moment of impact. In such a case they will be found lying in the roadway, dead on arrival or critically injured at the very least.

When occupants have been ejected from the vehicle, injury patterns from the side windows of the vehicle offer an important clue. The side windows are made from tempered glass, which breaks into small, angular fragments on impact. These fragments typically inflict small, superficial cuts to the side of the face of the occupant. Therefore, the location of these cuts can be used to determine who was driving and who was the passenger. In countries where vehicles drive on the right-hand side, the driver (who sits on the left side of the vehicle) will receive side-window cuts on the left-hand side of the face, and the front-seat passenger will have cuts on the right-hand side of the face. In countries where people drive on the left (and drivers sit on the right side of the vehicle), this pattern is reversed.

Examining the Vehicles

Once the occupants have been removed from the vehicle and the scene has been photographed, the vehicles involved in the accident are placed on flatbed trucks and taken to a garage for a detailed examination. Every aspect of the vehicles is examined by mechanical specialists, including tires, brakes, transmission and electrical systems, to determine if these were within normal operational parameters. The results of these investigations may be used in a legal setting to determine whether the accident was caused by driver's negligence or by vehicle malfunction. In some situations, the site where the accident occurred is closed off to the public in order to reenact the accident, to try to determine more precisely how events unfolded. Motor vehicle accident reenactments are most often conducted in cases involving homicide or wrongful death due to criminal negligence.

The Risks of an External Examination

The external examination is an effective method of reducing the workload of a coroner where the cause and manner of death are clear, and in apparent natural death cases where the family is strongly opposed to an autopsy.

However, at times choosing an external examination may come back to haunt the pathologist. Sometimes cases thought to be natural deaths and therefore only subjected to an external examination, after further investigation and as a result of information from new witnesses coming forward, prove to be non-natural deaths. In some of these cases, the body must be exhumed.

Exhumations are very uncommon, and to proceed with an exhumation requires authorization from the relevant government agency, as well as religious authorities, if the body has been buried in consecrated ground. Occasionally applications for exhumation are granted, usually for cultural or family reasons, where it can be shown that the deceased has not been buried in the correct location. More rarely, an exhumation will be granted because of questions that have arisen regarding the cause of death.

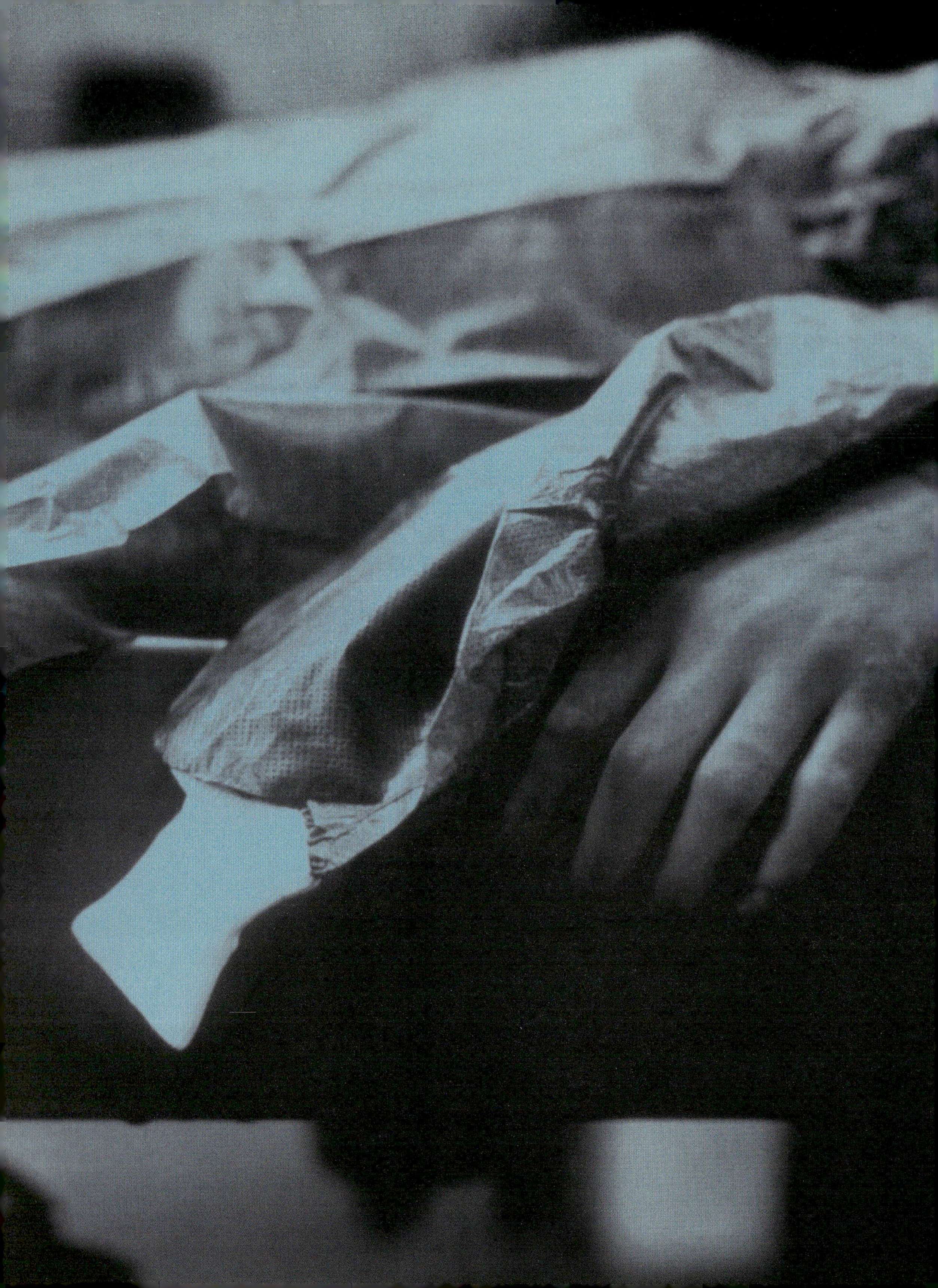

Chapter 4

The Complete Internal Examination

The complete autopsy is the most thorough physical examination that a person will ever undergo. Almost every facet of the deceased's health — or ill health — will be revealed as the forensic pathologist investigates not just the body's external surface, but also its interior organ systems, hoping to determine beyond doubt the ultimate cause of death.

Opening up the Body

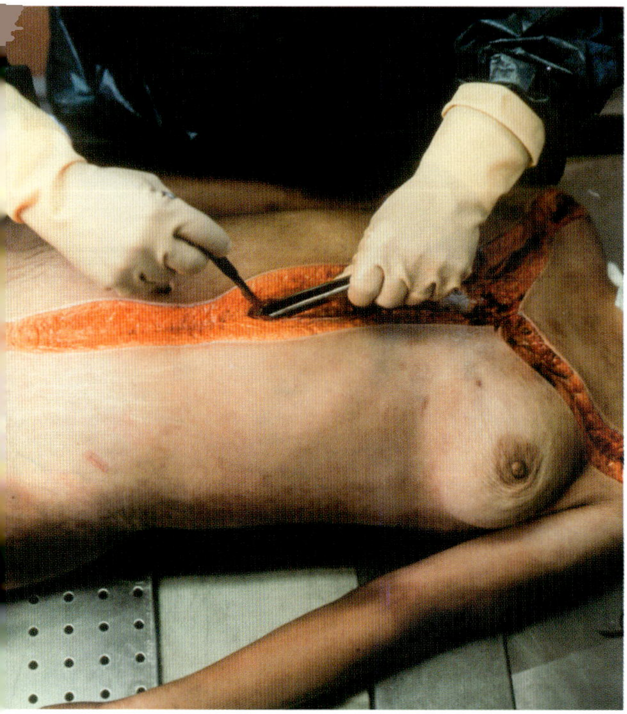

Above An autopsy technician makes the Y incision on a 20-year-old woman who has been dead for two days.

Non-natural deaths that appear suspicious in any way, or medically unexplained and mysterious deaths, will undergo a complete postmortem forensic examination. A complete examination consists of the external observation described in the last chapter, with a few modifications, followed by a detailed examination of the internal organs. Obviously, completing this process requires the autopsy team to open up the body.

The internal examination begins with an initial Y-shaped incision. This extends from the upper left chest region near the shoulder and angles downward toward the tip of the sternum (breastbone). A similar incision is made on the right side. These two incisions intersect at the xyphoid process, located at the end of the sternum. From there the incision extends downward along the midline of the body to the symphysis pubis (a point in the groin just above the genitals), curving slightly around the umbilicus (navel). Care needs to be taken not to injure the underlying organs. The three flaps of skin separated by the Y, together with their subcutaneous fat tissue, are then dissected from the underlying musculoskeletal structure, exposing the chest plate and the internal abdominal organs. This dissection process produces very little bleeding, since there is no blood pressure.

Methods of Internal Examination

There are two methods of conducting an internal examination. The Virchow technique (described in this chapter) is where the organs are removed one by one, while the Rokitansky technique involves in situ dissection of the organs, which remain connected and are then removed together as a block.

The Y Incision: Accessing the Internal Organs

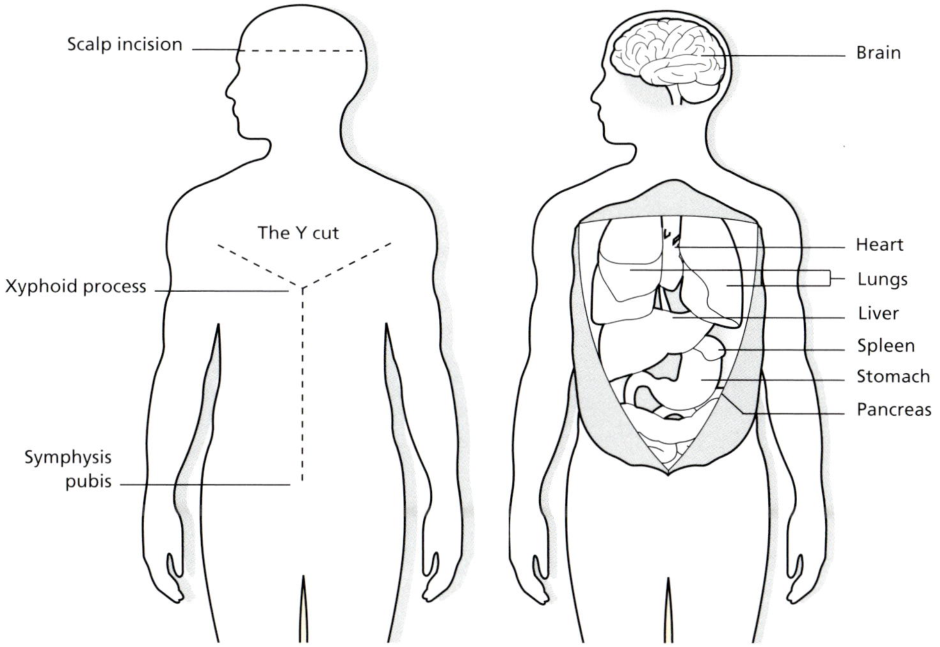

The locations of the Y incision and the main incision for removing the scalp. The illustration on the right shows the key internal organs that will be investigated in the postmortem examination.

Basic Torso Characteristics

Taking in the overall characteristics of the open torso, the pathologist measures the depth of the fat pad in centimeters at the umbilicus (navel), while the exposed ribs and sternum are examined for fractures and any deformity. It is not uncommon, especially among the elderly, for the ribs and the sternum to have been fractured as a result of cardiopulmonary resuscitation (CPR). The pathologist also notes the position of the diaphragm, the muscle that divides the chest-cavity organs from those of the abdominal cavity. Normally this muscle is positioned at the level of the fifth rib. Using rib cutters, the ribs and sternum are freed and then removed as a single bony plate, exposing the heart, lungs and liver.

The internal organs are usually examined in the following order: heart, lungs, liver, hemolymphatic organs (spleen and lymph nodes), pancreas, gastrointestinal tract, kidneys, prostate, neck organs, central nervous system, then musculoskeletal parts.

Tools of the Trade

Despite great advancements in most fields of medicine, the tools of forensic dissection resemble those of medieval medicine, having changed little in the past hundred years. A scalpel, rib-cutters, forceps, scissors, large single-edged knives, syringes, a hammer and chisel and a circular bone saw are the key tools used to conduct the internal examination of a body.

Scalpels are used to make all the initial incisions into the soft tissues. The ribs and sternum are removed using rib-cutters, which may be made of surgical steel or may even be the same sort of pruning shears that can be picked up from a local hardware store. The internal organs are removed by cutting them free from the body with scissors and scalpels, while removal of the brain requires a circular bone saw, hammer and chisel to open up the skull. Forceps are used to grip organs and other soft tissues, and syringes of several sizes are used to collect samples of body fluids.

Once all the organs have been removed, they are cut into sections using a large single-edged knife.

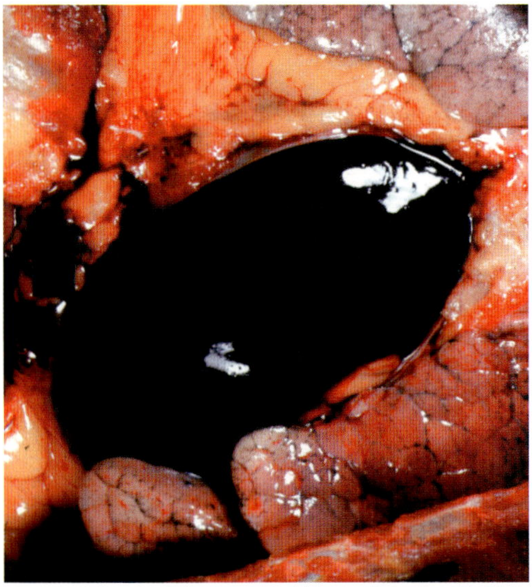

Above Severe blunt-force trauma has caused this heart to bleed extensively into the pericardial cavity surrounding it.

Heart

The first internal organ examined is the heart. It is located beneath the sternum (breastbone) and is enclosed by a thin membrane called the pericardium. Normally within the pericardium there is a little fluid; however, if there is excessive fluid or blood within this space, it will place pressure on the heart and prevent its proper functioning. Therefore, when the pericardium is examined, the pathologist starts with a small incision into the membrane to determine the amount of fluid surrounding the heart. Excessive fluid in the pericardial space may indicate a severe blunt-force trauma suffered in the chest region, or it may have been caused by CPR. The pericardium is then fully opened, exposing the heart.

Opposite Some of the tools used in the internal examination. From the top: saw for opening skull, rib-cutters, scalpels, scissors, wedge and dura-stripper for removing the layers covering the brain, hammer and hook for opening the spinal column. The syringes are used to collect body fluids. On the left is a dissection knife.

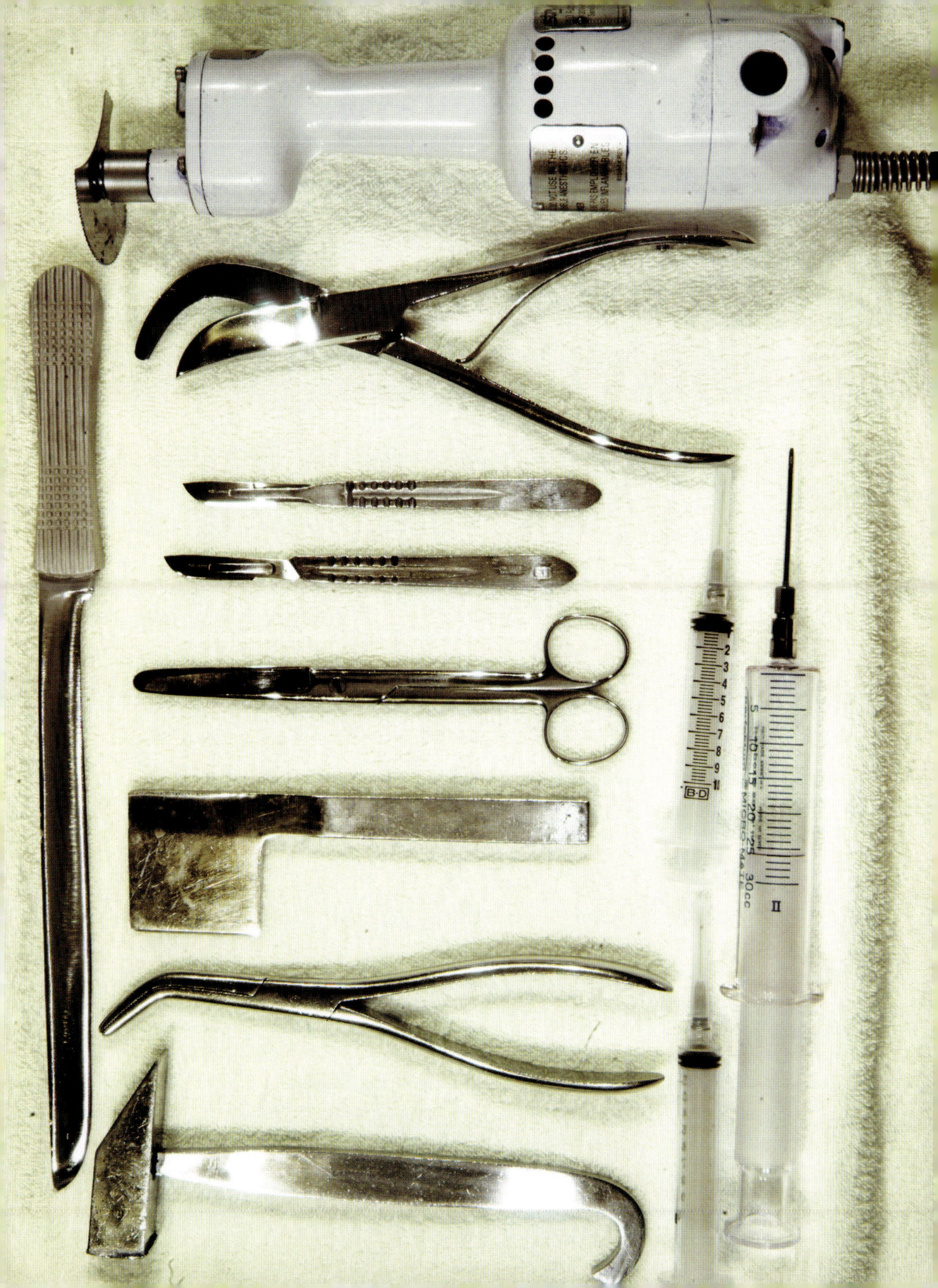
B-D
30cc

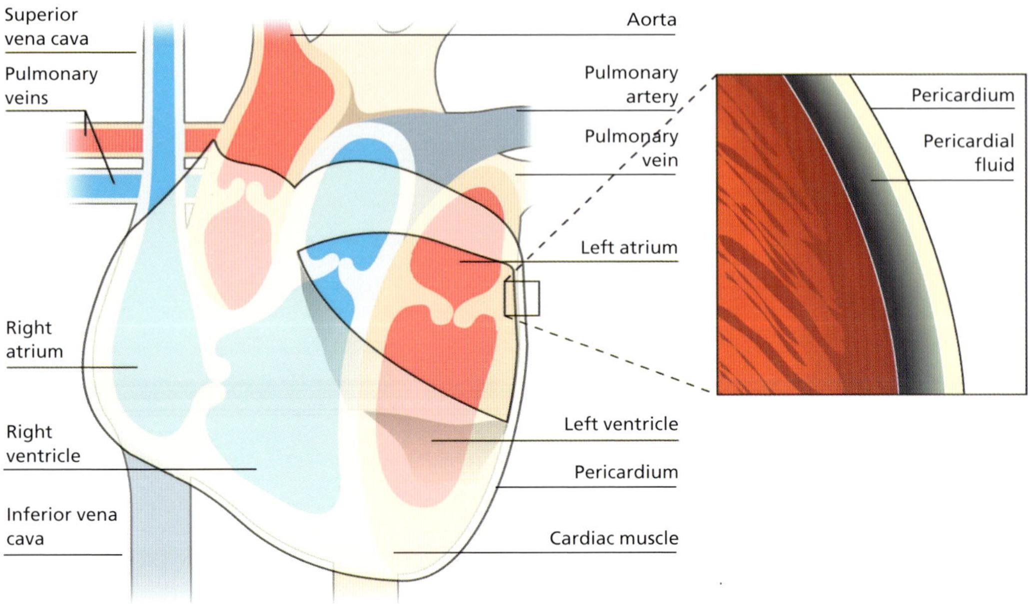

Above Diagram showing all the key functional elements of the human heart. Blockages, injuries or abnormalities discovered in any part of this organ are likely to have been involved in the cause of death.

The aorta is the main artery that takes blood out of the heart to circulate around the body, and the pathologist now inserts a large-bore syringe into this tube to collect blood for analysis. The heart is examined in situ, then removed by cutting the aorta, the superior and inferior vena cava (the main routes for blood returning to the heart after circulation) and the pulmonary arteries and veins. Then the heart is weighed, as its weight offers clues to the cause of death. The heart is also measured, and if it is unusually large, this may indicate myocardial disease such as hypertension, valvular heart disease or ischemic heart disease. The forensic pathologist examines the four chambers of the heart (right atrium, right ventricle, left atrium and left ventricle), noting the color (dark red or cherry red) and amount of clotted blood within each. The thickness of the ventricle walls is also measured. In an average-sized individual, the right ventricle wall is normally 0.1–0.15 inches (2.5–4 mm) thick, and the left is 0.6–0.7 inches (15–18 mm) thick; the left ventricle is considerably more muscular because it is the chamber that pushes the blood all the way around the body. Thickening of these walls, or hypertrophy, may be an indication of heart failure. The circumference of the heart's four valves (tricuspid, pulmonic, mitral and aortic) is measured and each one examined for evidence of thrombi — solid masses of blood that form because of inflammation or infarction of the heart muscle that can be a cause of death.

The heart muscle receives its blood supply from three coronary arteries (right coronary artery, left coronary artery and circumflex artery), which are examined by multiple cross-sectioning — i.e., they are cut into slices like a loaf of bread. The pathologist is looking for evidence of pathological changes such as atherosclerosis or calcification. Atherosclerosis is the most common pathology of the human heart, a disease characterized by the formation of plaques composed of lipids, collagen and calcium that block and stiffen the arteries' smooth muscles. Atherosclerosis is generally caused by too much cholesterol in the diet, smoking, hypertension and diabetes.

The pathologist estimates the percentage of blockage in the three coronary arteries, ranking this figure into the category of *minimal* (less than 20 percent), *moderate* (20–50 percent) or *severe* (over 50 percent). The myocardium (heart muscle) is described in terms of consistency (firm or soft) and color (red-brown, tan, pale) and any gross signs of scarring are noted.

Lungs

The respiratory system begins at the nasal and oral cavities, which lead to the pharynx (throat), past the larynx (vocal cords) and down the trachea (windpipe), which then divides into the right and left bronchi that enter the lungs. The primary function of the lungs is to eliminate carbon dioxide and absorb oxygen, providing a chemical environment in which cells can live healthily. This gas exchange takes place in a network of tiny alveolar (air sac) capillaries.

The lungs are first examined in situ. The forensic pathologist runs his hand along the perimeter of the lungs, searching for any adhesions (where the lungs have stuck to the internal walls of the chest), which can be caused by prior surgery or tumors. Healthy lungs should be free-floating. The surface of the lungs is described in terms of its color, normally pink to light reddish tan to purple. They are then separated by cutting the primary bronchial attachments and weighed.

Weight can offer clues to the pathology of the lungs. Diseases causing chronic obstructive pulmonary disease (COPD), or emphysema, result in lungs below the normal range, while pulmonary infections such as pneumonia produce heavier-than-normal lungs. The interior of the lungs is examined first by cutting along the path of the bronchioles to expose the smaller airways. Then cuts are made along the long axis of the lung to expose the maximal amount of internal surface area. Each lung is sectioned from top to bottom across the organ and examined for congestion, tumors, infarcts (localized areas of dead tissue caused by a lack of blood supply), infections and edema (swelling). Representative samples from the different lobes of the lung are placed in formaldehyde and later sent to histology for preparation.

Common Natural Causes

The majority of pathology seen in the lungs among autopsy cases is from natural causes. The most common natural diseases include pulmonary embolism and respiratory diseases such as bronchitis, pneumonia and emphysema.

Pulmonary embolism results from a "deep-vein thrombosis" blood clot that forms in the veins of the legs, then travels in the blood stream and blocks the pulmonary artery that feeds blood to the lungs. This condition is typically seen among individuals who are immobilized for a long period of time, which can be caused by long plane flights, but is also often the case with individuals who have suffered significant trauma or burns. It is also seen among very obese individuals.

Where the deceased has suffered from a respiratory disease, the lungs are characterized by an enlargement of the air spaces, appearing as if they have been over-inflated.

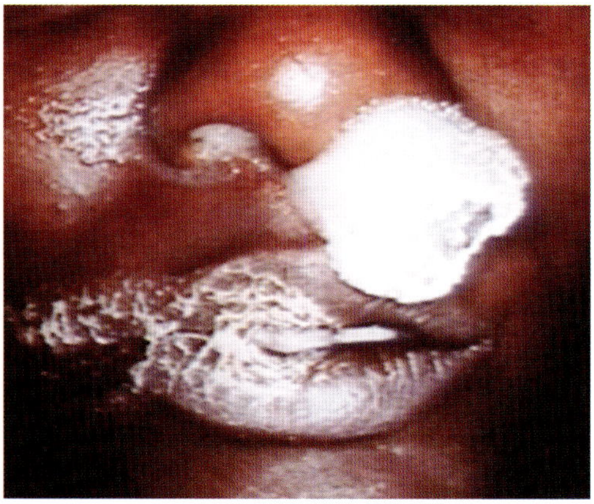

Above Foam exuding from the nose and mouth indicates drowning when the body has not remained submerged. This may be the case where a fluid other than water has flooded the lungs.

Death by Drowning

When a dead body is found in the water, the lungs may reveal whether the victim drowned or was already dead before entering the water. In cases of drowning, the lungs and airways may be full of water and the lungs swollen (though this is not always the case, as sometimes the airway spontaneously closes to stop water entering). Laboratory pathologists can also perform tests to determine whether single-cell algae living in the water can be found in the victim's respiratory system. If none of these indicators is present, then the forensics team will continue searching for another cause of death.

When a person has drowned, but the body has not remained submerged in water for one reason or another, the drowning will be revealed by a foamy exudate around the nose and mouth.

Trachea

The larynx and trachea (throat) are opened longitudinally from the rear and the interior is examined. The thyroid gland is dissected away from the trachea with scissors, weighed and examined in thin slices, as this may give clues to hormonal disorders.

The trachea also needs to be checked for soot or any other residues. Such residues in the upper airways would be one of the first signs of death by smoke inhalation, which could be confirmed by toxicological analysis of the blood.

Liver

The largest internal organ, the liver, is examined next. The external surface is described in terms of contour (smooth or glistening) and color (brown, yellow, reddish brown). The liver is lifted in situ to expose the gallbladder, from which bile is collected for analysis. Then the liver is removed and weighed before being placed on the examination table in a facedown position to expose the gallbladder. The gallbladder is opened and the amount of fluid inside is measured. If it contains gallstones, the number and size are noted.

The liver is dissected and examined for evidence of fatty change, cirrhosis and infection. A fatty liver is one of the signs of alcohol injury. Visually the liver will appear normal, but the microscope will reveal that fat has gathered in the cells; this condition is reversible if diagnosed early, but if left untreated can lead to liver failure. Cirrhosis, on the other hand, is caused by ongoing alcohol abuse, and is visually identifiable. It causes an enlarged liver with nodules and fibrous tissue that result from the cells of the liver dying off under the effects of alcohol. This condition can also be fatal.

Poisoning

Even more grave damage to the liver is exhibited as postnecrotic cirrhosis, which means that large areas of liver cells have died, giving the organs a knobbly appearance. This can be caused by hepatitis, but may also be interpreted as a sign of poisoning.

Kidneys

The kidneys are removed, weighed, cut lengthwise in half and examined. The pathologist examines the removed kidneys for nephritis, cystic disease or degenerative changes. In some cases degeneration or failure of the kidney may indicate chronic cocaine abuse.

The ureters and bladder are also examined. The urinary tract is opened and searched for stones. The bladder is examined for signs of congestion, hemorrhage, inflammation or ulcers.

Spleen

The spleen is removed from the rest of the abdominal organs, weighed, sliced and

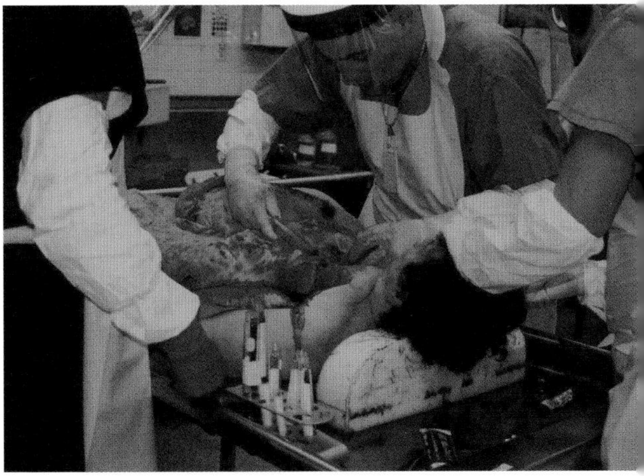

Above Blood is removed from the heart using a large-bore syringe, then sent to a forensic toxicologist for chemical analysis.

examined. An enlarged spleen may be a sign of infection, congestion or tumors.

Where the deceased has been the victim of a serious assault or accident, the spleen is often damaged, as it is unprotected by the rib cage. Internal bleeding from the abdominal organs, rather than the actual failure of an organ, will often be the cause of death.

Pancreas

With the liver removed, the oblong pancreas is exposed. The pancreas's primary function is to secrete hormones and digestive enzymes. The most important hormone released is insulin, which regulates blood sugar levels. The most common disease associated with the pancreas is diabetes, a failure in this sugar-regulatory function. The symptoms associated with diabetes can be seen only microscopically, so multiple cross-sections must be made of this organ and sent to the lab for analysis if the pathologist suspects that this disease may have played a part in the death.

Gastrointestinal Tract

The stomach and small and large intestines are the last internal organs examined and removed from the abdominal cavity.

The small and large intestines are examined externally for tumors, ulcers, obstructions and gangrene. The intestines are opened using special intestinal scissors. This is always done over a sink, as the contents of the intestines are extremely malodorous, being made up of foodstuffs in various states of digestion.

Stomach Contents

The stomach lies directly beneath the diaphragm in the left region of the upper abdomen. It contains recently digested food in a low pH (acidic) environment, and is connected to the mouth via the esophagus. The stomach is removed from the body by severing its connections to the esophagus above and duodenum below, then it is opened and the contents are emptied into a shallow container. Stomach contents are described and estimates of the weight and amount of fluid, food and other materials are noted. In cases of death from ingested drugs, the stomach is examined to recover the tablets. This may aid the pathologist in ascertaining whether the death was an accident or suicide. A large number of pills recovered from the stomach would be a strong indication of a deliberate suicide attempt as opposed to an accident.

Unusual Stomach Contents

Individuals with a history of psychosis may have swallowed indigestible objects such as keys, coins, toys or other small metal and plastic objects.

Where the victim has been involved in drug trafficking, examination of the stomach contents may reveal an attempt to hide narcotics by swallowing them in plastic bags: if the bags break, this will likely cause death by overdose from the drugs within.

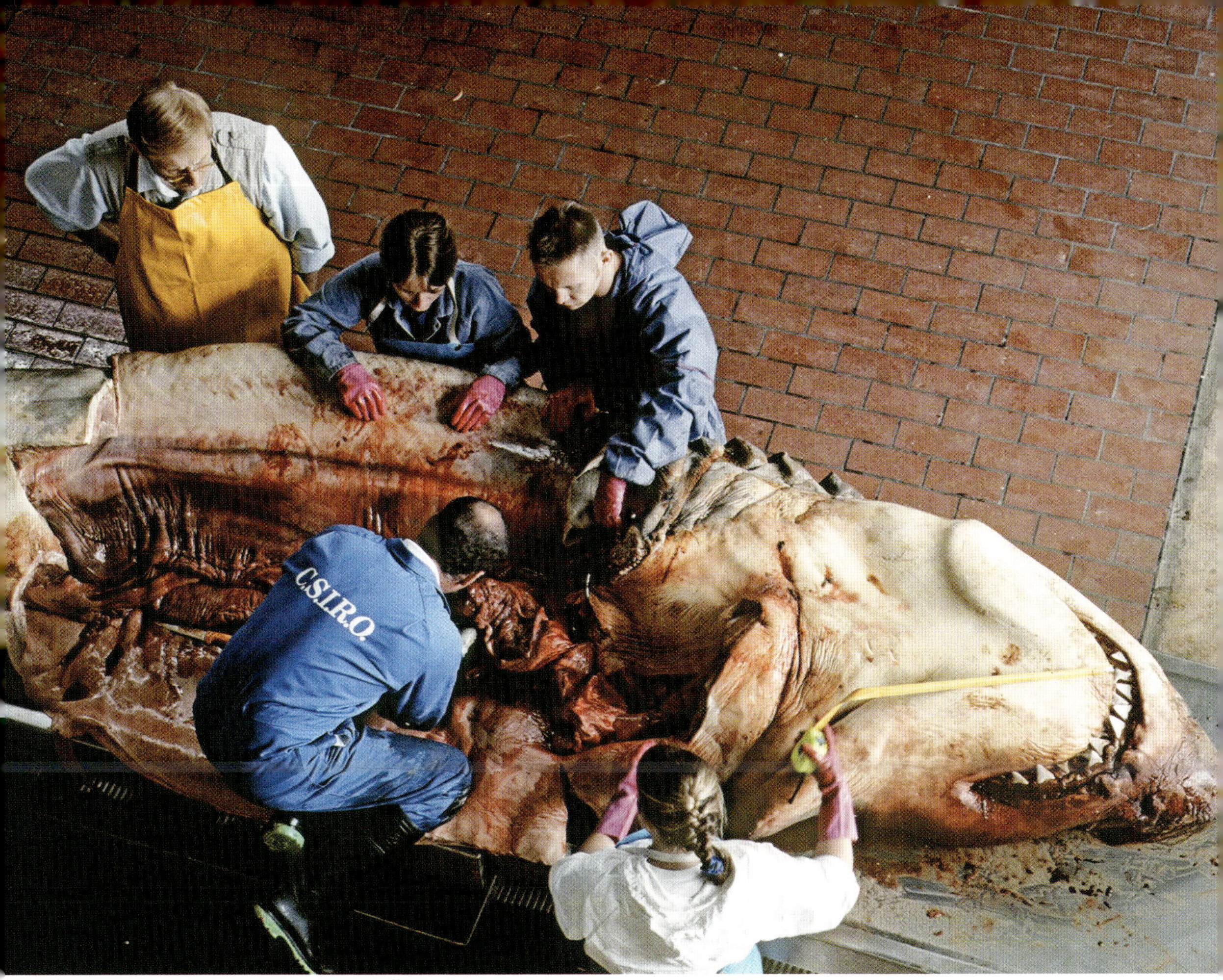

Above Examining the stomach contents of a shark. This investigation, conducted by marine biologists, reveals not what killed the shark, but who the shark may have killed. Great white sharks such as this one, caught off the coast of South Australia, occasionally have human remains in their stomachs.

Stomach Contents and Time of Death

On average the stomach processes and vacates a meal in 2–3 hours. Therefore, if the time of the victim's last meal can be determined, this can be used as a basis for estimating the time of death. For example, if an individual eats an average-sized meal at 1:00 p.m. and is found dead that evening, food in the stomach in a fairly intact state would indicate that the death occurred before about 2:00 p.m. However, if the stomach was empty, the death would most likely have occurred after 3:00 p.m.

However, various peripheral factors must be considered in estimating the breakdown of stomach contents. Different types of food are digested at different rates, the amount of fluid consumed affects the process, as does alcohol, and even psychological stress can alter the rate of digestion.

Central Nervous System

Once the organs of the chest and abdomen have been removed, attention is focused on the central nervous system, which is made up of the brain, brainstem and spinal cord.

Brain

A head block is used to raise the head above the shoulders, then an autopsy technician uses a scalpel to make an incision starting behind the right ear, encircling the back of the head and ending behind the left ear. The skin of the scalp is then peeled forward and the lower portion is drawn down toward the neck to expose the skull.

The skull is carefully examined by the pathologist for any signs of blunt-force trauma. If the victim has thick hair, trauma to the head may not have been seen during the external examination. A special vibrating circular saw is used to cut open the skull, leaving the dura mater, the material that lines the inside of the skull, still in place (the saw is designed to cut bone but not soft tissue). The pathologist observes the brain in situ, looking for signs of infection or hemorrhage. The most common brain infection is meningitis, which is indicated by a viscous ooze in the space between the brain and the skull. Hemorrhages can be caused spontaneously (non-traumatic) by hypertension or an aneurysm (rupture of a thinned artery), or by blunt-force trauma to the head.

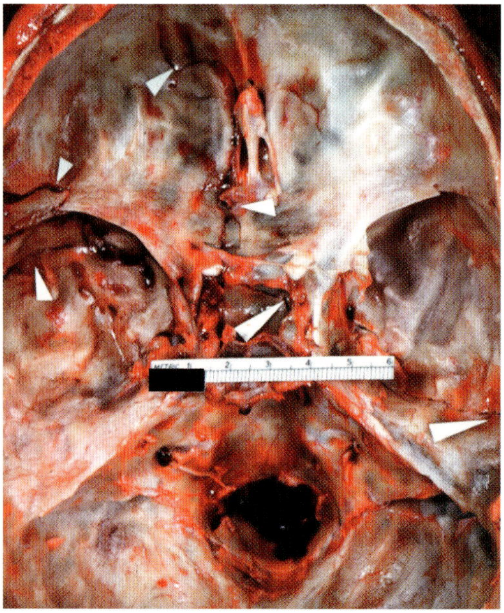

Above The inside of the skull, or *calvarium*, after the brain and brainstem have been removed. The white arrows show fractures in the skull, resulting from severe blunt-force trauma.

The technician next removes the brain by cutting it away from the brain stem and records its weight. After the dura mater lining the inside of the skull is removed, the skull is examined for signs of old or new fractures and injuries. The brain at this point is relatively soft, with the consistency of Jell-O. The brains of infants are the most fragile, as are the brains of individuals who have suffered

Layers Protecting the Brain

Scalp — a layer of skin, blood vessels and nerves, as well as the hair that grows out of it

Skull — the thickness of the skull varies, with the thickest areas located in the front and rear, while the thinnest area is at the top

Dura mater — the outermost of the cranial meninges, or protective tissues

Arachnoid — the middle layer of protective tissue

Subarachnoid space — a space between the arachnoid and the pia mater, which is filled with a few ounces of cerebrospinal fluid, a clear, colorless liquid that functions as a shock absorber for the brain and spinal cord

Pia mater — innermost of the protective tissues

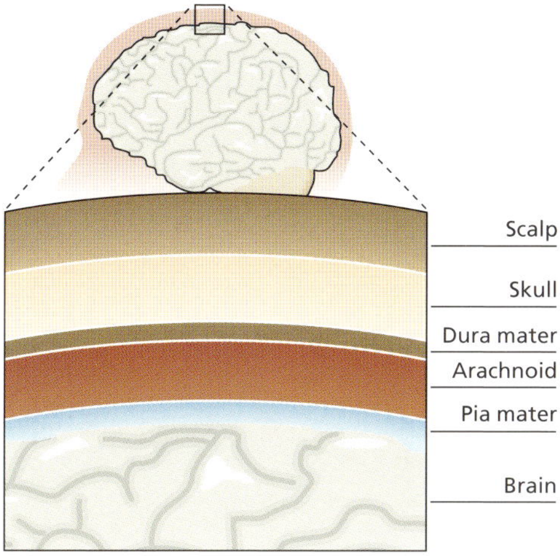

numerous strokes or a neurogenic disease such as Alzheimer's. Because of its fragility, the brain is suspended upside down by a string in a bucket of formaldehyde for 10–14 days. This process, called fixing the brain, causes it to become harder and therefore easier to cut into neat cross-sections. Just imagine trying to cut cross-sections of Jell-O!

Spinal Cord

There are two methods for removing the spinal cord, each with its own advantages and limitations.

The posterior method has the advantage of allowing complete exposure of the spinal cord, including the spinal canal and the roots and ganglia of the spinal nerves, in situ. The posterior method requires placing the body face-down on the table and making an incision down the midline of the back, from the base of the skull to the base of the spine, while also cutting away the muscles surrounding the spine. Then a circular saw is used to cut both sides of the vertebrae so that they can be partially removed, exposing the spinal cord and its surrounding dura mater.

The anterior approach works from the opposite side, cutting open the spinal column from the front after the internal organs have been removed. To free the spinal column a broad chisel must be wedged underneath, exposing the dura mater, nerve roots and ganglia. This method is less labor-intensive and does not require an additional skin incision, though it does not expose the nerve roots as completely as the posterior method.

TYPES OF SKELETAL FRACTURE

- Complete: bone is broken into two pieces
- Partial: bone is not fractured all the way through
- Closed: broken bone does not break through the skin
- Open: broken bone protrudes through the skin

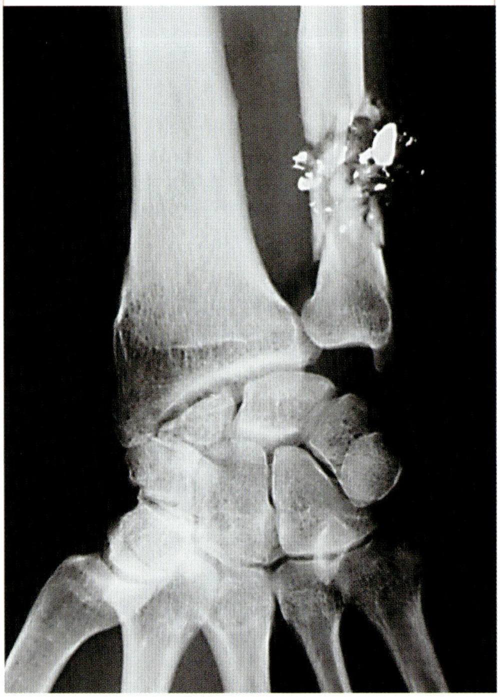

Above A complete fracture of the ulna bone in the wrist. The bone has been fragmented because this fracture was caused by a bullet.

Skeletal System

The adult skeleton consists of 206 bones. Part of a complete autopsy involves examining all the major bones and cartilage in the arms, legs, head (skull, jaws and nose), ribs, sternum, pelvis and vertebral column. These are examined, both visually and by X ray, for gross deformities, fractures, dislocations and compressions.

Skeletal fractures give the pathologist clues about a possible physical assault, fall or other accidental injury. If an individual is found dead from severe physical trauma in a public place, and there are no witnesses to the events that led to this person's death, the possible causes are many. However, X rays and detailed postmortem examination may reveal the cause.

For example, X ray results from the legs might reveal a fracture of the right tibia while external examination shows several impact marks on the skin, one at 15 inches (38 cm) and another at 13 inches (33 cm) above ground level. These findings would indicate to the pathologist that the leg was struck by a car bumper: The man was the victim of a hit-and-run. Each car manufacturer keeps detailed records of the profile for the front end of each car they produce, including the top and bottom heights of the bumper, lights and grill. These profiles can be matched against the injuries on the body so that the make and model of the car involved can be narrowed down.

Sewing up the Body

Once all the internal organs have been removed and the physical evidence (bullets, fingerprints, trace evidence) has been collected, the body cavities are ready to be sewn up. The thoracic and abdominal cavities are suctioned dry of fluids and then packed with absorptive papers. Those organs that haven't been stored in either the stock or histology jar are placed in a red biohazard bag, a small amount of formaldehyde is added, then the bag is tied up and placed in the chest cavity. The chest plate is placed over the bag, then the flaps of skin from the Y incision are sewn together using a baseball-type stitch with a large, curved needle and thread. The top of the skull is replaced and the two flaps of scalp are repositioned and sewn together. The naked body is washed, toweled dry, wrapped in a clean sheet and placed in a body bag. The bagged body is then placed on a gurney and retuned to the morgue's cooler until the funeral director arrives to claim and prepare it for a funeral and burial or cremation.

Above The microtome machine is used to cut organs into very thin slices so that light can pass through them more easily for microscopic examination.

Processing of the Organs and Fluids

Two representative sections of all the internal organs are placed into formaldehyde-filled jars. The larger, "stock" jar is used to store sections for long-term future reference, so if a question about the cause of death arises, the pathologist has additional tissues to retest or provide to an independent laboratory for processing. An example of this would be when the family believes that the death was caused by cancer but the autopsy did not list cancer on the death certificate. The lung sections from the stock jar could be tested to confirm or refute this belief. The organ sections in the stock jar are saved for five years.

A smaller jar is used to submit sections of each organ to the histology department, where they are trimmed into small square sections that will fit into microtome cassettes. The microtome is a machine that cuts the tissues into very thin sections, which are then mounted on glass microscope slides for further examination.

The body fluids collected during the autopsy (blood, bile, urine, eye fluid) are sent to a forensic toxicologist (see Chapter 5) for analysis.

Histology

Histology is the microscopic study of tissues and individual cells.

Histologists create microscope slides from organs retrieved from the body. These slides can be stained with a wide variety of chemicals in order to highlight different features of the tissue.

Special Cases

The vast majority of autopsies are conducted on recently deceased, unembalmed individuals. However, sometimes the examination is conducted on an embalmed body. There are three circumstances where this occurs.

1. The death was never reported to the coroner's office and the body was taken to the funeral home for embalming. While preparing the body, the funeral director notices bruises or other injuries that warrant further investigation. Most funeral directors have a good understanding of what type of cases fall under the coroner's jurisdiction. When they see a possible autopsy case, they report their findings to the coroner's office. If the death requires forensic investigation but funeral arrangements have already been made, the coroner may allow the embalming to be completed. Then, after the viewing by family and friends, the body must be brought to the morgue for investigation.

2. Sometimes a death will appear to be natural and raise no red flags for the attending physician, and the body will therefore be buried. However, days, weeks or even years later, evidence comes to light that strongly suggests an unnatural death. In these cases the body needs to be exhumed and an autopsy is conducted.

3. The rarest of circumstances is when a body undergoes a forensic examination and is embalmed and buried, yet is later the subject of disputes over cause or manner of death. In some cases these disputes will be raised by the family of the victim, and they may hire a private forensic pathologist to exhume the body and conduct a second postmortem examination. However, authorities do not easily grant permission for an exhumation, and the various administrative and service costs for the family are high.

If the body is going to be exhumed because of either the family's wishes or a court order, arrangements are made with the cemetery to have the coffin excavated, and the coroner's van will be used to transport it to the morgue.

Case Study WHEN THE WOUNDS TELL THE STORY

The phone rang at the coroner's office at 3:15 a.m., and the investigator was told by the police homicide division that a body had been discovered in the middle of a street. The victim, an unidentified white female between 20 and 25 years old, had already been pronounced dead by paramedics. She appeared to have suffered several penetrating wounds to the chest region, and was lying on her right side in a semi-fetal position. She was dressed in a light-colored top, dark-colored skirt and one dark-colored high heel; a matching shoe was located 18 feet (5.5 m) from the victim on the sidewalk. No purse was located at the scene.

A special photographic van from the coroner's office arrived on the scene. The scene photographer set up floodlights near the victim and where the shoe was found; when the lights were switched on, a blood trail became visible, with drops leading from the shoe toward the victim. These blood drops were photographed in close-up and as a broad pattern.

THE INVESTIGATION

After all the photographs had been taken, the body was examined for the first time. Her core temperature was 98.3°F (36.8°C), while the ambient air temperature was 79°F (26°C), indicating that the victim had been dead for only a few hours, possibly less then an hour.

Back at the morgue, the external examination revealed that the left hand had several incised defense wounds across the palms, and two fingernails were broken. The fingernails of the right hand had material embedded under them, which was photographed, collected and transferred to the serology and DNA divisions of the forensic lab for analysis. The material recovered appeared to be skin and possibly some blood.

The clothing was examined, revealing two cuts in the blouse corresponding to two apparent stab wounds. A specialized forensic nurse (see Chapter 5) investigated for evidence of sexual assault, but found no indication of such an event. The now naked victim was photographed again, and multiple close-up images were taken of the stab wounds. Two penetrating wounds were located in the left upper chest region. Externally, each wound was described in terms of its position, size and shape. Wound #1 was located in the left chest, 20 inches (51 cm) from the top of the head and 3.5 inches (9 cm) to the left of the midline of the chest; it measured 0.9 x 0.15 inches (2.3 x 0.4 cm). The margins of the wound were regular and linear. Wound #2 was located in the left chest, 23 inches (58 cm) from the top of the head and 5.5 inches (14 cm) to the left of the midline of the chest, and measured 0.12 x 0.04 inches (0.3 x 0.1 cm). The margins of the wound were regular and linear.

There was a break in the case. A woman living only two blocks from where the victim was found called the police station after seeing pictures of the victim on television. It was her daughter. The mother provided the name and address of her daughter's boyfriend, a white 28-year-old electrician. She mentioned that they had been fighting a lot in the past few weeks.

The detectives arrived at the boyfriend's place of employment. When told of the death, he appeared surprised and said he had no idea that his girlfriend of three months was dead. While each individual reacts differently to this type of news, the reaction to being told of a death for the first time is significantly different to the usual response on being informed of a the death that

continued overleaf

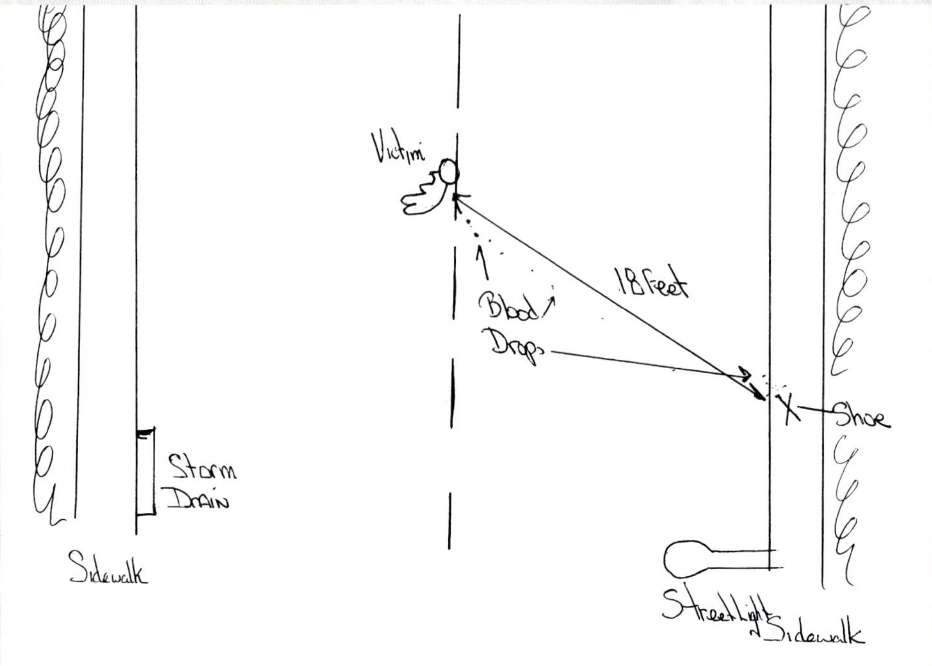

Above A death investigator made this sketch of the crime scene.

is already known or expected. The boyfriend's physical response to the news included crying and expressive body language that appeared to the detectives to be more in character with someone who is already aware of the death. But he said that he had not seen his girlfriend in two days. A search of his house yielded the following items: clothing in the back of the closet, a pair of black sneakers, a folding knife from his work-belt and a dark shirt recovered from the garbage. The dark shirt was noticed because it appeared brand-new and smelled of bleach.

During the questioning the detectives also noticed that the suspect had three parallel vertical wounds on his face. When questioned about them, he said that his friend's cat had scratched him. When asked the name of this friend, he had a hard time remembering the name. A DNA sample was collected from inside his mouth with a long cotton-tipped probe. The collected clothing, knife and DNA sample were all delivered to the crime laboratory for analysis. The suspect was placed under arrest on suspicion of homicide and taken to the county jail for processing.

AUTOPSY EVIDENCE

Back at the morgue an X ray of the chest was taken in case fragments of the weapon had broken off inside the victim. An internal examination was commenced, taking care not to transect (cut across) or go near the two wounds when cutting open the body.

Wound #2 appeared to have gone through the skin but failed to pass through the muscles of the rib cage. But with the chest plate and ribs exposed, one penetrating wound (wound #1) was seen to cut though the intercostal space between the third and fourth ribs. After the rib cage and sternum were removed, this wound was measured to be 0.2 x 0.16 inches (0.5 x 0.4 cm). The weapon had passed through the pericardium, the thin membrane that surrounds the heart, causing 3 ounces (60 ml) of blood to exit the heart into the pericardial space, the area between the heart and the pericardium. Blood had also been pumped out of the heart and into the left pleural cavity, the space around the lungs, where approximately 1.5 pints (700 ml) had collected. The path of stab wound #1 was through the entire thickness of the chest, perforating the muscles of the third intercostal space, piercing the pericardium and creating the wound to the heart. The total depth of this wound was about 5 inches (13 cm), and its path was upward and to the right.

FORENSIC TRACE EVIDENCE

The suspect's black sneakers were photographed and examined. They appeared very clean, and testing for the presence of blood on the top of the shoes was negative. However, painstaking testing in the spaces within the treads of the shoe was positive for blood, with a blood type matching that of the victim. This was the first physical evidence that placed the boyfriend at the crime scene. His knife was first fingerprinted, then photographed in the opened and closed positions, and then tested for blood. The knife blade and handle were very clean and negative for the presence of blood. However, a small amount of blood was detected within the well where the blade sits when the knife is in the closed position. This blood also matched the victim's. The detectives were told of the lab results, and they immediately began to focus on the boyfriend as their main suspect.

CONFRONTED WITH THE EVIDENCE

At the county jail, the suspect, with his lawyer present, was confronted with the forensic evidence. Against his lawyer's advice he confessed to being with his girlfriend that night, but stated that the fatal stabbing was an accident. He stated that the two of them had been having relationship problems over the previous few weeks. That night they had been walking down the street near her home, when she told him she did not want to see him any more. He claimed:

> *I tried to kiss her and she slapped me. I got very angry and pulled out my knife just to scare her. She screamed and I got scared and stabbed her once. She ran into the middle of the street and I ran after her. I was still holding the knife and I ran into her by accident. She fell to the ground and was bleeding a lot. I did not know what to do so I took her purse and put it into the storm drain to make it look like a robbery gone bad. It was an accident.*

That was his version of events, but the defense wounds and the depth of the internal stab wounds told a different story. He was charged with criminal homicide.

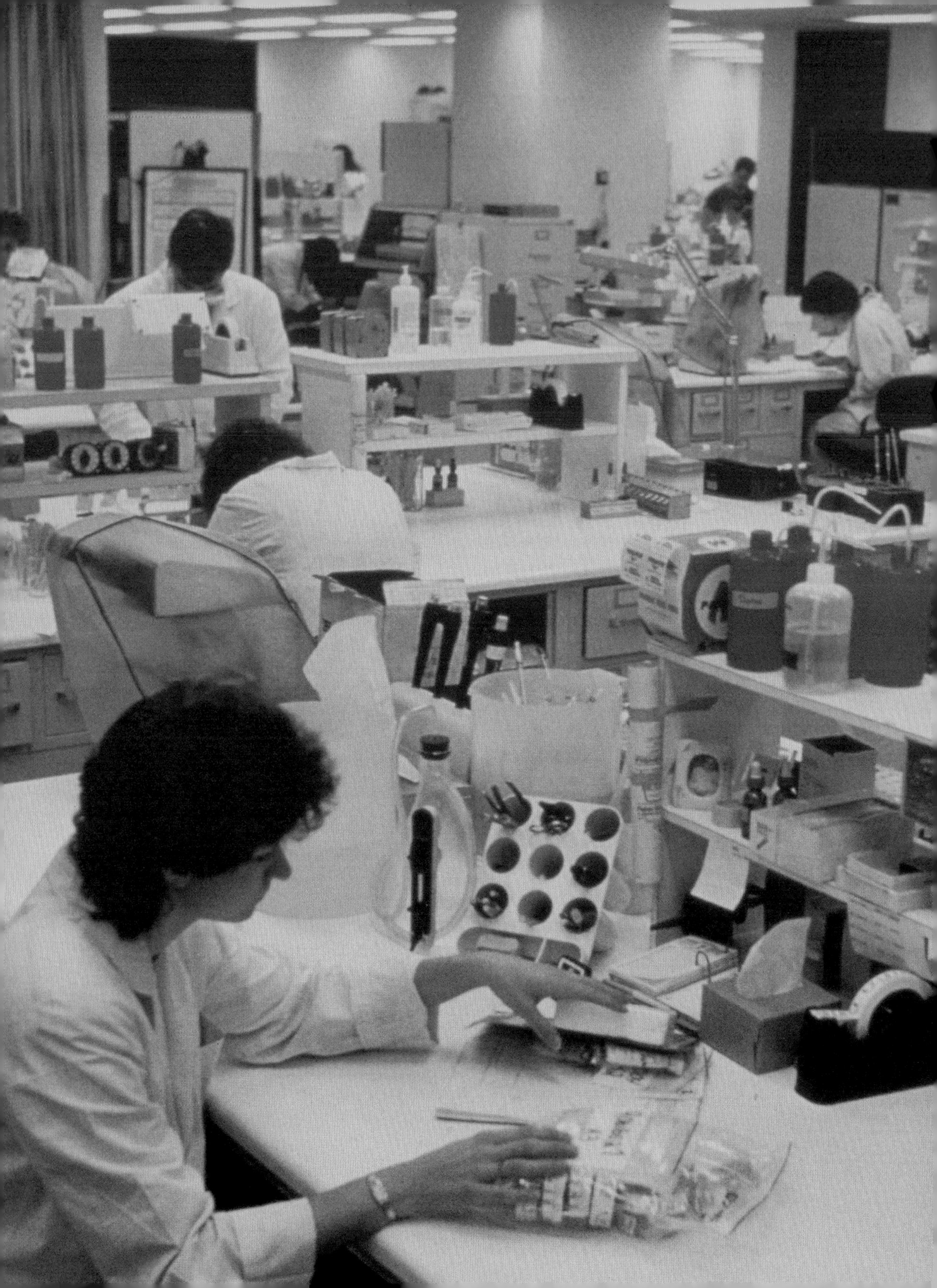

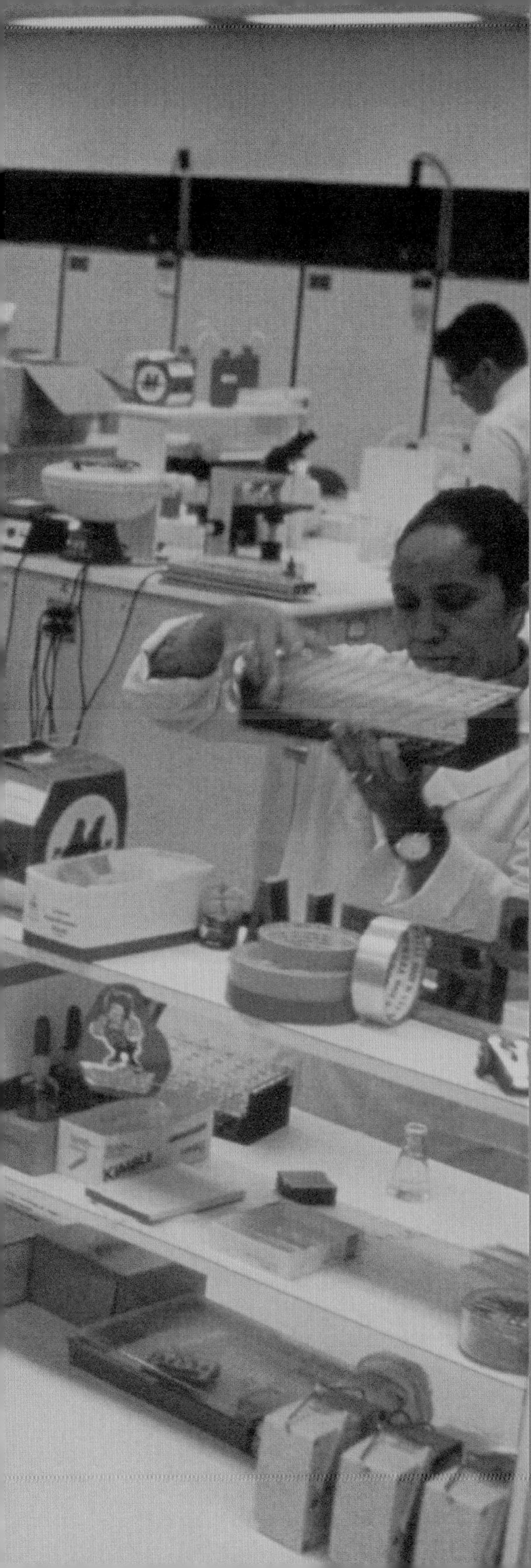

Chapter 5

When the Specialists Step In

Forensic specialists work on the cutting edge of crime-fighting technology. They employ the latest scientific methods to reveal details of events that would otherwise have remained shrouded in mystery, hypothesis and opinion.

The Need for Forensic Specialists

The cause and manner of death cannot always be determined by the forensic pathologist's examination. Fortunately, however, the pathologist can call on a range of other specialists who might assist in this goal. This chapter explains the roles of several well-recognized forensic specialists, as well as some of the emerging ones. One of the earliest specialties, forensic toxicology, dates back to the late 1600s, while modern forensic ballistics (firearms) examination can trace its origin to 1835, and forensic serology emerged in the early 20th century, following the discovery of the ABO blood groups. The more recent forensic specialities involve the training and use of cadaver dogs and the emergence of forensic nurses, forensic entomologists (insect specialists) and epidemiologists.

Above Mathieu Orfila, the "father of toxicology."

Great Names in Forensic History

The achievements of modern forensic science have been made possible only by remarkable scientific minds that througout history have turned their skills toward solving crime. A few of the major innovators are listed below.

James Marsh (1784–1846) — developed a test for showing the presence of arsenic. He first applied his test in 1832, in a murder trial where a man was accused of killing his grandfather with arsenic-laced coffee. At this time the test was still imperfect and did not secure a conviction.

Mathieu Orfila (1787–1853) — improved on previous methods of testing for arsenic, especially within a dead body. He published the *Treatise on General Toxicology* and is often referred to as the father of toxicology.

Henry Faulds (1843–1930) — a Scottish scientist who, while working with ancient clay pots, noticed the way that fingerprint impressions left in the clay had lasted thousands of years. From this observation he went on to conclude that every human being has a unique pattern of ridges making up their fingerprints.

Alec Jeffries (1950–) — developed methods for "genetic fingerprinting" of human beings at Leicester University in the 1970s. In 1988 Jeffries' method of DNA identification led to its first conviction, of the rapist and murderer Colin Pitchfork.

Forensic Toxicologist

The forensic toxicologist deals with the harmful effects of chemicals on humans. While it is forensic analysts who perform the actual testing of biological samples, to identify and quantify the amount of the chemical present, toxicologists determine the relationship between the exposure to a chemical and the noxious effects on the body. These chemicals may have been ingested, inhaled, injected or absorbed through the skin, and they may have been taken either deliberately or accidentally, or in some cases inflicted on a person without their knowing, in cases of homicidal poisoning.

The toxicologist is provided with the blood, urine, bile and eye fluid collected from the body and a copy of the death investigation report. This report sometimes offers clues to the drugs that should be tested for out of over 20 million registered compounds. Other clues are gathered from the labels on prescription bottles and statements from witnesses at the scene as to what substances may have been ingested. The methods for drug screening range from a simple spot test (where a reactive chemical is used to test for a particular suspected substance) to highly sensitive and sophisticated screening methods such as gas chromatography and mass spectrometry (see pages 105 and 106).

Blood-Alcohol Concentration

Alcohol is one of the most common toxic substances ingested by humans, and it is especially frequent as an accidental cause of death or contributing factor. Alcohol is almost always taken by ingestion (drinking), and is absorbed into the bloodstream through the stomach and small intestine. The amount of alcohol in the blood is measured by gas chromatography, and the level detected is compared to general human medical standards that determine the physiological effect on the body. From the time that the alcohol was absorbed into the blood to the time of death, it is generally accepted that the concentration of alcohol will have decreased at a rate of 0.015–0.020 percent per hour.

Spot Tests

A spot test is any method that checks for a particular drug or toxin that the forensics team suspects might be found in the blood sample. Spot tests are quick, simple color-change tests using a chemical that has a known reaction to the suspected substance; but they are not 100 percent reliable, so additional lab testing is required to confirm the identity of a suspected substance.

Testing for Legal Compounds

Once illegal substances have been investigated and alcohol levels checked, the body fluids are tested for common legal compounds — i.e., pharmaceutical drugs. All pharmaceuticals have therapeutic, toxic and lethal ranges for their dosage, and for any drug identified in the body of the deceased, it must be determined in what range the level falls. The difference between therapeutic and lethal ranges varies greatly among compounds. For example, with lithium the difference between the therapeutic and lethal levels is a factor of less than 4, meaning that one would have to take only 4 times the recommended dosage to die. The factor is over 7 for the drug acetaminophen, meaning that it would be considerably more difficult to overdose on this drug than on lithium.

Homicidal Poisoning

Occasionally toxicological screening processes may reveal substances that have no natural or likely accidental way of entering the body. Totally unexpected results, such as lethal levels of arsenic in a case that was thought to be death from illness, may be revealed. If the toxicologist has any reason to suspect that the victim was poisoned deliberately, then multiple samples (especially blood, kidney and liver) must be tested for the suspected substance, using an advanced technique such as mass spectrometry.

Blood-Alcohol Concentration and Symptoms

BAC %	Symptoms
0.010–0.050	Slight physiological impairment
0.050–0.070	Euphoria, decreased reaction time
0.080	Legal intoxication (in the United States and most parts of Canada)
0.080–0.100	Impairment to reaction time, response, attention, vision and motor coordination
0.100–0.200	Increased impairment to reaction time, sensory-motor activities, response, attention and vision Drowsiness, disorientation, loss of coordination, staggering and slurred speech
0.200–0.300	Staggering, lethargy, aggression Passing out
0.300–0.400	Impaired consciousness, stupor, unconsciousness
0.400–0.500	Unconsciousness, coma, death likely
>0.500	Death

Therapeutic, Toxic and Lethal Levels of Selected Pharmaceuticals

Drug	Therapeutic (mg/l)	Toxic (mg/l)	Lethal (mg/l)
Acetaminophen (Tylenol)	10–20	150	>160
Darvon	0.23–1.07	0.3–0.6	>1
Diazepam (Valium)	0.02–4.00	5–20	>30
Lead	0.4	0.4–13.7	>11
Lithium	4.2–9.7	13.9	>34
Magnesium	12–32	80–120	>200
Phenobarbital	10–40	40–60	>80
Xylocaine (Lidocaine)	1.5–5.0	7–20	>25

Above The mass spectrometer. This large and sophisticated piece of toxicological analysis equipment identifies substances by calculating their molecular mass. This mass is calculated by turning the molecules into charged ions, then accelerating them in a vacuum and deflecting their paths using a magnetic field. The degree to which they are deflected provides a calculation of mass, because a heavier ion will be deflected less from its trajectory than a lighter one.

Arsenic was the most popular substance used for homicidal poisonings in the 19th century, and remains so today. The main reasons for this are that it is lethal in very small quantities (200 milligrams or above) and, previously, because it could be found in household items. Arsenic was an ingredient in flypapers and could be extracted from these fairly easily.

Lethal Arrhythmia

If the results of the toxicological analyses are negative for legal and illegal compounds, or if drugs detected are below the threshold expected to cause death, then the forensic pathologist has several options in completing the death certificate. The immediate cause of death could be listed as sudden cardiac failure due to a lethal arrhythmia, and the manner as natural. An arrhythmia cannot be detected during the autopsy, and so it always remains a possible cause where no other can be detected. It is an altered activity of the normal cardiac cycle, an out-of-rhythm beating that disrupts the supply of blood to the cells. It results from a range of diseases or abnormalities that affect the activity of the cardiac muscles.

A pathologist may often have to choose between listing cardiac arrhythmia as the cause of death and simply listing the cause and manner as undetermined.

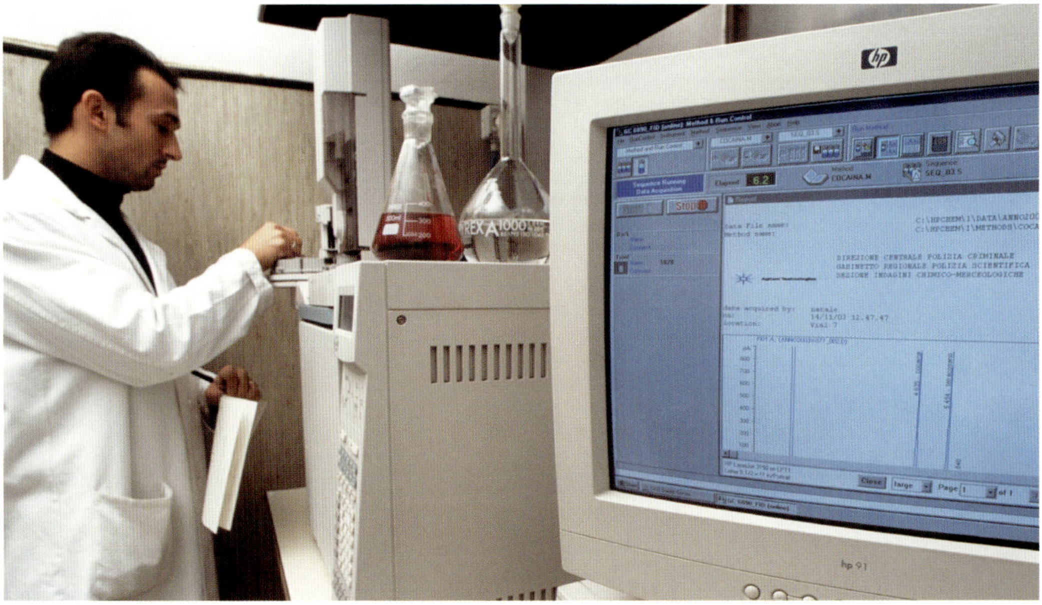

Above A forensic toxicologist operating a gas chromatograph, a machine that is extremely sensitive to small traces of chemical substances.

Case Study A YOUNG MAN WHO NEVER WOKE UP

At approximately 8:00 a.m. one morning a 28-year-old white male was found by his roommate lying faceup in bed and unresponsive. The roommate called paramedics, who arrived within 10 minutes. They declared the victim to be beyond medical treatment and pronounced him dead at 8:25 a.m.

THE INVESTIGATION

Death investigators were called in and, on arrival, obtained the following information from the roommate:

> *Last night we had a small party with five or six friends. Only alcohol was served. I last saw him alive around 2:30 a.m. talking to his girlfriend. I heard that they had a major fight last night. I saw her leave around 3:15 when I was cleaning up, and I thought I heard him snoring at around 4:00. I went to sleep soon after that, then awoke around 8:00 and discovered him unresponsive.*

Investigators visited the victim's girlfriend and informed her of the death. She became visibly upset and acknowledged that the two of them had a fight at the party.

The deceased's residence was messy, with beer cans in the garbage and some on the coffee tables. The victim was lying on a single-sized bed faceup, with no signs of struggle or foul play. The room was searched for drug paraphernalia and prescription medication bottles, but none were located. According to the roommate the victim had no significant past medical history. In addition, no suicide note was found at the scene. The roommate said the victim had been employed for the past five years as a painter and enjoyed his job; the roommate also provided next-of-kin information. His mother was called at 9:30 a.m. and informed of the death.

AUTOPSY EVIDENCE

The external examination revealed no signs of injury or intravenous drug abuse, so an internal examination was commenced. The man's heart was found to weigh 12.5 ounces (350 g), which was within the normal range. There were no occlusions (blockages) of any of the three coronary arteries, nor were there any signs of old or recent infarction of the heart muscle. The surface of the liver was smooth and dark reddish brown in color, with a weight of 3.3 pounds (1.5 kg), all of which indicated a healthy and normal liver.

At this point in the investigation the examination of the internal organs had revealed no disease or traumatic injury that could explain the cause of death. With no obvious cause of death, the pathologist signed the death certificate as "pending toxicology."

TOXICOLOGY RESULTS

Six weeks after the autopsy the results of the toxicological analyses arrived at the office of the forensic pathologist. The analysis of blood samples revealed a blood-alcohol level of 0.407 percent, well within the lethal range. Based on this, coupled with the circumstances surrounding the incident, the death was judged to be a case of accidental alcohol poisoning.

Forensic Serologist

The primary function of a forensic serologist is the examination and analysis of body fluids such as blood, saliva, semen and urine found on evidence collected from the scene or on the body. The science of forensic serology is based on the fact that certain genetically inherited characteristics present in an individual's blood can also be found in some of the other physiological fluids mentioned above, and so fluids found in a forensic investigation can be used to create a genetic profile. The foundation for these technologies was laid in 1901 with the discovery of ABO blood groups; at around the same time proteins were identified that first enabled laboratory workers to differentiate human blood from animal blood.

One of the first tasks of a serologist is to determine if the presumed sample of red material is actually blood. This test is usually conducted by using a reagent called phenolphthalein, which will turn bright pink if blood is present in the sample. This is a very easy test and is frequently carried out at the scene. If the sample is blood, the next step is to determine the ABO blood group. The serologist also looks for other genetic markers, such as protein or enzyme compounds, in the body fluids, as these can be used to confirm or deny a match with another sample.

ABO Blood Groups

Every person's blood fits into one of four blood groups: A, B, AB and O. These categories indicate whether the blood contains the A marker in its genetic makeup, the B marker, both markers (AB group) or neither (O group).

Distribution of ABO blood groups varies according to geographic and racial origin; in every part of the world, the people native to that region have quite a different statistical breakdown of ABO blood groups. For example, over 90 percent of native South Americans and Central Americans have the O blood type, while less than 5 percent of native Australians, North Americans or South Americans are of the B group. The A blood type is most common among natives of Western Europe, Scandinavia and Arctic regions, as well as certain groups of Australian Aboriginals.

Because of this variable distribution of blood types, serological analysis can be seen as a clue toward the ethnic origin of the person from whom the blood came. However, since these are merely statistical tendencies, rather than absolute rules of distribution, this can only be taken as a clue, rather than a fact.

Opposite The forensic serology lab at the U.S. Federal Bureau of Investigation (FBI) in Washington, DC.

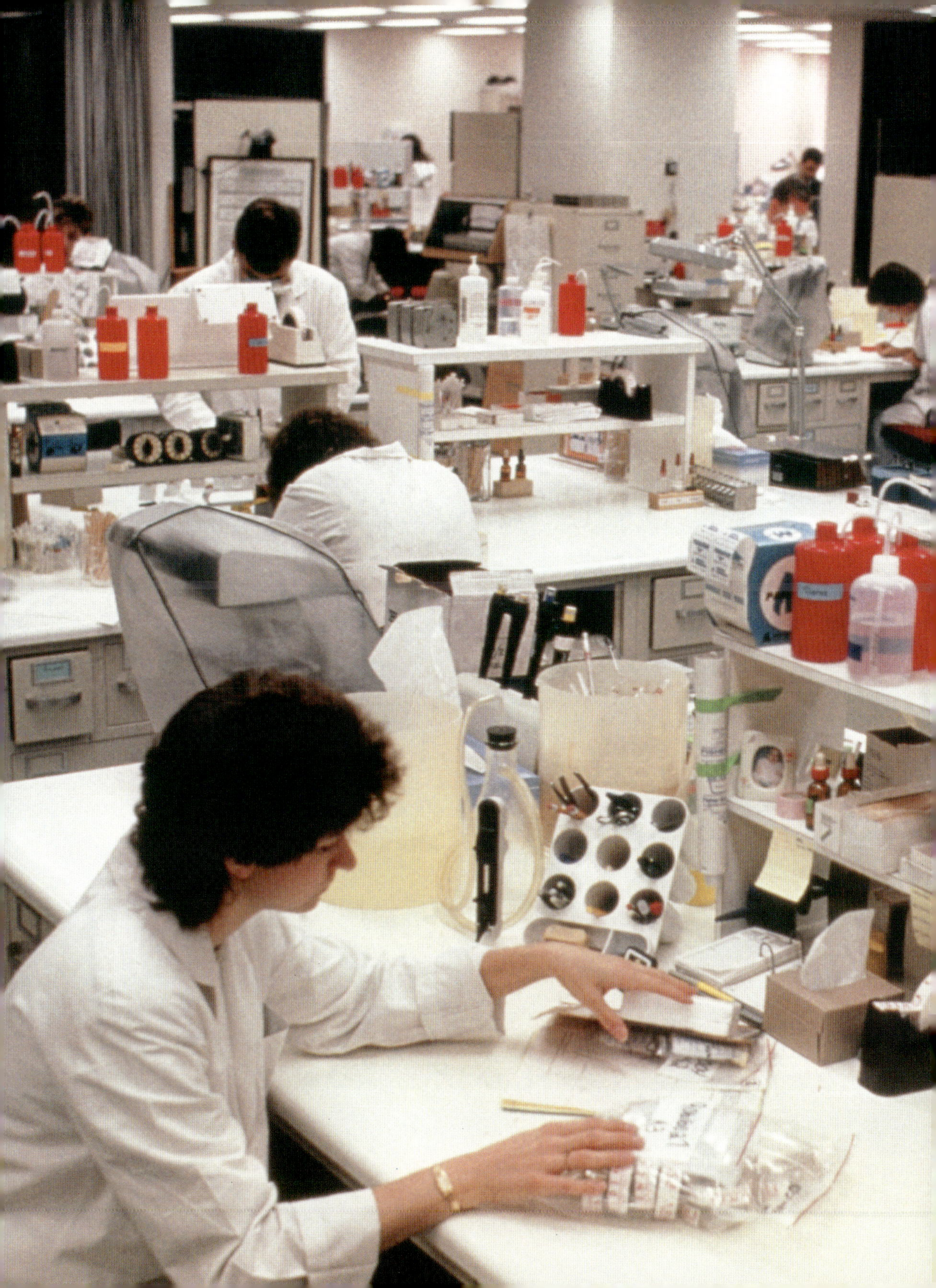

Firearms Examiner

The responsibilities of firearms examiners include determining the operational level of a weapon, testing weapons, describing the features of bullets and cartridges, comparing bullets and cartridges from one scene to others, and conducting gunshot powder residue testing. When a handgun is fired, a primer is struck, igniting the gunpowder. This results in the bullet, together with burned and unburned powder, being ejected from the end of the barrel. This powder can be deposited on the hands and clothing of the shooter, on the victim, and on individuals close to the shooter.

There are several types of firearms:

- handguns
- shotguns
- rifles
- assault rifles

The barrels of all handguns and rifles are rifled, that is, a spiral groove is cut into the length of the barrel. This rifling causes the bullet to spin when it leaves the barrel. Shotguns, on the other hand, have a smooth barrel.

The most common type of gun among the civilian population is the handgun, and among handguns there are four basic types available:

- single-shot pistols
- derringers
- revolvers
- automatics

The basic components of gun ammunition are the primer, the cartridge or case containing the gunpowder, and the projectile bullet itself. The sequence that results in the firing of a bullet is as follows: the hammer is pulled back; the trigger is pulled; the hammer strikes the primer, which ignites the powder, which then propels the bullet down the barrel with extreme force. The bullet is projected from the barrel at a velocity between 810 feet (247 m) per second up

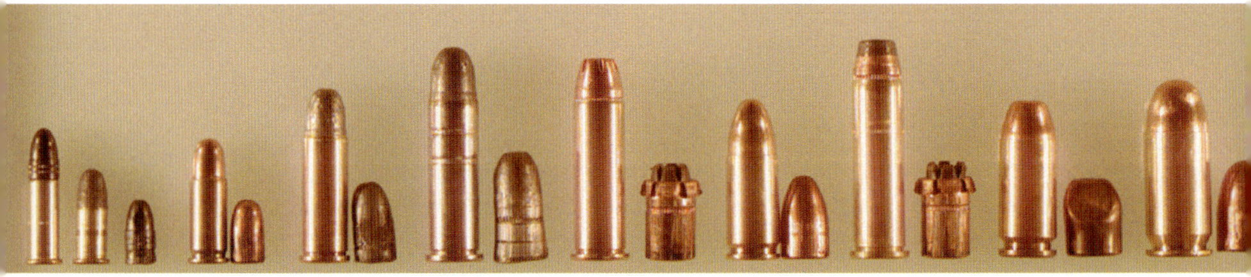

Above A range of bullets, each one displayed in its complete state and as it would typically appear after test-firing into the water tank.

Above A small-caliber, automatic handgun at a crime scene. The blood spatters indicate the direction of fire and can therefore be used, in combination with the bullet wound examination techniques described in Chapter 3, to establish where the assailant was positioned at the moment of the shooting.

to 4,110 feet (1,253 m) per second, depending on the type of firearm.

Examining a Weapon

The first thing a firearms examiner does before examining a weapon is to send it to be checked for latent fingerprints. After this, the serial number of the weapon is noted and the examiner determines whether the weapon is operational. If the weapon is incapable of operating, no further tests are conducted. But if the weapon is found to be operational, it is test-fired into a plastic water tank, which enables recovery of an undamaged bullet and a cartridge. The features of the bullet are examined with a special type of instrument called a comparison microscope, allowing the marks on the surface of the bullet (lands and grooves) to be compared against other bullets that may have been presented as evidence. This close comparison helps the firearms examiner to determine if two bullets were fired from the same weapon.

Examining a Bullet

Bullets are photographed, weighed and have their caliber measured. Under the microscope, the degree of twist exerted by the gun can be seen in the raised distortions and indented grooves that have been cut into the bullet as it traveled down the barrel. These are known as lands (the raised parts) and grooves (the indented parts). The bullet will have either a right twist or a left twist depending on the manufacturer. When a bullet is found at a crime scene or in a dead body, all the various pieces of information about its lands, grooves and twist allow the firearms examiner to fairly reliably determine what sort of gun was used to fire the bullet, and whether two bullets were shot from the same gun.

By accessing scene reports on the position of the victim, and connecting this information with the path of the entry wound, the firearms examiner is able to establish a model for the trajectory of the fatal bullet and the range from which the weapon was fired.

Bullet Wounds

When a bullet strikes the human body, it pushes the skin inward slightly, stretching it, then perforating the layers of skin to enter the bone and tissue beneath. Because the skin is stretched before being perforated and then returning back to its original position, the diameter of the entry wound is often slightly smaller than the diameter (caliber) of the bullet that caused it.

The pressure of the bullet passing through soft tissue causes a temporary cavity to open up around the path of the bullet. This cavity only lasts for about three microseconds, before contracting again as the pressure is released, leaving the tissues damaged and hemorrhaging.

The distance from which the bullet was fired has a significant effect on the nature of the wound, as described in Chapter 3.

National Ballistics Information

In the United States, class characteristics collected from bullets and cartridges are entered into the National Integrated Ballistic Information Network (NIBIN), which was established in 1997.

The NIBIN system links firearm evidence from different jurisdictions around the country, compiling digital images of bullets collected from crime scenes and bullets test-fired from recovered firearms. The system can be used to conduct a nationwide search to determine if identical bullets or cartridges have been discovered at other crime scenes. When two images match up, this strongly suggests that the two crimes were committed with the same weapon.

Opposite A comparison of the effects of three common bullet types: .357 Magnum, 7.62 mm as used in some automatic rifles, and a 12-gauge shotgun cartridge. These illustrations show the shape and depth of wounds that would be inflicted on a victim, and the manner in which fragments of ammunition disperse in the flesh.

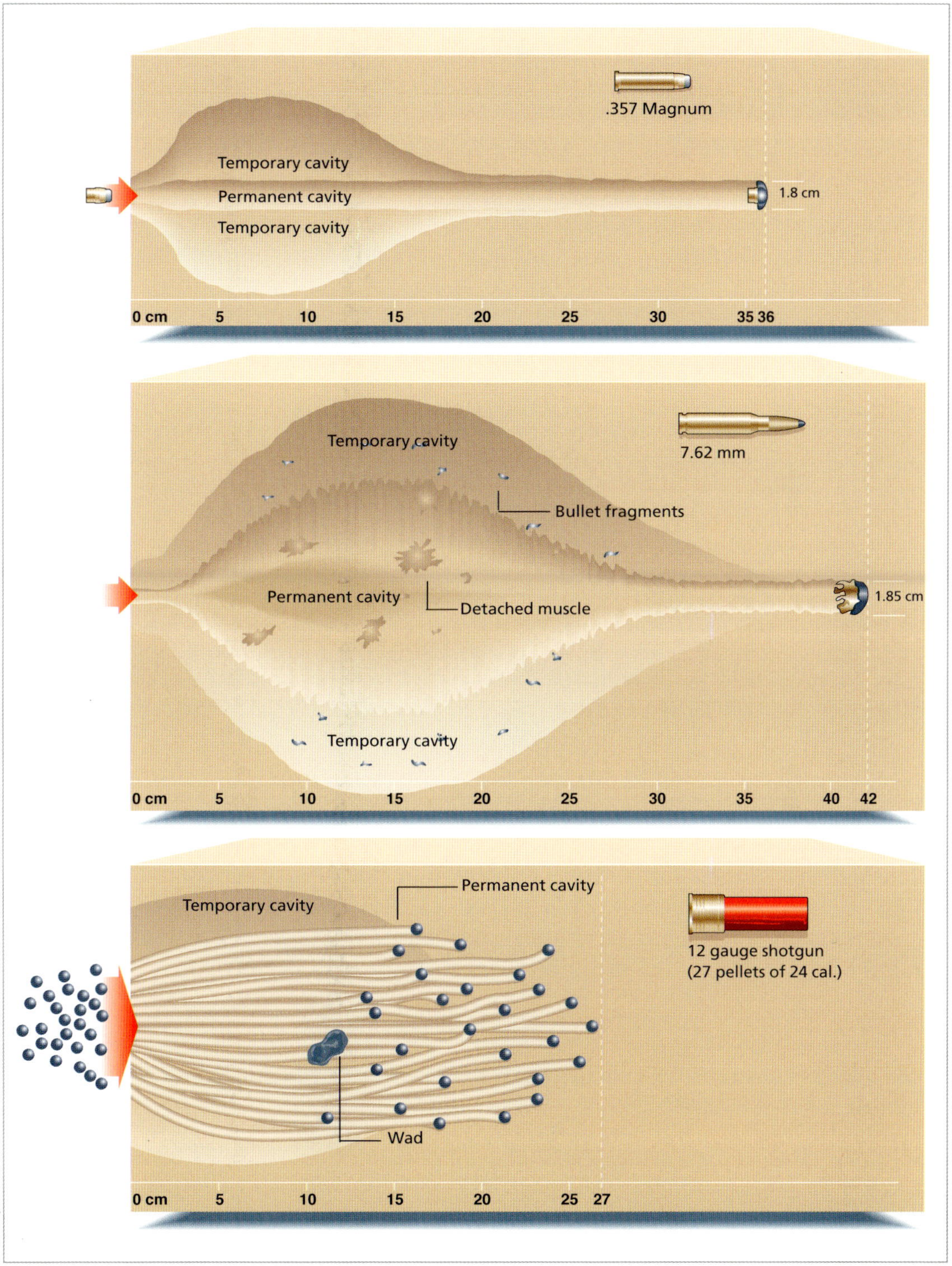
.357 Magnum
Temporary cavity
Permanent cavity
Temporary cavity
1.8 cm
0 cm
5
10
15
20
25
30
35 36
7.62 mm
Temporary cavity
Bullet fragments
Permanent cavity
Detached muscle
1.85 cm
Temporary cavity
0 cm
5
10
15
20
25
30
35
40
42
Permanent cavity
Temporary cavity
12 gauge shotgun
(27 pellets of 24 cal.)
Wad
0 cm
5
10
15
20
25
27

Case Study FRIENDS AND ENEMIES

According to the police and paramedic reports, two friends had been out target shooting in a backyard when the gun went off by accident, hitting a 25-year-old male in the back. The shooter, a 23-year-old male, gave the following statement to the police at the emergency room:

We were shooting my 9 mm automatic handgun at plastic bottles placed on a log in my backyard. My friend was walking down to set up more bottles when the handgun went off. I was holding the handgun and I thought it was empty and was about to reload it when it went off. I immediately called 911.

THE INVESTIGATION

The police took custody of the weapon and conducted an atomic absorption analysis (AAA) test (see Chapter 3) on the shooter. Unfortunately, the victim died in the emergency room. The victim's clothing, AAA results and the weapon were all transferred to the forensic lab, while the body was transferred to the morgue.

The forensic team found that the victim's gray T-shirt had an irregular hole and a small amount of dark foreign matter around the hole. The firearms examiner observed the autopsy, in which a wound was located in the lower neck region, at the back of the neck. The shape of the wound was circular and there was powder tattooing, consisting of reddish brown to orange-red lesions surrounding the entrance wound. The firearms examiner called the police officer and asked him if the shooter had stated how far away he was standing when the weapon went off, and at what angle the firearm was held. The shooter had claimed to be 6–8 feet (1.8–2.4 m) from his friend, and that the gun was at his side pointing upward when it went off. The examiner informed the officer that this would have been physically impossible, and that this was most likely not an accident but a homicide.

THE FINDINGS

The firearm examiner's report stated that the powder tattooing seen on the victim was consistent with a handgun located 1.5–2 feet (0.5–0.6 m) from the point of impact. The distribution of the powder and the shape of the entrance wound were consistent with the barrel of the weapon being very close to the entrance. To make matters even more suspicious, the autopsy report showed the path of the bullet to be from back to front, slightly downward and toward the left.

The shooter was charged with criminal homicide. During the trial, evidence was presented that he had been having a relationship with his friend's wife and wanted his friend out of the way. He had thought he could make it look like an accident. The postmortem examination of the bullet wound and the firearm examiner's testimony were sufficient to secure a guilty conviction, and the victim's "friend" was sentenced to life imprisonment.

Trace Evidence Examiner

The trace evidence division of the crime lab analyzes trace substances and objects, some of which may be visible to the naked eye, but some of which will be revealed only under microscopic examination. It is often in these, the tiniest details of the case, that the truth will be revealed.

Trace evidence includes hairs, fibers, paints, explosives, soil, glass and any other tiny physical detail that may reveal the facts of the case. The founding principle of trace evidence, known as Locard's exchange, states that when there is an interaction between two individuals (or objects) there is an exchange of physical material, and this material can be treated as evidence of the interaction. In addition, this principle also holds true for interactions between individuals and the environment. In accordance with Locard's exchange, a physical assault will result in hairs, fibers, skin cells and blood being transferred as trace evidence from the assailant to the victim, and vice versa. The use of a firearm will leave evidence of the gun on the shooter's hand and evidence of the shooter on the gun. This principle can be extended to an infinite range of situations and interactions.

Detection and Collection Methods

Trace evidence must first be detected so that it can then be collected. Methods of detection include visual searches, using various types of illumination such as ultraviolet light, lasers or high-intensity white light, and the use of magnification (and therefore the classic image of the detective's magnifying glass).

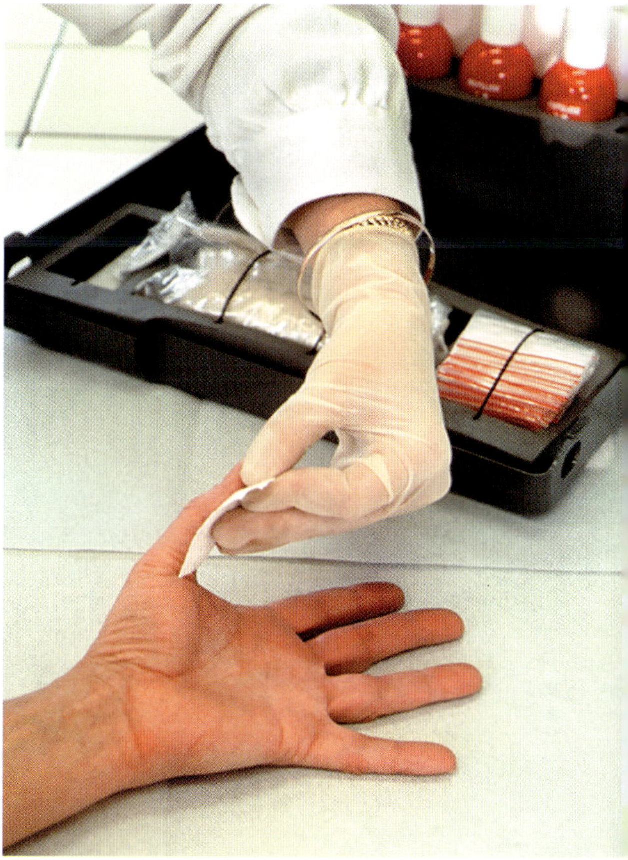

Above One method of collecting trace evidence by "lifting" is the use of medical swabs on the body of the victim. In this case the hand of a homicide victim is being tested for gun powder residue.

Once evidence is located there are several techniques for collection: picking, lifting, scraping, vacuuming, sweeping, combing and clipping. Picking means collecting evidence by using forceps. Lifting uses an adhesive tape to collect material by repeatedly and firmly patting or rolling the tape over the area to be sampled. To dislodge trace evidence from a surface where it is firmly settled or stuck, scraping with a spatula is employed. The loosened material is then collected into clean envelopes. To collect trace evidence from a carpet or bedspread a special vacuum cleaner equipped with a filter trap is used. All trace substances in the material are drawn in and collected at the filter, from which they can afterward be removed and sent for analysis.

Postmortem Trace Evidence

In the process of the postmortem examination, trace evidence may be collected from various parts of the body, such as the hair or the fingernails. Evidence caught among the hair is recovered by running a clean comb or brush though it. To recover evidence from under the fingernails, the undersides can be scraped or the nails can be entirely removed using scissors or clippers. Removed fingernails are packaged in clean paper, placed in labeled envelopes and then sent for analysis.

Lab analysts have several methods for examining trace evidence, depending on the nature of the material. For example, synthetic fibers such as nylon, rayon and polyesters can be identified using a specialized microscope. The microscopic examination can determine the fabric type, the cross-sectional shape and signs of elongation resulting from stretching of the fabric. A comparison microscope can then be used to compare the fiber sample from the suspect or crime scene to clothing fibers from the victim. The analysis of other types of trace evidence may fall under the specialization of serologists, DNA experts, sexual assault nurse examiners or ballistics experts.

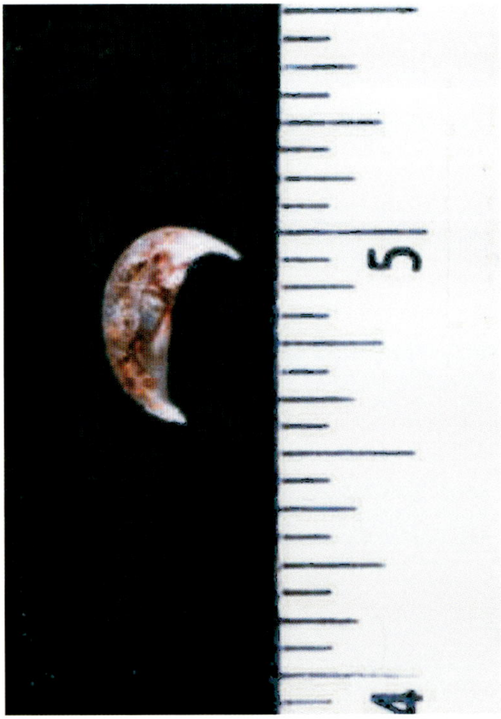

Above A fingernail removed from a homicide victim. Trace evidence under the nail may identify the assailant, either by serological testing or by DNA.

Sexual Assault Nurse Examiner

A forensic nurse is a registered nurse who has received special training in evidence collection and the preservation of death-related material. There are several sub-specialties of forensic nursing, including clinical forensic nurses, forensic psychiatric nurses and sexual assault nurse examiners (SANEs).

A SANE conducts a forensic examination checking for evidence of possible sexual assault. The nurse's main tool is the colposcope, which allows for a magnified visual inspection of the internal genitalia, revealing any bruising, tears, abrasions or lacerations that may have occurred during a rape, as well as any body fluids, hair and other trace evidence that might have been deposited by the assailant. At the end of the examination the SANE offers an opinion as to whether a sexual assault occurred, and may present this evidence as an expert witness in court. These nurses conduct their examinations on both living victims and on dead bodies that may have been the victims of a homicidal assault.

Case Study CAUSE FOR SUSPICION?

A nursing-home supervisor called the coroner's office reporting the death of one of their residents, a 76-year-old black female. The nurse called the coroner's office because the deceased was found in her bed at the 7:00 a.m. room check with her incontinence pants pulled down around her ankles. The coroner's office called in a SANE to meet them at the nursing home to conduct an assault examination.

The death investigators arrived at the scene first and collected background information about the circumstances of the death. When the SANE arrived she was provided with a summary of the events leading to the discovery of the victim, then proceeded with an external physical examination, followed by a magnified inspection of the internal genitalia using the colposcope. She did not observe any recent injuries, bruising or lacerations. Neither was any trace evidence such as semen or hair identified. At the end of the examination the nurse informed the death investigators at the scene that in her opinion there was no physical evidence of a sexual assault or abuse.

The incontinence pants around the ankles were not by themselves an indication of a sexual assault; elderly individuals, especially those suffering from dementia (often caused by Alzheimer's), may pull their pants down at inappropriate times. The elderly lady had in fact died of natural causes.

Forensic Entomologist

Not all bodies are discovered shortly after death. A number are found in advanced stages of decomposition, with maggots or other insects making use of the remains for nutrition.

Literally moments after a death, flies arrive on the body to lay their eggs. These eggs develop into several larvae (maggots) before they form into pupae, and then emerge from the pupal state as adult flies. The maggots can be used to determine the time the eggs were laid and therefore the estimated time of death.

The forensic entomologist is an individual specially trained in the life cycles of insects, as well as methods of identification, preservation and how these facts can be used to determine the time of death of an individual. The entomologist collects live maggots from the body and allows them to become adult flies, the species of which can then be identified. Each fly species has a specific life cycle, immigration patterns and feeding behaviors. Once the fly species has been identified, an estimate as to when the eggs were laid can be determined. In these cases, the time of death cannot be determined in terms of hours or days, but rather in terms of weeks, months or season that the death occurred.

Below Colored scanning electron micrograph of a female blowfly laying eggs. Blowflies are one of the species most commonly attracted to decaying human flesh.

Life Cycle of the Fly

Understanding the life cycle of flies, as shown below, is the key the forensic entomologist uses to estimate the time that has elapsed since death. The stage of life that flies on the body have reached shows how long the body has been vulnerable to fly infestation. For example, the presence of fly pupae would suggest 10 to 20 days elapsed since death.

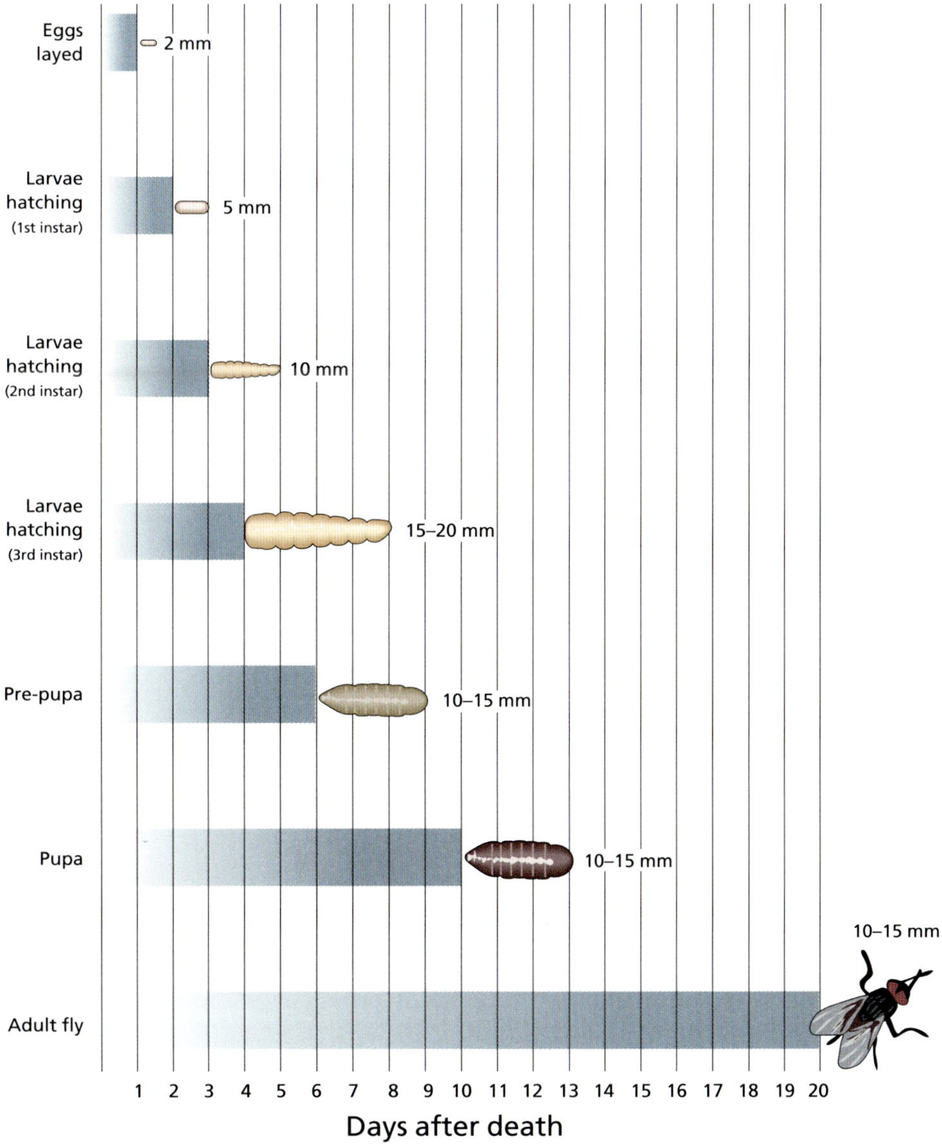

Forensic Epidemiologist

Not all forensic scientists are directly involved with the death scene investigation, the autopsy or the processing of evidence. The newest field to emerge in forensics is that of epidemiology — a specialization in providing detailed statistics about the dead. The forensic epidemiologist must detect the emergence of new, lethal and illegal drugs; document fatality trends; identify populations at risk of death; link behavior to specific deaths; and provide relevant data to outside agencies such as the Food and Drug Administration (FDA), the Federal Bureau of Investigation (FBI) and the Centers for Disease Control (CDC).

Epidemiological method isolates the risk factors that are involved in the distribution, causation and control of disease in the human population. A forensic epidemiologist concentrates on a particular section of the population and examines the patterns and distribution of deaths from homicide, suicide, accident and natural causes within that group. For example, a forensic epidemiologist would be interested in the distribution of homicide cases by time, place and motive — do people commit murder more often in the evening or the morning; at home, work or in public; against a stranger, friend or an acquaintance; out of anger, greed, revenge or jealousy?

Odds of Dying for Citizens of the U.S., 1995

Event	Odds of dying during a year	Lifetime odds of dying
Pedestrian	1 in 45,117	1 in 588
Car occupant	1 in 18,752	1 in 244
Drowning	1 in 544,551	1 in 7,100
Fall	1 in 20,728	1 in 270
Firearm	1 in 331,092	1 in 4,317
Dog attack	1 in 10,912,800	1 in 142,279
Lightning	1 in 4,262,813	1 in 55,578
Suicide	1 in 9,343	1 in 122
Homicide	1 in 16,154	1 in 211

Forensic epidemiologists are also concerned with distinguishing personal, biological or socioeconomic characteristics that place certain individuals at an increased risk of disease. For instance, does living in proximity to a chemical facility increase the likelihood of dying from cancer, or are those individuals who develop cancer more genetically susceptible? This relatively new specialty will increase our knowledge of intentional and unintentional injuries and death and thereby improve the health and safety of the community. Forensic epidemiologists are typically employed at coroners' offices or health departments, or as forensic consultants and expert witnesses.

Forensic epidemiologists have played key roles in the investigation of sudden infant death syndrome (SIDS), silicone breast implants and poisonings.

Death Statistics

From the work of the forensic epidemiologist we gain an overall picture of the statistical facts for how, when and where people die — and who is most likely to die in which circumstances, in terms of their age, sex and ethnicity. The figures of these statistics vary significantly from one country to another, although there are certain broad patterns that appear in all developed countries.

Causes of death can be divided into main categories, which are, in order of prevalence: natural death, accidntal drug overdose, suicide, falls, motor vehicle accident and homicide.

Natural Death

Typically, natural deaths by illness or infirmity represent around 40 percent of the coroner's caseload, making them the single most likely general category. Natural deaths are further subcategorized according to the bodily system in which the malfunction occurs. The most prevalent are circulatory system deaths (especially heart disease), followed by respiratory failures, then diseases of the nervous system (especially the brain).

Humans of both sexes and all ethnicities are naturally prone to die from disease, and of course the older the body gets, the more likely it is to succumb.

Overdose Death

Drug overdose is the second most prevalent category, including overdoses of illegal narcotics and legal pharmaceuticals. Victims of drug overdose are most often white males, and the substances most often responsible are cocaine and heroin.

Epidemiological data about drug overdose deaths are passed on to the police to help them analyze the trafficking of drugs: which drugs are being sold in which areas, any unusually potent supplies that may have become available, and any new drugs that appear among users and dealers.

Suicide

Epidemiologists collect data on suicide, which they then pass on to community health and mental health organizations.

Information is recorded on the method of suicide and any past attempts. Perceived or stated reasons for suicide are also recorded: relationship problems, economic problems or health problems. All of this information helps to identify who is at risk of suicide, and therefore to offer them better care and protection.

Males of middle age are generally at greatest risk of suicide, and the vast majority take their lives while alone in their own homes.

Falls

Information on falls is collected: who, where and how. The demographic group most at risk is women over 75 years old, most of whom fall fatally within their own residences.

Motor Vehicle Accident

This cause of death is subject to detailed epidemiological analysis as part of governments' efforts to reduce the prevalence of fatal accidents. Some of the major risk factors to emerge from epidemiological data are not wearing a seat belt, alcohol intoxication, being the driver and being male. After drivers, pedestrians are the most likely group to die in a motor vehicle accident, and the most dangerous time of day is late afternoon or early evening.

Homicide

Homicide is less prevalent than all the other causes of death listed above, and is often associated with other criminal activity. The demographics for homicide victims vary widely from country to country, according to the social tensions in each. Epidemiological patterns of homicide are carefully monitored, as they may give an indication of broader criminal or social trends.

Sudden Infant Death Syndrome

Sudden infant death syndrome (SIDS) is the tragic death of a previously healthy infant during the first year of life, with no detectable cause of death. Neither the death scene investigation, autopsy nor toxicology analysis can provide evidence for a cause. The medical community has been puzzled and has very little comfort to offer grieving parents as to how or why their infants died.

However, epidemiological analyses of the circumstances surrounding the thousands of infant deaths have started to develop some patterns and risk factors among a large percentage of the deaths. The forensic epidemiologists reviewing the death investigation reports have noted two factors — the majority of the infants were placed to sleep in the facedown position, and there is also a statistically significant tendency for infants co-sleeping with their parents to become victims of SIDS. While the work of forensic epidemiologists has not explained the physiological reasons behind SIDS, it has significantly reduced the death rate. In the early 1960s there were approximately 25,000 SIDS deaths per year in the United States. Today,

Above Evening and nighttime are particularly high-risk times of day for motor vehicle accidents. Drug or alcohol usage heightens the risk.

following the "Back to Sleep" campaign, the figure is now under 5,000 a year.

Mass Poisoning

One of the roles of the forensic epidemiologist is to track the number of deaths by cause and manner of death for that jurisdiction and to note increases from the normal or expected numbers for each type of death. The forensic epidemiologist, using several years' worth of data, can determine the range of deaths expected to be seen during a year. This method can be used to detect intentional or unintentional poisoning on a large scale. If a coroner's office typically sees two deaths per year from gastrointestinal bleeds, but suddenly comes across 15 cases within a couple of weeks, an investigation would be triggered. The locations of residences and workplaces of the victims would be mapped to look for patterns, which might reveal that a water or food supply was being contaminated. This might turn out to be a case of food poisoning through poor hygiene standards in a food production plant, or deliberate mass poisoning, even calculated chemical terrorism, by use of toxic agents.

Cadaver Dogs

Another of the more recent forensic specialties to emerge is a canine, rather than human, ability. The first dog trained exclusively for a cadaver search by law enforcement was put to work in 1974 by the New York State Police, who were investigating a series of homicides in Oneida County that involved multiple buried victims in a large, heavily wooded area. The dog involved was a yellow Labrador retriever trained at a military research facility in Texas, and it soon found its first cadaver, a college student buried at a depth of 4 feet (1.2 m).

Above A cadaver dog and its tranport van, at the scene and ready to search.

Realizing that cadaver dogs could turn out to be very valuable forensic assets, police expanded their training programs to include dogs taught to find bodies below ground, above ground or hanging, and even drowned victims.

Selection and Training

A very important consideration for choosing the type of dog for cadaver search is that the dog must have a strong "prey drive." This can be tested when the dog is a puppy, by observing its enthusiasm for chasing a ball or toy that has been thrown across a room. A dog that shows extreme interest in these objects and a need to retrieve them for the handler shows excellent potential for a search dog career.

Cadaver dogs use a form of search called air scenting. This differs from a tracking dog, which follows a specific, individualized scent on the ground or through brush. Air-scenting dogs work from what is known as a scent cone, the area over which the target's scent is dispersed through the air. The dog has the ability to pick up the scent of decomposing human remains from up to a quarter of a mile away and home in on that scent at its strongest point of origin, that being the actual deceased individual.

A human's scent undergoes a transformation at the time of biological death. Live scent is specific to each individual human on the planet, but when a body begins to decompose, it begins to emit a generic scent that all human remains have in common. These stages of decomposition fall into five general categories: fresh (or newly deceased), bloating, decaying, liquefying or skeletal remains. Bodies that have been submerged in water also have a distinguishing odor caused by a substance called *adipocer*, a grayish, soapy substance also known as "grave wax." Bodies left in hot, dry environments will mummify and give off a musty smell for the dog to follow. From an early stage of training the cadaver dog must be trained to recognize the scents that accompany each of these stages of human decomposition.

During initial training the dog is introduced to the scent of human remains. One way to do this is to set up "training blocks," which are concrete cinder blocks with holes in the top where scent can be placed. A scent is placed in one of the numerous blocks in the training area and the dog is introduced to each of the blocks and allowed to sniff them. When the dog sniffs the block with the scent it is rewarded with lots of praise and given a favorite toy or ball. The dog also has to be taught to indicate its findings by movements of its head, ears, eyes, tail, whole body or even breathing patterns. This sets up communication between the cadaver dog and its handler, so that they can work together as a team to find bodies.

As training progresses, the scent is placed in more difficult areas, perhaps buried an inch or two below ground in an open field, or placed under a cover of

The Passive Alert

One of the most important aspects of the cadaver dog's work is the task of signaling correctly when it has discovered the odor of a decomposing body. The dog must be carefully trained so that it indicates the presence of the odor at the precise moment when it finds the odor at its strongest point, and not at any other time.

The dog must also be trained to use a correct signaling method. Standard signals are either sitting down or lying down; these are referred to as "passive alerts" and are important because the dog must not alert in any way that might disturb crucial evidence.

leaves or debris. The dog learns to use its sense of smell to please the handler and be rewarded. The dogs are also trained not to alert to scents the handler is not interested in finding, such as decomposing animal remains, food, previous dog markings, etc. To accomplish this, the dog is placed back on the block work previously mentioned, and in one of the blocks, for example, a carcass of a dead animal will be placed. When the dog shows the least bit of interest in this scent, it is strongly corrected away from it, told "Leave it," and encouraged to continue down the line of blocks to the human-remains scent.

K-9s

Another type of cadaver dog is the forensic K-9, which is trained to a more advanced level of scent detection. A K-9 is able to indicate to its handler items that have previously been in contact with a human body. For instance, the handler may be called to a section of highway where the occupant of a fleeing vehicle was noticed to throw a murder weapon, such as a knife, out the window of the vehicle. A skilled K-9 would be called in to locate this knife, which might be covered in the victim's blood. Forensic K-9s may also be used for vehicle searches, for instance, if police have been given a tip that leads them to believe that a body may be in the trunk of a vehicle, and this vehicle is now parked in a lot with numerous other vehicles. The K-9 would be walked around the perimeter of these vehicles and would show a trained indication wherever it picked up a cadaver scent emanting from within.

Human and Animal Limitations

There are limits to what a cadaver dog can do. One can never conclude that there are definitely no human remains in an area, because the dog may not have picked up the scent because of weather conditions or air movement between the scent and the dog. Sometimes the handler may have failed to interpret the dog's signals and behavior. These limitations in the work of the cadaver dog must be acknowledged to prevent police and forensic teams from having unrealistic expectations about the search and the meaning of its results.

Opposite A cadaver dog in training, being introduced to the scent of decomposed human skeletal remains.

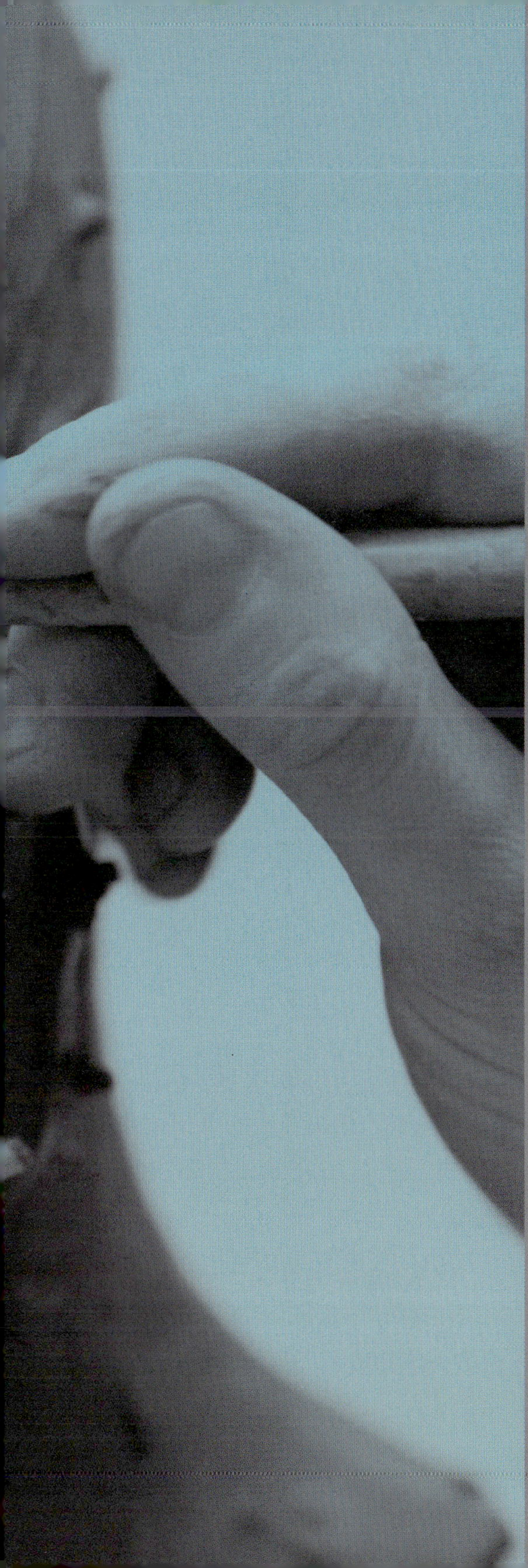

Chapter 6

The Determination of Identity

Police sometimes have trouble obtaining the true identity of a living person, but the dead can be much more difficult. A dead body cannot tell you its name, where it is from or who are its next of kin. Instead, forensic techniques are required, whether they be simple methods based on inquiry and questioning, or more sophisticated scientific methods.

Determining Identity

LEVELS OF IDENTIFICATION

- **Positive Identification**
  The antemortem and postmortem data match in sufficient detail to establish that they are from the same individual. At the same time, there are no irreconcilable discrepancies.
- **Possible Identification**
  The antemortem and postmortem data have consistent features but, because of the quality of either the postmortem remains or the ante-mortem evidence, it is not possible to positively establish identification.
- **Insufficient Evidence**
  The available information is insufficient to form the basis for a conclusion.
- **Exclusion**
  The antemortem and postmortem data are clearly inconsistent. However, exclusion may deductively lead to a positive identification in certain circumstances, where forensics experts can work out who the body is by working out who it isn't.

Why is it so important to make a positive identification? The reasons include

1. to establish the death of that individual for official, statistical and administrative purposes;
2. to allow the discharge of legal claims and obligations such as property, estates and debts;
3. to allow claims for life insurance, survivor's pensions and other financial matters;
4. to allow the initiation of legal investigations and inquiries into criminal or suspicious deaths;
5. to provide relatives with definitive proof of the death of their loved one, allowing them emotional closure.

Methods for establishing positive identification fall into visual, medical and technical categories. Visual methods include viewing of the body by those who knew the living person, clothing recognition, and matching the body against official identity documents. Medical methods include the use of fingerprints, X-ray comparison (dental and other sites), surgical prostheses, medical implants and evidence of disease conditions. The most technical methods of identification rely on

Opposite Thai officials attempt to identify bodies in the aftermath of the Indian Ocean tsunami disaster, December 2004.

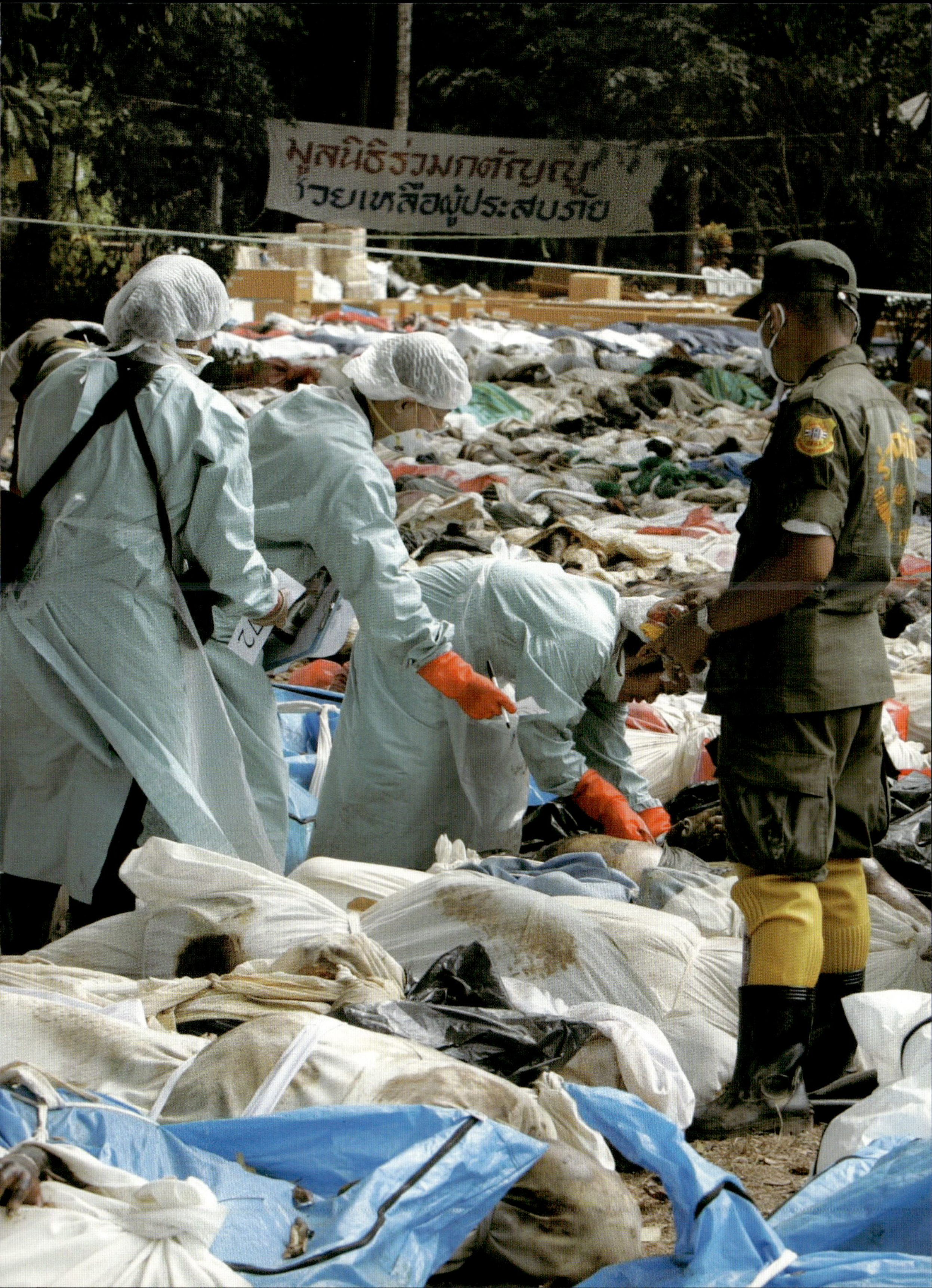
มูลนิธิร่วมกตัญญู
วยเหลือผู้ประสบภัย

skeletal analysis, DNA comparison or facial reconstruction. The method employed is dictated by the circumstances of the death and the condition of the body.

Visual Identification

One of the most frequently employed methods of determining identity is through visual comparison. Typically this is done by the next of kin viewing the body, either in person or via a closed-circuit monitor, to determine that it is in fact their mother, father, spouse, etc. However, recognition of the recently dead is not always easy, because death can cause significant alteration in the features. There have been cases where parents and spouses doubt or even deny the identity of their nearest and dearest in these circumstances.

If there is no immediate family, then close friends or neighbors may be able to establish the identity of an individual. Another method of visual identification, where there is nobody present who knows the deceased, is to compare the body against the image on a driver's license or other official photo-identity card.

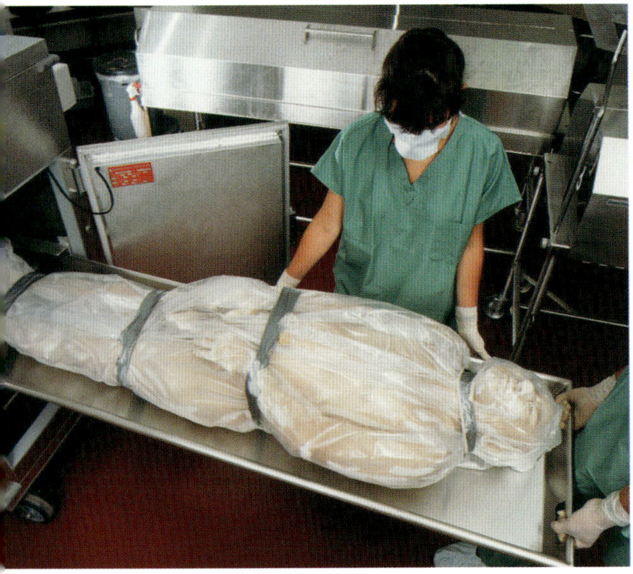

Above The body of a white male is removed from the cooler, in the hope that next of kin can make a visual identification.

Tattoos

Tattoos are created by injecting pigments under the epidermis into the layer of skin underneath. Black pigments are the most resistant and least likely to fade.

Tattoos encompass a broad range of styles and imagery. Because of their uniqueness, tattoos can be used to make a positive identification even in cases where the body is in advanced stages of decomposition. Professionally applied tattoos are permanent, and even where a body is decomposed, burnt or has been submerged in water, pathologists can still usually find a suspected tattoo by scraping away the outer skin to find the ink still present in the dermis underneath.

The face is often the primary target in the decomposition process, thereby making a positive identification through facial recognition difficult or impossible. However, the back, chest and arms (where tattoos are often applied) are less affected by the decomposition process, so this may become a backup method for visual identification. Photos of the victim depicting tattoos are sometimes compared to those taken during the postmortem examination.

Tattoos applied in jail or at home are not as useful for postmortem identification as professional tattoos, since amateur methods generally don't manage to get as much ink lodged permanently under the skin.

Clothing and Personal Effects

In cases where the features of the head have been so distorted that positive identification is impossible or highly traumatic for the next of kin, the clothing worn by the victim can be used to make a positive identification. These circumstances include cases such as suicide by shotgun wound to the head, an individual hit by a train, or victims of exposure to chemical agents. Detailed description of the clothing includes the type, color, size of the collar, trouser length and the nature of the fabric. Laundry marks and tailor's labels can also help to identity the owner. The next of kin are asked to describe the clothing worn by their loved one to determine if it matches that worn by the victim. However, if the clothing lacks uniqueness, this is not a strong method.

Personal effects found on the body can also aid in identification.Wallets or purses are inspected for a driver's license, social security card or credit cards. In addition, rings, watches and necklaces may be engraved, or may be identified by family members as having been worn by a particular individual.

Above When a body is badly decomposed, distinctive items of clothing may present one of the best chances of making an identification. In this case, green buttons on a dress are visible despite the body having been buried underground for years.

Limits of Visual Identification

While visual comparison provides a quick and efficient method of identification, there are many circumstances in which it is impossible. Visual identification usually requires relatives or close friends to help make the determination. In small towns and close communities this is usually possible, but in cities with a large, transient population, the coroner's office will often need to turn to other methods. And except for when distinguishing tattoos have survived, visual methods are virtually useless in identifying decomposed bodies.

Medical Identification

Fingerprints

Fingerprints are composed of patterned ridges on the tip of each finger and thumb. The human body forms these marks at 17 weeks of gestation, and they survive without change for the rest of the individual's lifetime.

Developments in Fingerprinting

The use of fingerprints as a means of identification is an ancient method. Its earliest recorded use is on clay tablets for business transactions in Babylon between 1000 and 200 BCE. In the 14th century CE a Persian government physician realized that no two fingerprints are an exact match, while in 1823 nine fingerprint patterns were first published by Professor Johannes Evangelist Purkinjii at the University of Breslau, Prussia.

The first modern-day use of fingerprint identification was made in 1870, and the technique soon gained further fame after it was used to identify the murderer in Mark Twain's *Life on the Mississippi* (1883). The first real-life use of fingerprint identification to solve a crime was by Argentinian police in 1892, when they identified a woman who had murdered her two sons. The woman had cut her own throat in an attempt to blame another, but her bloody print on a doorpost proved her identity as the murderer.

In 1905 the U.S. Army started fingerprinting its troops; by 1908 both the Navy and the Marines had followed suit. In 1924 the FBI established an identification division, initially collecting prints on cardboard cards, from which matches were searched for by visual inspection. In 1999 the Automated Fingerprint Identification System (AFIS) technology was created, computerizing fingerprints and allowing an automated search among millions of records.

Fingerprints for Corpse Identification

Aside from the identification of criminals, fingerprints can also help in the identification of unknown dead bodies.

Above The seven main classifications of fingerprints. Every human print either fits one of these types, or displays a mixture of these characteristics.

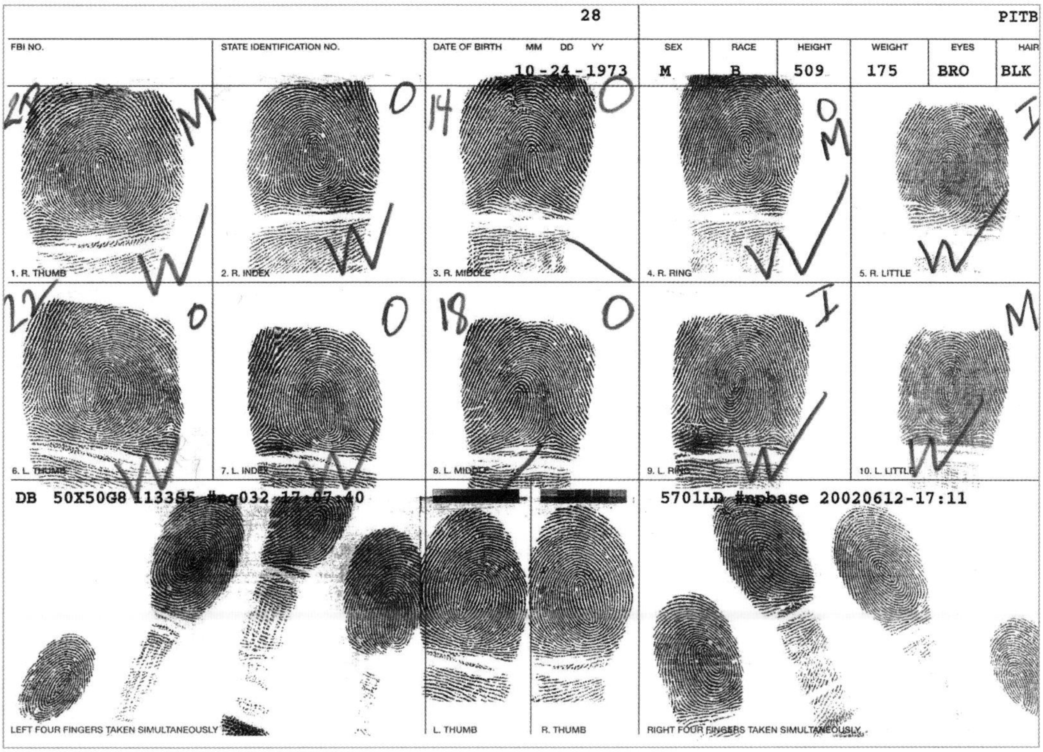

Above A full set of fingerprints, showing each finger separately, as well as all together.

Individuals who are found naked, without identifiable clothing or tattoos, and in a moderate stage of decomposition may be most appropriately identified by their fingerprints.

If the search of the victim (clothing and effects) and a thorough scene investigation fail to identify an individual, the forensic pathologist will call in a latent-fingerprint examiner to take fingerprints. The technique of fingerprinting the recently dead is similar to that used on the living: the basic equipment consists of an inking plate, a cardholder, printing ink (heavy black paste) and a roller. The ink is spread in a thin, even coat over the tips of the fingers, then the thumb, index, middle, ring and little finger of each hand are rolled on a card. Next, impressions of the fingers and the thumb are taken simultaneously without rolling.

If the victim is in the early stages of decomposition, the hands may be in a clenched position and rigor mortis of the fingers may have set in. Under these conditions, attempts are made to straighten the fingers, first by the application of force; if that fails, deep incisions between the thumb and index finger can be attempted. If the stiffening cannot be broken, it may be necessary to cut off the skin. Another problem encountered with decomposed fingers is excessive wrinkling. This condition can be corrected by injecting a tissue-building substance underneath the skin.

Fingerprinting Decomposed Bodies

In the advanced stages of decomposition, three conditions are encountered: putrefaction (rotting), mummification (drying out) or maceration (water-logging). In any of these circumstances the outer skin may detach from the finger. If the fingers are mummified they are removed and placed in a solution to rehydrate them. This process can take several hours, or even weeks. The skin of fingers immersed in water first absorbs water and swells, then starts to loosen from the flesh within a few hours. These changes are reversed by applying alcohol, benzene

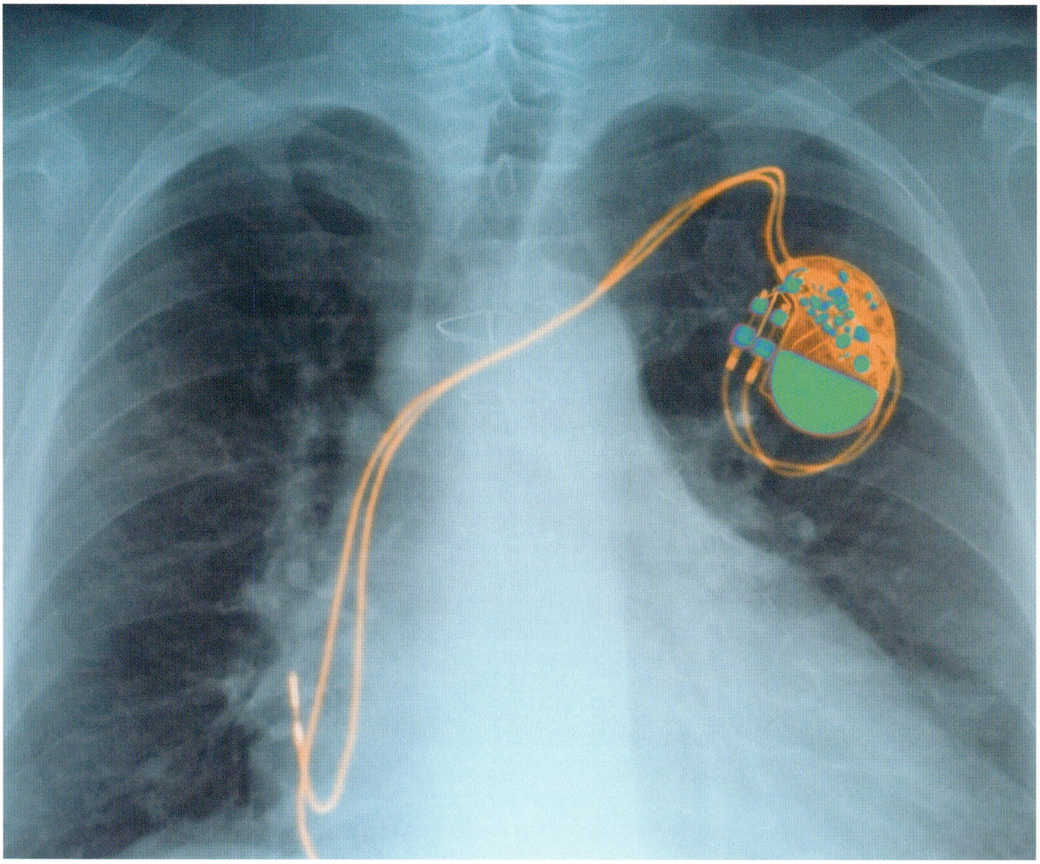

Above Colored X ray showing a pacemaker that has been surgically implanted inside the body. If matched with medical records, this might be used to identify the deceased.

or acetone to the fingers, thus allowing prints to be taken.

Fingerprinting is a highly effective means of identification. However, there are two common limiting conditions. First, the fingerprints of the unidentified victim must be on file with either a law enforcement, government or military database. Second, fingerprint identification is often not possible if the body has sustained extensive burns.

Implants and scars

Another form of medical identification is through the location of surgical implants such as pacemakers, breast implants, surgical pins or plates during the internal examination of the body. In addition, procedures such as bypass surgery, stomach stapling and removal of the appendix can be matched to medical records and used to identify the individual.

All medical implants bear a serial number. Once the implant has been located and removed, the manufacturer can be contacted to determine the name, date of implant and other medical information regarding the individual patient.

Disease Conditions

The internal examination of the organs can reveal medical conditions such as gallstones, silicosis, asbestosis and various congenital anomalies. These conditions can be identified even in decomposed bodies. If these conditions had been documented during the individual's life, the forensic evidence can be compared against medical records to assist in the identification process.

Case Study IDENTIFYING A LOST SOUL

A demolition crew preparing to bring down an abandoned building were doing their final walkthrough when a worker discovered what appeared to be the charred remains of a human being. Police, death investigators and a forensic photographer were called to the scene.

The victim appeared to be a male dressed in only a shirt and shorts, providing little to help with the identification. Facial recognition and fingerprinting were ruled out by the advanced state of decomposition, besides which there were no leads for next of kin. At the forensic labs the body was X-rayed from head to toe, revealing that the right ulna in the forearm had a metal implant. This bone had previously sustained multiple fractures, requiring it to be surgically repaired by installing a 10-inch (25 cm) metal plate.

The plate was removed during the autopsy and revealed the name of the manufacturer and a serial number. The makers of the plate were contacted and provided the name, address and the date that the plate was implanted. This information was used to contact the next of kin, who confirmed that the victim was a chronic drug abuser and had been a drifter for several years.

Skeletal Identification

One of the most complicated circumstances for a forensic pathologist is the determination of identity when the remains are nothing more than a collection of bones, either a whole or an incomplete skeleton. In these cases an outside expert such as a forensic anthropologist is typically called in to answer several key questions:

1. Are they bones?
2. Are they human bones?
3. What is the sex?
4. What is the stature?
5. What is the race?
6. What is the age?
7. How long has the victim been dead?

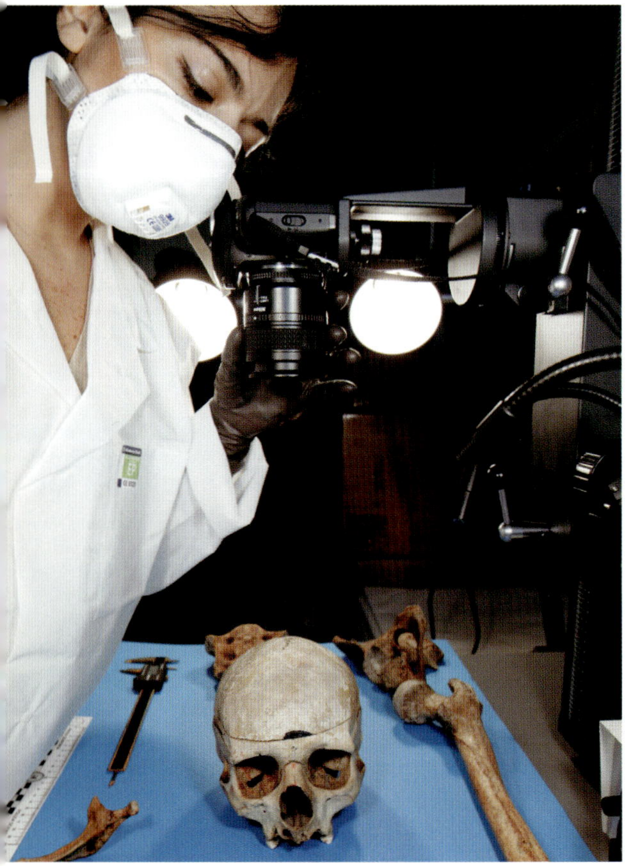

Above Rulers, calipers and cameras being used to measure all the dimensions of a skull.

To the untrained eye, including those of police, many objects can resemble bones. Stones, plastic and hardwoods have been confused with skeletal remains. Each year around the beginning of the hunting and hiking season, the police and coroner's offices are flooded with reports from outdoor adventurers who are convinced that they have found human bones; the vast majority turn out to have come from small animals.

Sometimes human remains are found by passersby in uninhabited areas, but even then it may not turn out to be a case of suspicious circumstances. In one case a human mandible was found in a wooded area behind a large medical school. Upon close examination by the forensic pathologist, it was determined to be a discarded lower jaw that had been used for teaching in the medical school's dental department.

Occasionally human skeletal remains are discovered that require a full forensic investigation. The skeletal remains are collected, along with the immediately surrounding soil to ensure that even the smallest bones are included. At the coroner's office the bones are laid out on a clean white sheet and assembled into their normal anatomical positions. The first role of the anthropologist is now to determine the sex, race, age and stature of the victim. Sex and, to a lesser degree, race can be determined from the skull. Sex can also be confidently determined from the pelvis bone if it has been recovered. The femur (the long bone of the thigh) gives an approximate calculation of the individual's height.

If candidates for possible identity of the remains have been identified, and if antemortem X rays of these candidates' skeletons are available, the forensic team can use the skeletal remains to attempt a positive identification. At the morgue an X ray is taken that closely matches the position and angle of the antemortem X ray. Then the two are overlaid and examined for similarities. For example, if chest X rays were taken for a physical checkup, a similar type of chest X ray would be taken from the skeletal remains. Signs of old fractures or abnormalities of the bones (e.g., sclerosis) increase the accuracy of this method of identification.

THE HUMAN SKELETON

- Adult humans usually have about 206 bones, but a baby is born with approximately 270.
- Males tend to have slightly thicker and longer limbs.
- Women tend to have larger pelvic bones in relation to body size, narrower rib cages, smaller teeth and less angular jawbones.

Photo Superimposition

Another method of identification compares skeletal remains against photographs of a possible candidate for identification. A famous case in which photo superimposition led to an identification involved Dr. Josef Mengele, who had been a notorious camp doctor at Auschwitz during the Nazi Holocaust. It was believed that Mengele left Germany and later died in Brazil on February 7, 1979, being buried under the alias of Wolfgang Gerhard.

The remains of "Wolfgang Gerhard" were exhumed six years after his death. The age and sex of the remains matched the facts about Dr. Mengele, so the skull was measured and used to conduct a photo superimposition. Two photographs of Dr. Mengele were available, one of when he was 27 years old and another at age 60. The dimensions of the "Wolfgang Gerhard" skull were imposed on the hard landmarks of these photographs, and experts found it to be an exact match, ending one of the greatest mysteries around the Holocaust war criminals.

DNA

DNA (deoxyribonucleic acid) has received significant media attention for the criminal cases where it has been used to link an individual to a crime scene, has exonerated the innocent or has excluded suspects. However, DNA also plays a role in identifying the dead. It is the latest and perhaps the most revolutionary method of identification.

DEOXYRIBONUCLEIC ACID

- DNA is the foundational building block for an individual's entire genetic makeup. It controls biological development not just in humans, but in all living things.
- DNA is composed of two strands of sugar and phosphate molecules that form a double helix, bound together by links formed by adenine, thymine, cytosine and guanine.
- DNA can be extracted as forensic evidence from blood, semen, skin cells, tissue, organs, muscle, bone, teeth, hair, saliva, mucus, perspiration, fingernails, urine and feces.

DNA has advantages over the other methods of identification. It is a highly stable compound, having been recovered from badly decomposed bodies, charred bodies and even thousand-year-old mummies. And only a tiny amount of this compound is required for analyses and comparisons. But the most powerful advantage is the fact that every human being has a unique DNA profile, along with the fact that normally this DNA makeup is completely consistent throughout the body of every individual, where it is present in every single cell. The DNA profile from the skin is identical to the profile from the blood, saliva or hair from the same individual.

DNA for Identifying Bodies

Though it is not difficult to extract DNA from unidentified human remains, matching it to a missing person may be more difficult. Where a possible candidate has been identified, the DNA from the remains can be compared against DNA gathered from traces of organic matter left in the candidate's home or on possessions. If no candidate has been focused upon, the DNA profile can be compared to the profiles in the Combined DNA Index System (CODIS), an electronic database containing DNA profiles from federal, state and local crime labs across the United States and operated by the FBI. CODIS can compare the DNA profile of the unknown person to all those stored electronically within its system.

Using the CODIS system has one major limitation. The system only contains DNA profiles of individuals convicted of sex offenses, rape, murder, child abuse and other violent crimes, although some U.S. states also include those convicted of other felonies. Therefore this system is helpful for identifying unknown remains only if the deceased turns out to have had a (recent) criminal record.

DNA in the Aftermath of 9/11

In the aftermath of the 9/11 terrorist attacks, over 19,000 samples of human remains were recovered from the 2,700 victims. From these samples over 1,500 victims have been positively identified to date using DNA matching. This was almost the only effective method for identifying remains that were largely unrecognizable.

Under instruction from forensic authorities, family members of possible victims of the attack supplied DNA samples to be compared against remains recovered from the scene; the best samples generally came from hairbrushes containing hair. The same system was used to a lesser extent after the Indian Ocean tsunami in December 2004, and has also been used to determine the identity of the remains of soldiers recovered from Korea and Vietnam.

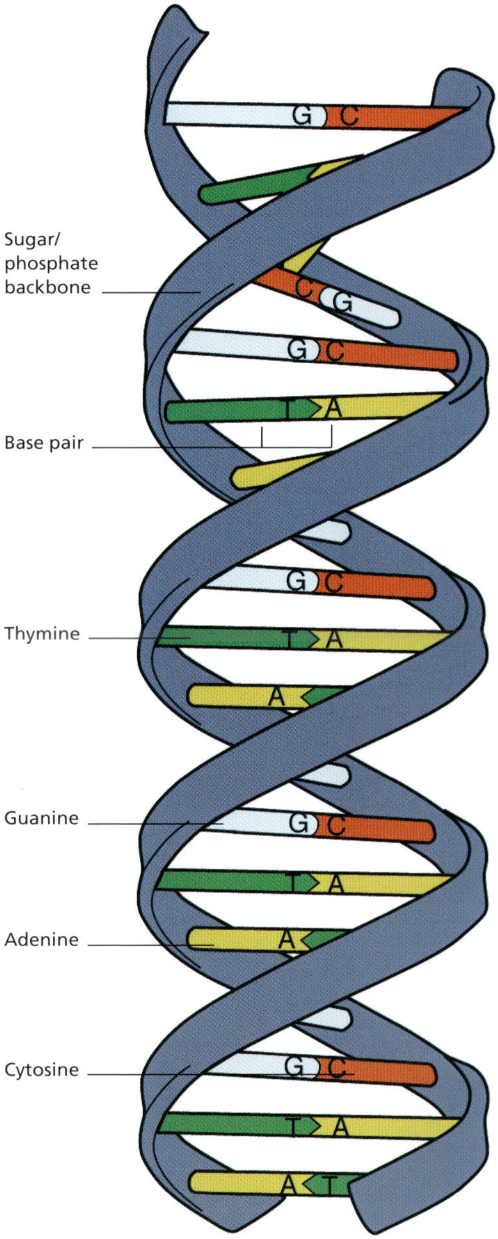

Above The structure of the DNA "double-helix" molecule. An actual DNA strand has many more base pairs than this.

Dental Comparison

Under special circumstances the coroner's office must call upon the skills of a forensic odontologist to determine the identity of individuals. Victims who are burned beyond visual recognition, in advanced stages of decomposition or skeletonized may yet be identified through dental comparison.

A forensic odontologist is a dentist who applies this medical expertise to death investigations and other matters of law. A forensic odontologist's functions range from identification of a single human's remains to those of hundreds of victims after a mass disaster, assessment of bite marks, and collection of any DNA samples that might be found in blood or saliva around an apparent bite mark.

A key role of the forensic odontologist is to provide an expert opinion regarding the likelihood of a match between antemortem and postmortem dental X rays, which may provide a positive identification of the deceased. The main skill required for this task is to be able to recognize and compare patterns.

Durability

The dental area is so important in the determination of identity because the teeth and jaw can resist even the most severe circumstances, such as fire and extreme trauma. Artificial dental restorations such as fillings and bridges are also very tough, and frequently remain completely intact even in the most decomposed corpses. The durability of teeth is primarily due to the enamel (the outermost covering of the crowns of teeth) and the cementum (the outer covering of the roots of teeth).

Unique Teeth

The other important factor for identification purposes is the uniqueness of human dentition. A full set of adult teeth consists of 32 teeth, each with five surfaces, thus providing 160 possibilities for individual variations of surface anatomy and dental restorations in configuration, size, shape, material and wear patterns. Other distinctive structures used for antemortem versus postmortem X ray comparison include maxillary sinus patterns (the area above the upper jaw) and orbital outlines (the shape of the eye sockets). In addition, factors such as decay and missing or extra teeth all increase the level of certainty of a match.

Dental prosthetic replacements (dentures, bridges, partials), even where they don't reveal an individual identity, can potentially yield information such as geography of origin, approximate date of

Opposite Skull and bones in a forensics lab. The damage to the skull suggests that the deceased was the victim of a violent assault.

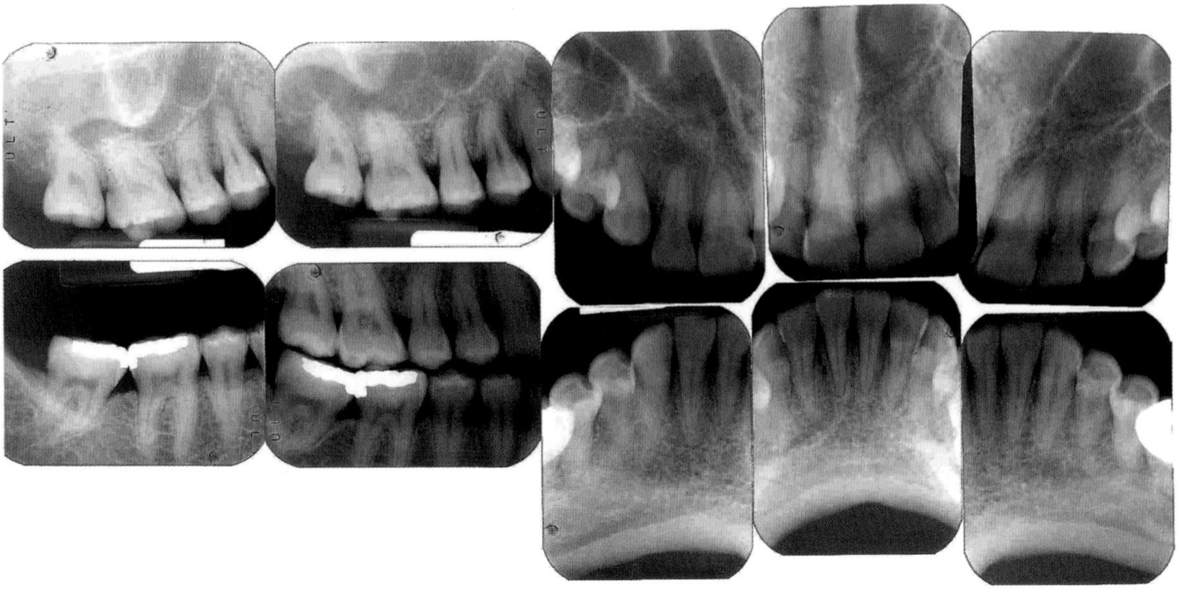

Above A full set of antemortem dental X rays showing all the teeth in the mouth.These are compard with postmortem records by the forensic odontologist.

construction and even linkage to a particular dentist or dental laboratory. The level of dental work can also offer a clue to the socioeconomic status of the deceased, as elaborate dental work tends to be quite expensive.

Dental Data

The limitation of dental identification is that it requires antemortem dental X rays to compare to the postmortem X rays. Most countries have many more dental records on file than fingerprint records, but nonetheless there are many individuals for whom dental records will never have been made because of lack of health insurance, fear of dental procedures or omissions by dentists.

In terms of data searching and matching, a major downfall of dental identification is that, unlike fingerprints, dental records are generally not in a centralized and searchable database. The coroner's office must therefore provide the odontologist with a short list of individuals who might be a possible match, and each of these possible matches must have antemortem dental X rays to compare with the postmortem images. If a hiker or hunter comes across a skull with teeth, there is nothing an odontologist can do until possible lists of names are generated from the police and forensic investigation.

Society now places a high value on being able to establish positive identity for all individuals, dead or alive. Dental data collected into a central and searchable system could, along with fingerprint and DNA information, offer us a near-perfect system for achieving this in all cases.

Case Study OBTAINING CLOSURE

An intense fire raced through a 50-year-old three-story brick home. The age of the structure and the drop ceilings that had been recently installed made the fire hard to extinguish. Across the street paramedics were trying to comfort a highly anxious woman. Her two children, a five-year-old girl and her seven-year-old brother, were still trapped in the building. Despite the firefighters' best efforts, the children could not be saved.

After the fire was completely extinguished and the fire captain determined that the scene was safe to enter, two firefighters entered the home to recover the bodies. A firefighter located two very badly charred bodies in the second-floor bedroom. The bodies were placed in black body bags, labeled A05F-41305 and A05-41306, and transported to the morgue.

Because of the state of the bodies, positive identification could not be made via visual, fingerprint or skeletal features. To positively identify the male and female victims, dental comparisons were required. The family's dentist was contacted and asked to send the most recent X rays of the children's teeth. When these arrived, the autopsy technicians positioned the two victims so that similar X rays could be taken of the remains. A forensic odontologist then compared the antemortem to the postmortem films and positively identified which victim was the boy and which was the girl. This allowed the coroner's office to fulfill one of its primary duties, namely, providing positive identification of the remains, helping the mother to reach emotional closure and to put the remains to rest under the correct headstones.

A Database of Humanity

Identification methods such as fingerprint and dental comparisons are effective only inasmuch as the characteristics of the deceased can be compared against a database of possible matches. The more complete the database, the better the chance of determining identity.

In various countries around the world, there have been national efforts to have all children fingerprinted (with the print cards being retained by the parents) or to have all citizens' dental records collected together in a searchable database. But in light of the limitations of fingerprinting, a national DNA database would be even more useful in providing a rapid, accurate and definitive method of identifying human remains. We might even imagine some time in the future when there will be comprehensive DNA records of all citizens in every country — perhaps even a system for the international sharing of data. In many senses this would provide a mode of legal identification that would be much more secure than identity cards or passports, both of which can be faked by professional forgers.

Not everyone will necessarily embrace this technology, however. Civil rights advocates may question to what extent we would want to have our most personal information and identity at the disposal of government authorities. This is part of an ongoing debate between the need for security and the need for liberty.

Unidentified Bodies

There are always a certain number of deceased individuals for whom identity cannot be ascertained by any of the standard methods. One last resort is the new technique of facial reconstruction, which may be used under extreme circumstances, when all other attempts have failed. Modeling clay, small sticks, modeling tools and plastic eyes are used to create a three-dimensional face, allowing visual recognition by members of the public, family or friends.

Where a skeletonized skull has been recovered, facial reconstruction begins by estimating the correct tissue thickness on all parts of the face, using information from a large database that covers variables of age, race and gender. Modeling clay is then applied in a layer over the bone, using supporting sticks to hold up the clay and tissue-depth markers to show how thick the clay should be.

The method is part science and part art, using demographic and lifestyle information to add imaginative details. The end result is a three-dimensional bust complete with skin tone, eyes, eyebrows, lips, ears, hair and scars. The resulting bust is shown on news broadcasts and in newspapers and police flyers.

John Does and Jane Does

Individuals who cannot be identified by any available method are frequently known as "John Does" and "Jane Does." Often the attemps to establish identity fail because their lifestyle or circumstances have meant that they have had little contact with family, government authorities, medical personnel or any of the other agencies that store information on people.

Some jurisdictions now have Internet sites that publish information on unidentified bodies, in the hope that Web browsers may be able to provide the missing links required to solve the case. Morgue authorities in cities and counties often have anywhere from a handful up to several dozen unidentified bodies on file at any one time; in large cities, the number tends to be higher. Some of these bodies may have been in storage and awaiting identification over a period of decades. It is estimated that in the United States there are over 4,000 of these unidentified bodies on file, and in storage, at any one time.

For the coroner's office, the presence of long-term unidentified dead places an unwelcome burden on storage space and administrative resources. There is also the problem of progressive decomposition of the stored bodies.

Right Facial reconstruction artist modeling the facial muscles with clay. The wooden pegs are marked to show correct depth of muscle tissue.

Case Study UNIDENTIFIED WHITE FEMALE

During the early morning hours a couple was fishing from a small motorboat. As they rounded the bend in the river, they noticed a red object bobbing by the shore. As they motored closer, they discovered that the object was a body wrapped in a blanket secured by tape. They immediately called emergency services. A short time later several police officers, homicide detectives and two deputy coroners arrived at the scene and pulled the body to the shore. After a detailed external examination the blanket was unwrapped to reveal a body in an advanced stage of decomposition. It was transported to the coroner's office for examination.

THE INVESTIGATION

The body was of a white female, an apparent victim of a homicide. She was dressed in a short-sleeved blue top, denim pants and pink underwear. The clothing and a search of the pockets revealed no unique or identifying markings, and visual recognition was impossible because of the advanced decomposition. The hands had been protected sufficiently by the blanket for a latent-fingerprint examiner to get a set of prints of the victim. These were sent to the FBI laboratory, but the lab called back a few hours later to say that the prints did not match any on record.

The next step was to issue an "all-points bulletin" (APB) to the media, describing all known characteristics of the female victim. The APB included in particular a description of the clothing, the height, weight and hair color, and the comment that there were some scars. Shortly after the APB was broadcast, the police received several calls from people looking for their lost loved ones. In one case a mother was looking for her daughter who had been missing for several weeks, and who matched the APB description. Upon further questioning by the police it was discovered that her daughter had poor dental hygiene. An examination of the unknown victim revealed teeth with expensive dental work, thereby ruling out a positive match.

The next day, the missing persons division of the police department contacted the coroner's office to inquire if the victim had any tattoos, hoping that they had found a match in a missing teen. Even though the body had been in the water for a substantial period of time, a tattoo of a rose could still be made out on the victim's skin. But the missing teen had a tattoo of the number 13 on the small of her back, excluding this candidate from the identity search.

The skull was totally devoid of flesh, making easier the examination of the upper and lower jaws by the forensic odontologist. The odontologist noted that the dental work was a type typically done in Europe, suggesting the possibility that the victim might be an undocumented alien. However, without a comparison set of antemortem dental records, this method could not be used for obtaining the identity of the individual.

CASE REMAINS OPEN

With all the traditional methods of identifying this individual exhausted, the coroner's office turned to facial reconstruction. A reconstructed model of the woman's face was created by the experts, then shown on local and state news media, billboards and flyers at local stores. The public was instructed to contact their local police if they had any information on the identity of the unknown female, but to date her identity remains unknown.

Protocols for Unidentified Bodies

When all attempts to establish identity have failed and efforts to match the body against missing persons records do not lead to successful resolution of the case, there may eventually come a point when the body must be disposed of.

In some morgues there is an established maximum period for which a body can be stored while attempts are made to establish identity. This period is as short as six months in some jurisdictions, after which the body will be cremated. The morgue may feel that this policy is necessary simply because of the smell caused by old and decaying corpses and the development of insect infestation, even though the body has been stored correctly and kept cool. If time-limit disposal methods such as this are considered necessary, it is in any case not the end of any possible investigation, since the postmortem information that has been gathered from the body still remains on file in documentary and digital form.

In times of war, disaster or civil unrest, morgues will be placed under particular pressure and may need to dispose of bodies more quickly because of the number of unidentified dead being brought in. Lack of a stable electricity supply for keeping bodies cool may also become a problem in times of crisis.

Iraqi law states that a body must be held for two months to give relatives a chance to identify their loved one. But in recent years this period has often been shortened to just three weeks, due to the high rate of unidentified bodies being brought in.

The Body Farm

In Knoxville, Tennessee, there exists a very specialized and unique facility. Its proper name is the University of Tennessee Forensic Anthropology Facility, but especially since Patricia Cornwell published a bestseller based on it, it has been more commonly known as "the body farm." The facility was established in 1971 by the forensic anthrolpologist William Bass, and the insights gained there have since been crucial in solving a number of murder cases.

Some of the bodies that are studied at the body farm are deceased persons who have donated their bodies to science, but others are the unidentified and unclaimed corpses that cannot remain indefinitely in morgue storage.

The purpose of the body farm is to study in detail the effects of human decomposition, and therefore it plays a very useful role in the advancement of postmortem forensic science. At any given time the farm has about 40 bodies, kept in a variety of situations to observe how decomposition is effected in each and how it changes with the seasonal variations. Some bodies are buried or submerged in water, some are in the open air, some under canvas and some left in closed vehicles. This is all done in an effort to learn more about the processes that affect the human body after death.

Chapter 7

The Cause and Manner of Death

The end result of forensic investigative work is the issuing of a death certificate by the coroner. The forensic pathologist contributes the key information to this official document, integrating all the information collected and providing an opinion as to the cause and manner of death. The forensic pathologist draws on the information in the reports from the death investigators, paramedics, police and homicide detectives, as well as the medical records, the results of the postmortem toxicology test and microscopic examination of the tissues.

What Happens When You Die?

Alongside the timeless quest of humanity to understand death, there is also the matter of developing an anatomical understanding of the event. The ancient Greeks and Romans identified death by the absence of heartbeat and breathing and, right up until a few centuries ago, we had no more technical explanation of death than that. In medieval times a candle was held to the mouth; a flicker of the flame was an indication of life.

In 1742 J. Bruhier documented 52 examples of claims of live burial. This heightened the public's already sizable fears of premature burial and put pressure on doctors to establish reliable "signs of life." German doctors concluded that putrefaction was the only reliable indicator of death, and in 19th-century Germany *Leichenhaüser* or "corpse houses" were established, where corpses were kept until the bodies putrefied. Another response to the fear of being buried alive was the "safety coffin," equipped with apparatus that the "corpse" could use to signal to the world above that he or she was still alive. With the advances of modern medicine these fears disappeared, but a good definition of death was still lacking.

Before we can define death, some basic anatomical interrelationships between the brain, heart and lungs must be covered. The brain can be divided into the cerebrum, cerebellum and brain stem. The brain stem contains the medulla, the region that controls respiration and cardiac activity. Neural impulses from this region control the diaphragm and the intercostal muscles, which cause the lungs to expand. The heart operates independently of the brain to some extent, although the brain can influence heart rate.

What Makes You Dead?

Destruction of the brain stem will result in cessation of respiration, which in turn deprives the heart of oxygen, causing it to stop functioning. If the brain stem has been destroyed, it is possible to keep the body alive using life-support technologies that sustain the respiratory and other basic functions of the body; but this external support does not offer any means of healing or repairing the brain stem, and so is usually withdrawn after a period when recovery seems impossible.

The most common causes of brain stem destruction include direct trauma, such as a gunshot wound, or massive spontaneous hemorrhage. Individuals who suffer a fall, a motor vehicle accident or other severe trauma may not immediately show signs of brain injury. However, over a period of time there can be an accumulation of fluid that causes the brain tissues to swell, called cerebral

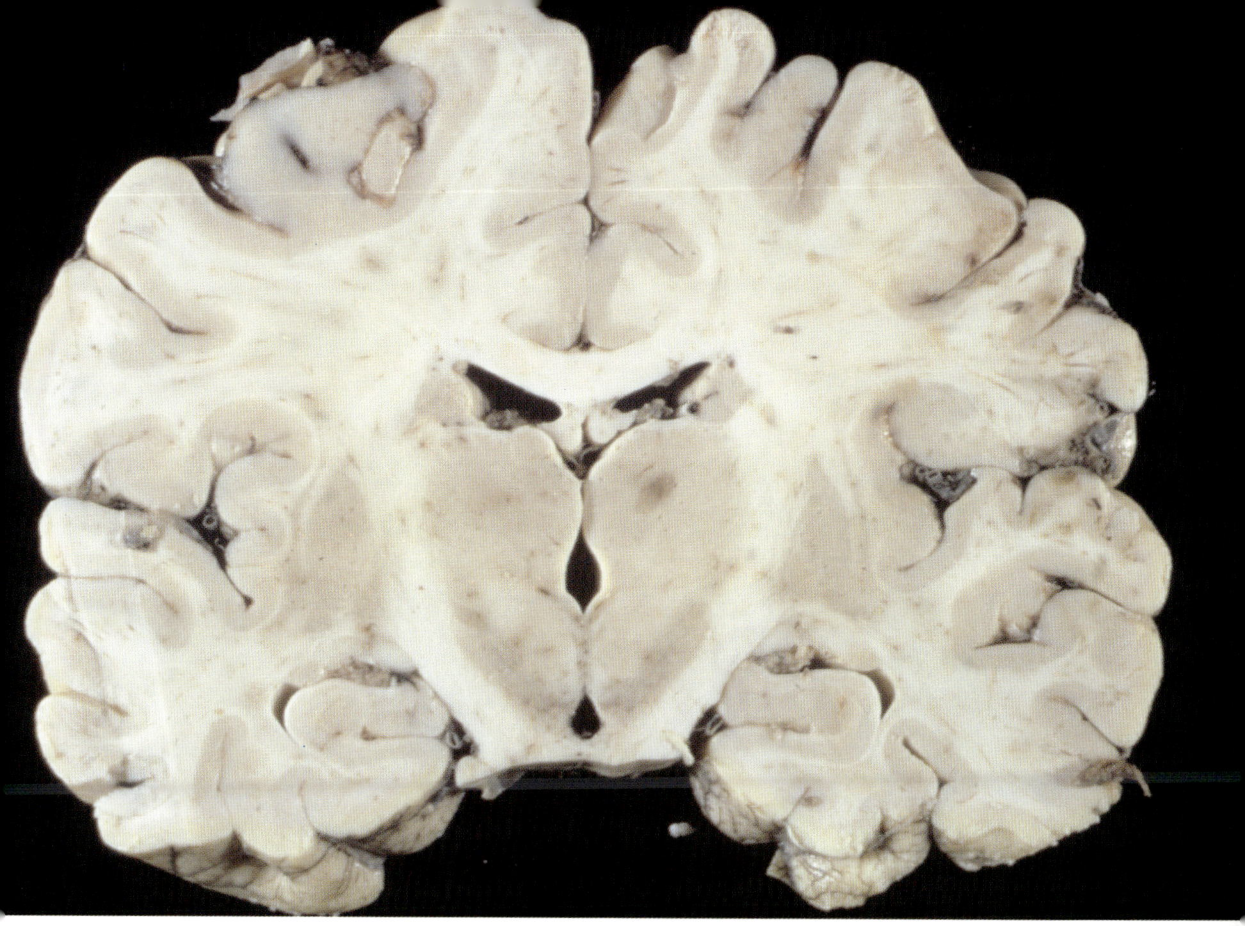

Above Section of a brain affected by cerebral edema. The brain has swollen with fluid because of trauma to the head, and the pressure from this swelling has caused compression of the central spaces (ventricles).

edema. This increasing edema places pressure on the brain. The brain is located in a closed cavity in which there is very little space for it to expand. Therefore when the brain swells, its lower portion, where the medulla is located, is compromised, leading to a decrease in respiratory and cardiac function that may result in death.

Thus a dead person can be defined as an individual with irreversible cessation of circulation and respiration, or an individual with irreversible cessation of all brain function, or brain death.

Brain Death

Advances in life-support technology such as mechanical ventilators and heart-lung machines have blurred the definition of death. These machines take over the biological functions of the heart and lungs. If an individual has suffered a massive head trauma but the heart and lung functions are being carried out by machines, that person is clinically termed *brain-dead* or *brain-stem-dead*. Brain death is therefore the point at which all functions of the brain have permanently and irreversibly ceased.

Case Study FIRE VICTIM OR MURDER VICTIM?

At 5:00 a.m. neighbors noticed flames coming from the house across the street and called the fire department. When they arrived, the two-story brick house was fully engulfed in flames. The fire chief was informed that the house was occupied by an elderly black woman. The flames were too intense to allow entry into the building, so a search and recovery was conducted after the structure was safe to enter. The search resulted in the discovery of an unidentified body in the upstairs hallway. Investigators from the coroner's office arrived at the scene to conduct their investigation, as did the fire marshal. The fire marshal's investigative team was assisted by an arson dog specially trained to locate accelerants such as gasoline or kerosene. Homicide detectives were also called to the scene.

At this point the possible cause of death could have been anything from heart disease, carbon monoxide poisoning, smoke inhalation, cyanide poisoning, stab wound or gunshot wound to manual strangulation. The manner of death could have been natural, accidental or homicide. The victim could have suffered a massive heart attack during an attempt to exit the house. She could have been overcome by high carbon monoxide concentrations or smoke in the air, causing her to become unconscious and then die. The fire could have ignited material that, when burned, released toxic compounds such as cyanide or other poisonous gases. The fire could have been set to conceal a homicide.

THE INVESTIGATION

At the morgue the victim was tagged Fire Victim #87-6912 and placed on the examination table. The body first underwent full-length, multiple-angle X rays to determine whether metal objects such as bullets or knife fragments were present. The body was photographed and the clothing was closely examined for holes or cuts, then removed and examined again for holes or cuts. The victim had sustained second- to third-degree burns over 80 percent of her body. The forensic pathologist asked one of the investigators to call for the forensic odontologist to come to the morgue, and also to determine if the victim's dentist could be contacted. If so, the dentist was to send the dental records and any X rays he or she might have to the morgue.

THE INTERNAL EXAMINATION

Burns affect the skin, and severe burns cause the skin to tear. Therefore, if the victim had been shot or stabbed, the entrance wound might have been difficult to locate externally. Fortunately, the underlying skin and organs usually remain relatively unaffected. So if the woman had been shot or stabbed, the path of the bullet or knife could be ascertained.

At the start of the internal examination, the Y incision was made and the skin folded back and examined for holes or cuts penetrating the underlying muscles. After the chest plate was removed, blood was collected and rushed to toxicology to test for carbon monoxide and other gases. In this case, the developed X rays showed no metal objects or fractures.

The lead homicide detective entered the autopsy suite and informed the pathologist that the arson dog had located gasoline residue on the back porch and that a small gas can was also found there. This discovery increased the likelihood that the case was a homicide and not an accident. At this point there was no anatomical evidence to suggest a gunshot or penetration wound. However, manual strangulation was still very possible.

The examination continued. The heart was removed and the coronary arteries were examined. The arteries showed severe atherosclerosis, with 80 to 90 percent occlusion of one artery and 50 to 60 percent occlusion of the other two major vessels. This finding supported a natural death from heart disease. However, the pendulum of cause of death can swing from natural to accidental to homicide as more information from different forensic investigators is collected and compared with other findings.

A call from the fire marshal informed the coroner's office that the gasoline and can discovered were most likely used for the small lawn mower that was also found nearby. He was still attempting to locate the origin of the fire. The pendulum swung toward a natural death.

Next, a junior homicide detective arrived at the morgue with information about a possible motive for a homicide. The victim's grandson had recently testified against a local gang member. Would the internal examination reveal evidence of a homicide, or confirm an accidental death?

THE CAUSE BECOMES CLEAR

Once the internal organs and the brain were removed, the investigation moved to the neck region. The pathologist observed the tongue and oral cavity, then removed the trachea. The trachea is opened by cutting down the middle to expose the airway. The pathologist wanted to determine if the victim was alive or dead at the time of the fire. The level of carbon monoxide in her blood and examination of the airway would answer this question. If she had been alive and was overcome by carbon monoxide and smoke, the blood level of carbon monoxide and the soot within the trachea would be definitive. Later, the toxicology analysis of the blood showed a carbon monoxide level of 87 percent. Soot was located in the victim's trachea. The victim had been alive during the fire and had inhaled the toxic carbon monoxide and the smoke.

Next, the forensic odontologist arrived. This specialist's role is critical in this type of case. The odontologist removed the lower and upper jaws, making X rays similar to the ones taken by the family dentist, then compared the postmortem and antemortem images. The identity of the woman was confirmed. She had had extensive dental work done that made the matching easy. With the positive identification completed, the next of kin were informed.

THE FINDINGS

At this point, based on the toxicological analysis and the soot within the airway, it could be stated that the cause of death was carbon monoxide poisoning and smoke inhalation. However, the manner of death was another matter. The pathologist pended the manner of death until he received supplementary reports from the fire marshal and homicide detectives. Two weeks later, the report from the fire marshal concluded that the fire had originated in the kitchen wall because of frayed wiring. Homicide detectives were unable to link any of the gang members to the scene and were convinced that the death was an accident. Therefore the pathologist issued a replacement death certificate with the manner listed as accidental.

The Death Certificate

The death certificate has two functions. The first is as a legal document certifying the cause and manner of an individual's death. This document is required in order for the next of kin to authorize cremation or burial, settle life insurance claims, family pensions and distribution of the deceased's movable and immovable property and obtain any bequeathed inheritance. A death certificate is also required to delete the decedent's name

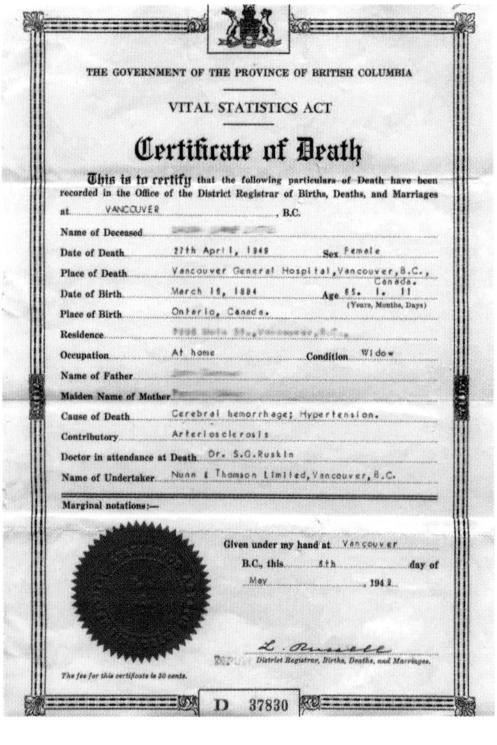
THE GOVERNMENT OF THE PROVINCE OF BRITISH COLUMBIA

VITAL STATISTICS ACT

Certificate of Death

This is to certify that the following particulars of Death have been recorded in the Office of the District Registrar of Births, Deaths, and Marriages at VANCOUVER, B.C.

Name of Deceased

Date of Death 27th April, 1949 Sex Female

Place of Death Vancouver General Hospital, Vancouver, B.C., Canada.

Date of Birth March 16, 1884 Age 65. 1. 11 (Years, Months, Days)

Place of Birth Ontario, Canada.

Residence

Occupation At home Condition Widow

Name of Father

Maiden Name of Mother

Cause of Death Cerebral hemorrhage; Hypertension.

Contributory Arteriosclerosis

Doctor in attendance at Death Dr. S.G.Ruskin

Name of Undertaker Nunn & Thomson Limited, Vancouver, B.C.

Marginal notations:—

Given under my hand at Vancouver B.C., this 6th day of May, 1949

L. Russell

District Registrar, Births, Deaths, and Marriages.

The fee for this certificate is 50 cents.

D 37830

Above A 1940s Canadian death certificate reporting on a natural death.

from titles to property such as homes, stocks or businesses. In addition, a death certificate must be presented if there are any legal or insurance claims involving an accidental death.

The second function of the death certificate is to provide an opinion as to the cause and manner of an individual's death. It is important to note that the cause and manner of death listed on the death certificate are not legally binding for any agency or individual other than the coroner's office or the coroner. In other words, it does not mandate, prevent or preclude any other type of action by any other individual, agency or public office, such as further investigation, an independent review of the conclusions or reexamination of the body.

The cause and manner of death sections of the death certificate represent an opinion — the best effort of the medical-legal officer to reduce to a few words the cause of death and a reasonable opinion as to the manner of death. The coroner's office should use reasonable medical probability in the formulation of opinions and in the certification of death, in the same way that clinicians make diagnoses and plans for treatment. The death certificate is a civil law document, not a medical scientific document.

As we have seen, all deaths of an unnatural cause fall under the jurisdiction of the coroner's office, and in these cases the death certificate can be completed only by a forensic pathologist and issued only by a coroner's office. Natural deaths with no unusual circumstances may be certified by an attending physician.

Who Sees the Death Certificate?

The information on the death certificate is also passed on to a number of agencies that use it for compiling fatality data. A copy of every completed death certificate is provided to the state's vital records office, which passes the data to the National Center for Health Statistics (NCHS). The NCHS, a division of the Center for Disease Control and Prevention, uses this collected data to document the health status of the general population and subpopulations by generating tables of the total number of deaths by age, sex, race and location (state and county), as well as by disease and by manner of death. The data are also used to monitor trends, identify health problems, determine life expectancies, provide research for biochemical and health studies and compare mortality rates in the United States to those of other countries.

Limitations of the Death Certificate

The death certificate is a very useful document in terms of obtaining information on critical features of the death, namely the cause and manner of death plus some basic demographic data. However, it is important to understand that the death certificate does not contain everything you need to know. For example, in deaths involving bullets, the caliber, number of times shot, location of entrance wound, path of the bullet, level of damage to the internal organs and location of exit wound are not listed on the death certificate. Instead, this information is contained in the final anatomic pathology report. The police report, if there is an arrest, will list the characteristics of the shooter.

In cases of suicide, the death certificate does not provide information as to whether the victim had attempted suicide before, whether a suicide note was left or the reason for the suicide. Instead, the death investigation report will contain the history of previous attempts and the methods used, while a copy of the suicide note is kept in the case file. If the death involved drugs, the concentration of the drugs and method of ingestion are not listed on the death certificate. Instead, the toxicology report lists all the drugs tested for and the concentration of each drug, while the death investigation report includes information on the method of ingestion.

Contents of the Death Certificate

The standard death certificate contains six main sections:

Decedent's Personal Data

This section contains the following demographic information: age, sex, race, marital status, date and place of birth, home address, occupation, highest level of education and whether the individual was a member of the armed forces. It also includes information about the place of death and next of kin.

Disposition
This section describes the method that will be used to dispose of the body, such as burial, cremation, donation for research or removal from the state where the death occurred. The name of the facility that will handle the disposition is also included.

Pronouncement
The time and date at which the individual was pronounced dead are recorded in this section.

Certification This section lists the personnel who can pronounce an individual dead, including first responders such as emergency medical technicians (EMTs), paramedics, police, nurses and hospital physicians, and indicates who certified the death in the case of this individual.

Cause of Death
The cause of death is the pathological condition (disease) or injury responsible for initiating the chronology of events — acute or prolonged — that produce death. This section of the death certificate contains two major parts: the immediate and underlying cause of death, and the conditions contributing to death. The section also lists the date, time and place of injury; a description of how the injury occurred; whether the injury occurred at work; whether an autopsy was performed; and the manner of death.

Manner of Death
The circumstances that brought about the cause of death (see following section).

Ruling on Russian Roulette

The circumstances surrounding the death play a key role in determining the manner of death. Take, for example, Russian roulette, where a single bullet is placed in one of the six chambers of a revolver. The participant then spins the chamber, places the weapon to his head and pulls the trigger. If the chamber is empty, nothing happens, and the process is repeated by the same individual or by another.

If the chamber contains a live round when the trigger is pulled, the cause of death is clear: namely, gunshot wound to the head. However, determining the manner of death depends heavily on the circumstances surrounding the death. If the victim was alone in his room playing this "game," the manner would most likely be ruled suicide — the logic being that when an individual places a loaded weapon against his head and pulls the trigger, resulting in death, it's a suicide. However, the death could be ruled accidental if the event occurred when a group of teenagers was drinking and playing the game as a way to impress friends at a party, without seriously considering the possibility of death.

Manner of Death

The manner of death is the fashion in which the cause of death came to be. There are five classifications of manner of death: natural, accidental, suicide, homicide and "cannot be determined," or undetermined. In addition, there is a temporary classification of manner of death called "pending investigation," or simply "pending."

Natural Death

Natural deaths are those caused by naturally occurring disease processes without trauma, such as cancer, heart disease, liver disease and so on. If the death is ruled natural, no criminal investigation is needed. However, a thorough examination of the facts leading to the natural manner of death must be undertaken.

Accidental Death

Accidental deaths are those that occur as a result of behavior or actions that unintentionally end in death. The most frequently encountered accidental deaths are from drug overdoses — most people taking illegal drugs are not trying to commit suicide — followed by motor vehicle accidents, falls and fires. A ruling of accidental death may result in continuation of the investigation, but in a different direction. Civil liability may be involved, and the coroner may be called upon to testify in a civil court. The amount of time devoted to this extended investigation will vary from one jurisdiction to another.

Suicide

Suicide is defined as the deliberate termination of one's own life. The most common methods of suicide vary by sex: males typically use firearms, while females typically overdose on pills. The manner of suicide will need thorough confirmation. In most cases that are ruled suicide, the determination will stand; however, occasionally new evidence brought out by an in-depth investigation will change the coroner's mind.

Suicide Notes

In general, only about 30 percent of those who commit suicide leave a note. These notes range from a few words to multiple pages to those that are left as computer files. Individuals leave suicide notes for many reasons: to explain the reason for their actions; to apologize to their loved ones; and, at times, to vent their anger toward someone who has hurt them.

Young people typically commit suicide after the loss of their "first love." Their notes express feelings of desperation, loneliness and heartbreak. The notes also sometimes express wishes, such as to be buried with pictures of the former girlfriend, a particular item of clothing or even a guitar.

During midlife the features of suicide notes change to reflect economic problems. Loss of a job, gambling debts or bad investments are typical reasons.

Near-the-end-of-life notes tend to reflect issues around health problems as increasing age brings increased physical and mental issues. For example, individuals suffering from severe arthritis or signs of progressive mental disease such as Alzheimer's may choose not to live with such a dire prognosis.

Homicide

Homicide is defined as the action of taking the life of another person. Based on this definition, all police shootings and all executions are homicides. The determination of first degree, second degree, third degree and other types of homicide is made by a court, not the coroner's office. However, evidence presented by the coroner regarding the manner of death may be a crucial factor in helping the court to reach a decision as to what type of homicide was committed.

Accidental Deaths

In the U.S. accidental death was the number-one cause of death among individuals aged between one and 34. In coroners' offices the most frequent types of accidental deaths investigated are drug overdose deaths, followed by motor vehicle accidents and falls.

Homicide or Suicide?

Detailed observations in the postmortem examination are often key to whether a death will be ruled homicide or suicide. There are a number of causes of death such as bullet wounds, stab wounds and poisonings that could be self-caused or caused by an assailant: the forensic pathologist gives an expert opinion as to which was the case.

For example, where death has been caused by stab wounds, a single deep wound suggests murder. If the wound is in the back, this is almost certain. By contrast, multiple incised wounds (wounds that are longer than they are deep) to the arms suggest a suicide. A self-inflicted stab wound to the neck is usually characterised by several superficial cuts, known as hesitation marks, as well as one deeper fatal cut.

Multiple stab wounds to the chest and head suggest a homicidal crime of passion, and may dissuade the judge from reaching a verdict of first degree murder, which would only be appropriate for a more calculated attack.

Another characteristic of stab wounds that will lead to a determination of homicide is the presence of defense wounds. These are usually small, fairly superficial wounds on the arms and hands, caused when a victim attempts to shield his or herself from attack.

Corpus delicti

Traditionally, in English common law and as adopted and applied in the United

States, the courts required that there be an identified dead body before an official charge of homicide could be filed against anyone. This was referred to as the *corpus delicti*. This legal requisite remained in place until well past the mid-20th century in the United States.

Such a formal requirement is no longer necessary. There have been several cases in which murder charges were filed despite the fact that the body of the alleged victim was never found.

It should be emphasized, however, that other areas of forensic scientific expertise might play a significant role in the ultimate successful resolution of such cases. DNA, blood-spatter analysis, hair and fiber comparisons, trace evidence, fingerprints, analysis of questioned documents and so on are extremely important in enabling law enforcement officials to pursue death investigations in which a body has never been found.

Undetermined

"Undetermined" is used when all avenues of investigation have been explored but a valid conclusion as to the cause of death cannot be reached. Even in the best-equipped forensic laboratory and after hours of investigation, the cause or the manner of death — or both — may occasionally remain undetermined.

As we have seen already, there are cases where no obvious cause of death is detected in the postmortem examination. In these cases the death certificate may be signed off as undetermined, though the cause may equally be attributed to lethal cardiac arrhythmia, as this condition cannot be detected after death. However, where this option is taken, the manner of death must be declared as natural.

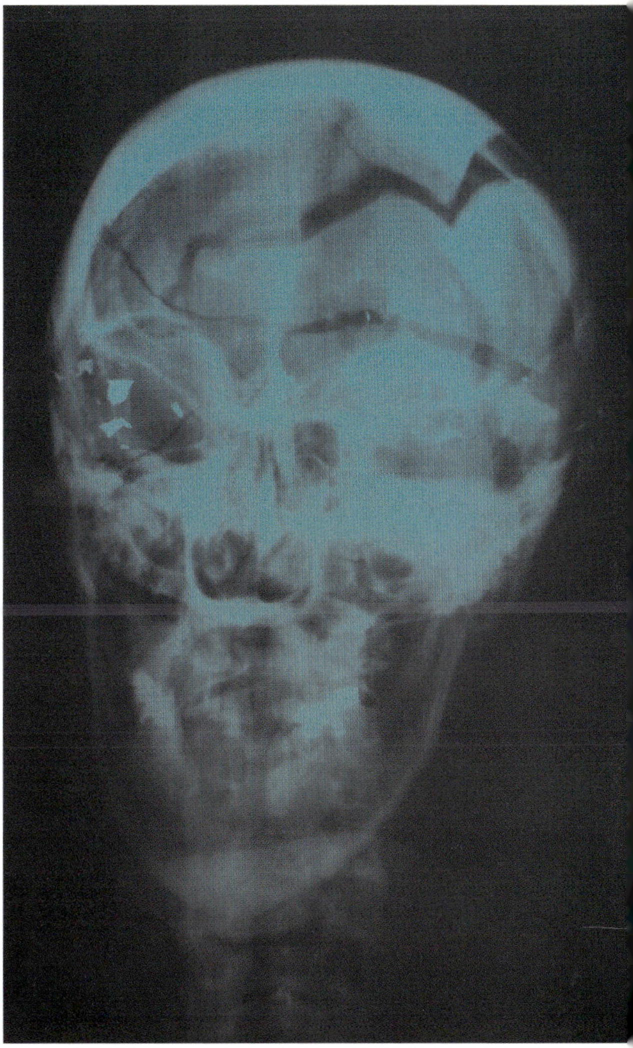

Above X ray of the head of a homicide victim. The highlights are fragments of metal broken off from a fatal bullet.

TYPES OF HOMICIDE

- **First Degree**
  The intentional killing of a human being, characterized by a plan and lacking spontaneity, and especially where the killer demonstrates a calculated attempt to get away with the crime.
- **Second Degree**
  Committed when the actor is the principal perpetrator of a felony. There exists an intention to carry out the felony, but not the intention to commit the murder.
- **Third Degree**
  All other kinds of homicides that cannot be categorized as intentional or as having been committed during the perpetration of a felony.
- **Voluntary Manslaughter**
  The killing of an individual without lawful justification while acting under sudden and intense passion resulting from a serious provocation by the individual killed.
- **Involuntary Manslaughter**
  The death of another as the direct result of an unlawful act committed in a reckless and grossly negligent manner.

Pending

"Pending" simply means that further testing or investigation is warranted before a definitive manner of death can be declared. Most states require that the death certificate be issued within 72 hours of discovery of the body, even if the cause of death is still unknown. If the cause of death cannot be established with reasonable certainty by this time, the coroner's office will issue a death certificate with the cause of death designated as "pending further action" or simply "pending." In most cases the pathologist will be waiting for the results of toxicological analysis, supplementary police reports or histology slides. Once a determination of the cause and the manner of death has been made, the coroner's office will issue a replacement death certificate. It is important to note that while the manner of death can be undetermined, it cannot be left indefinitely as pending, but must be changed in due course to one of the five manners already discussed.

Undetermined Deaths

Occasionally there are cases in which it is simply not possible to determine the cause and mechanism of death, or the time of death, with any degree of scientific certainty. Advanced decomposition, lack of clear evidence or a multiplicity of possible causes may all result in a death having to be signed off as undetermined.

Brain Hemorrhage

A brain hemorrhage is one cause of death that may sometimes leave the manner of death as undetermined.

For example, in one case, distraught parents brought their five-year-old child in to hospital, having woken up in bed with the child lying unresponsive between them. The child was pronounced dead.

Brain scans showed a subarachnoid hemorrhage, which could have been caused by natural conditions or by shaken baby syndrome. The autopsy examination was unremarkable except for the cerebral edema of the brain.

The cause of death was clear: namely, the injury to the brain. However, the manner of death could be natural if the bleed was caused by spontaneous rupture of an aneurysm, an accident if one of the parents had rolled over onto the child, or homicide if the parents had violently shaken the infant during one of his crying episodes. All three manners of death were possible, but there was no overwhelming evidence to support one manner of death over another.

Competing Theories

A further example shows how a body displaying multiple but inconclusive pathologies may have to be signed off as a case of undetermined death.

A 44-year-old white female was found lying in bed by her husband, completely unresponsive. She was pronounced dead at the scene by the paramedics.

Her only previous medical problem was mild hypertension and alcohol abuse. The death investigators noted a small bruise on one of the upper extremities, and there was some history of domestic abuse between the couple, though no charges had ever been filed. Further bruises were found, which were determined to be at least 7 to 10 days old.

The internal examination showed advanced liver disease, significant enough to have caused the death. However, the trauma and history of abuse could not be ignored. Then there was the possibility that the victim could have bruised herself while intoxicated, making it a natural death. So the manner of death could be either natural or homicide; however, as the available evidence failed definitively to establish a manner of death, it was signed off as undetermined.

Real-Life Forensics: Famous Cases

There is no time when postmortem investigations capture the public imagination more than when they successfully solve a notorious case. The following pages review a few of the most famous crimes of recent decades and explain the role postmortems played, either in convicting the killer or in leaving the casebook open.

There is often a significant amount of suggestive or circumstantial evidence linking a perpetrator to a crime. But securing a conviction requires clear scientific evidence about the cause and manner of death. It is only then that the accused can definitively be linked to a suspicious death, underlining the importance of the role of the forensic pathologist who carries out the postmortem examination.

Forensic pathologists are often used as expert witnesses in court since they are the ones who determine the cause and circumstances of death. Their role is to give evidence of scientific fact and an opinion based on professional knowledge and experience that the lay jurors will not have. It is important that the legal professionals find the right pathologist for the case in hand in order to maximize the use of the scientific evidence. To appear credible, the pathologist will need to be able to accurately and clearly summarize complex medical issues. In addition, it is important that they also state the limits of accuracy within which they are speaking, and what cannot be proved. Ideally, the pathologist should also be familiar with the legal system. This helps the pathologist to avoid situations where a lawyer may try to guide the jury to an interpretation the pathologist believes to be scientifically incorrect or unsound.

Despite these complex requirements, the evidence from postmortems has frequently been responsible for the conviction of violent criminals.

Above Ted Bundy, one of the most brutal killers of modern times, is thought to have killed between 40 and 50 women.

TED BUNDY

1978

> Case Details

By 1978, Ted Bundy had already been killing woman for at least nine years. He had eluded authorities repeatedly, and even after his capture in 1974 led to a sentence of 15 years' imprisonment he escaped and went on a rampage again.

In early 1978 Bundy attacked several women students staying in a sorority house at Florida State University, killing two and leaving another two seriously injured. He was eventually captured in Pensacola, where he had killed again, this time targeting a 12-year-old schoolgirl. Apprehending him proved particularly difficult as he used a series of stolen cars and violently resisted any attempted arrest.

> Postmortem Evidence

A forensic investigation was mounted, aiming to prove definitively that Bundy had been responsible for the murders at Florida State University, as well as the young girl in Pensacola.

One of the deceased, Lisa Levy, was found to have died from multiple blunt-force trauma to the head. This matched up with reports from one of the surviving students, who had seen a man fleeing the sorority house carrying what looked like a log wrapped in cloth. Levy had also been strangled and sexually assaulted. But most telling for the prosecution's case against Bundy were the bite marks found on Levy's buttocks and breast. Bundy was forced to have a cast made of his teeth, and a forensic odontologist found that his dental characteristics exactly matched the marks found on Lisa Levy.

The body of Kimberley Leach, the Pensacola schoolgirl, was not found until it was severely decomposed. However, blood and semen samples could still be found in her underwear, and these matched samples taken from Bundy.

> The Verdict

The testimony of the forensic odontologist sealed Bundy's fate, leading to a jury verdict of guilty for the murder of Lisa Levy. Despite numerous appeals, Bundy was eventually executed for his crimes in 1989.

1991 JOANN CURLEY

> Case Details

In August 1991 a Pennsylvania electrician, Robert Curley, was admitted to hospital with mysterious symptoms. He was suffering from nausea, as well as pains, numbness and burning sensations in his limbs. Before the cause of the symptoms was discovered, Curley's condition improved, and he was discharged at the end of the month.

However, nine days after his discharge Curley was back in hospital, with the same symptoms now at a more severe level. He began to recover again, and by September 22 was well enough to see his wife, brother and sister; but that night he deteriorated again and later died from his condition on September 27.

> Postmortem Evidence

Before Curley died, doctors had managed to establish that he was suffering from high levels of thallium in his system. He had been working at a building site where thallium salts were present and at first it was hypothesized that he might have accidentally been exposed to the poison.

However, postmortem toxicological analysis of his tissues showed a level of thallium in his system that could not have been present unless he had ingested it through eating or drinking. Since Curley had repeatedly sought medical treatment, the manner of death could not be ruled as suicide and the case remained open.

It was not until 1994 that a specialist in forensic toxicology made a full analysis of thallium levels in Curley's skin, hair and nails, from which a time line was created, showing the peak levels of thallium ingestion in the time leading up to his death. The results showed a curious set of peaks and troughs, suggesting repeated doses over a long period of time, with a final massive dose correlating with September 22. This was the day that his wife, sister and brother had visited him in hospital. His wife was the only person who had had access to him on all occasions when his thallium ingestion had peaked.

> The Verdict

On the basis of detailed toxicological analysis, Joann Curley was found guilty of murdering her husband. She received a sentence of 10 to 20 years.

JONBENÉT RAMSEY

1996

> Case Details

JonBenét Ramsey was a child beauty queen whose brutal murder on the night of December 25, 1996 shocked America. Right from the beginning, the case was characterized by conflicting reports and mysterious clues.

JonBenét's parents, Patricia and John Ramsey, were wealthy and respected residents of Boulder, Colorado. Though there was never any firm evidence linking them to the death of their daughter, they soon came to be treated by media and police alike as the prime suspects in the case. This was largely due to the curious fact that their daughter's body was found in the basement of the family home, while a three-page ransom note was also discovered. The postmortem examination raised more questions.

> Postmortem Evidence

A forensic pathologist found that JonBenét had suffered ligature furrows and abrasions to her neck, as well as showing petechial hemorrhages associated with strangulation. She also had skull fractures and brain contusions suggesting heavy blows to the head. Accordingly, the cause of death was found to be a combination of asphyxia and cerebral trauma.

A genital examination found signs of abrasion and inflammation, which could be taken as a sign of sexual abuse, though the pathologist was not able to reach a conclusion on this matter. Other experts, however, have claimed that her genital injuries suggest ongoing sexual abuse, occurring at least 72 hours before death. In December 2003, further examination revealed a blood sample in her underwear; however, the DNA of this blood has not yet been matched to any individual, despite ongoing database searches.

Above JonBenét Ramsey

> The Verdict

Patricia and John Ramsey were never charged over the case, while debate continues as to whether they should be considered the main suspects. The case remains open.

1998

DR. HAROLD SHIPMAN

> Case Details

The death of 81-year-old Katherine Grundy on June 24, 1998, did not at first seem to be suspicious in any way. Her doctor, Harold Shipman, had visited her just hours earlier at her home in Hyde, a suburb of Manchester, England. When friends found her dead they called him back and he pronounced her dead of natural causes, assuring them that an autopsy would not be necessary as he had been in recent attendance.

It was not until after Grundy's funeral that her daughter, Angela Woodruff, heard from solicitors claiming to have a copy of her mother's will leaving £386,000 (about $700,000) to Dr. Shipman. Ms. Woodruff believed this will to be fake, and took the case to the police.

> Postmortem Evidence

The body of Ms. Grundy had already been buried following the funeral, so an exhumation order was required to conduct a postmortem examination. An external examination of the body did not reveal anything unusual. It was only upon toxicological analysis of the tissues that crucial evidence came to light: it was revealed that Ms. Grundy had died from a morphine overdose, administered within a three-hour period before her death. This closely matched the time when Dr. Shipman was known to have visited her. Further exhumations were carried out on other deceased patients of Dr. Shipman, revealing high levels of morphine in each of the bodies.

Above Dr. Harold Shipman

In his youth, Shipman had watched his mother succumb to disease while under the soothing effects of morphine. But his apparent obsession with the drug would prove to be his downfall, as it is one of the few substances that remains in the body tissues over many decades.

> The Verdict

Grundy's death was ruled to be a homicide by morphine poisoning. Dr. Shipman was found guilty of her murder and 14 others, receiving multiple life sentences for his crimes.

CHANDRA LEVY

2001

> Case Details

On May 1, 2001, Chandra Levy, who was working in Washington, DC, as a congressional intern, went to Rock Creek Park. It is not known whether she simply went there for a walk or a run, or to meet with a particular person. She was never seen alive thereafter. The case soon became a focus for national media attention, and it was revealed that she had most likely been having an affair with Gary Condit, a Democrat member of the U.S. House of Representatives.

In spite of several lengthy searches of the park using cadaver dogs, the police did not find Chandra's remains. On May 22, 2002, nearly a year and a month after Chandra had last visited the park, a man followed his dog off the general path when his pet began digging in leaves for a turtle. There the man discovered a skull on a steep slope less than a mile from the Pierce-Klingle Mansion. Police and forensic investigators were called in and more skeletal remains were found.

> Postmortem Evidence

Based on dental records, the remains were positively identified later that day as those of Chandra Levy. However, there was very little evidence to help reveal how she had died.

External soft tissues and internal organs were completely absent, having decayed altogether. From the skeleton several bones were missing: the ulna, which is part of the forearm opposite the thumb; the left pelvis, which is quite large; a number of vertebrae; some foot bones, including one right phalanx; and some anklebones. With so little bodily matter to go on, even expert forensic pathologists and other forensic scientists were not able to reconstruct the circumstances of the death.

> The Verdict

The postmortem examination of the skeletal remains did not yield enough information to determine the cause or mechanism of death, or the time of death. However, in light of the suspicious circumstances surrounding the case, the District of Columbia medical examiner later declared the death to be a homicide.

Glossary

Atomic absorption analysis kit (AAA): This is used to detect traces of gunpowder residue.

Algor mortis: The cooling of the body after death.

Antemortem: Pre-death

Arachnoid layer: The middle layer of membranes covering the brain.

Arrhythmia: A departure from the normal cardiac rhythm of the heart beat.

Assault rifle: A type of rifle that is able to fire 20 or more rounds of ammunition.

BAC: Blood Alcohol Concentration — the amount of alcohol in the bloodstream.

Blow flies: A common type of fly that is especially attracted to dead bodies.

Cadaver dog: A dog specially trained to locate dead and decomposing remains.

Cause of death: The disease or injury that results in the cessation of life.

Cirrhosis: A general term used to describe diseases to the liver of various etiology (causes) such as alcohol abuse, drugs and hepatitis.

Clinical pathologist: A physician trained to analyze cells, body fluids and tissues by laboratory testing.

Close contact wound: A wound that occurs when the end of the barrel of a weapon is fired in very close proximity to the skin.

Coroner: Typically a lay person who is elected to run the coroner's office. The coroner's office is derived from the medieval English system.

Contact wound: A wound that occurs when the end of the barrel of a weapon is in contact with the skin of the victim.

Contusion: The collection of blood underneath the skin resulting from trauma; otherwise known as a bruise.

COPD: Chronic Obstructive Pulmonary Disease

CPR: Cardiopulmonary Resuscitation

Death certificate: An official document that lists the cause and manner of death of an individual. It is a legal requirement before release for burial.

Distant contact wound: A wound that occurs when the barrel of a weapon is more than 24 inches (61 cm) from the skin of a victim.

DNA: Deoxyribonucleic Acid

DOA: "Dead on arrival" — a term used by paramedics and hospital staff.

Dura mater: The layer of membrane protecting the brain that lies directly underneath the skull.

ECG: Electrocardiogram — a test that measures the electrical activity of the heart.

ETT: Endotracheal tube

Emphysema: Condition of the lungs characterized by enlargement of the alveoli.

EMT: Emergency Medical Technician

Exhumation: The digging up of a casket for the purpose of examination or re-examination of a body.

Fatty liver: A liver with an abnormal accumulation of fat within the liver cells.

Forensic anthropologist: Applies the theory and methods of anthropology to identify human remains.

Forensic entomologist: Specializes in the study of the life cycle and habits of insects and beetles, and how these relate to human cadavers.

Forensic epidemiologist: Applies statistical and demographic analyses to forensic issues such as homicide, suicide, accidents and the factors associated with those deaths.

Forensic pathologist: A physician specializing in the determination of the cause and manner of death.

Forensic odontologist: A dentist who applies the science of dentistry to the postmortem determinations of identity.

Forensic serologist: Analyzes body fluids such as blood, saliva, semen and urine to discover genetic traits.

Forensic toxicologist: Analyzes body fluids such as blood, bile, urine, eye fluid and stomach for drugs and other compounds.

Formaldehyde: A solution used to preserve internal organs.

Handgun: A small hand-held firearm; either a single-shot pistol, derringer, revolver or automatic.

Hemorrhage: A significant amount of blood that accumulates within a tissue caused by a ruptured or lacerated blood vessel.

Gas chromatography: Highly sophisticated technique used to identify precisely the chemical makeup of substances.

Grooves: The shallow furrows on the outside of a bullet, produced as it passes through the barrel of a gun. These marks are used to match the bullet to the gun from which it was fired.

In situ: As the organ appears within the body.

Jane Doe: A general name given to the remains of an unknown female individual.

John Doe: A general name given to the remains of an unknown male individual.

Lands: The raised marks on a bullet produced as it passes through the barrel of a gun.

Lethal level: The concentration of a drug or other compound in the bloodstream that can cause death.

Livor mortis: The collection or pooling of blood caused by gravity resulting in purple discoloration to the skin.

Locard's exhange: The principle that any interaction between two individuals or objects results in an exchange of physical material.

Medical examiner: A physician (forensic pathologist) selected to oversee the operation of a medical examiner's office and investigate sudden and unexpected deaths.

Myocardium: The heart muscle

Petechial: Pin-head areas of hemorrhage in the skin.

Pia mater: The closest layer of matter covering the brain.

Postmortem: After death

Rifle: A firearm with a bored barrel, designed to be fired from the shoulder.

Rigor mortis: The stiffing of the muscles of the body after death due to chemical changes.

SANE: Sexual Assault Nurse Examiner — a nurse specially trained to conduct a forensic examination for evidence of a possible sexual assault.

Shotgun: A firearm with a smooth barrel, designed to be fired from the shoulder.

Subarachnoid space: The space between the arachnoid and pia mater layers protecting the brain.

SIDS: Sudden Infant Death Syndrome

Therapeutic level: The concentration of a drug in the bloodstream that falls within the recommended level for treatment.

Toxic level: The concentration of a drug in the bloodstream that is seriously harmful to humans.

Umbilicus: The navel

Index

Page numbers in *italic* type refer to illustrations.

Acknowledgements

I wish to sincerely thank the entire staff of the Allegheny County Medical Examiner's Office for the assistance, support and knowledge they contributed to this book.

I am especially grateful to Joseph T. Dominick, who gave his special expertise and invaluable assistance to the writing of this book. Thanks is also due to Deputy Coroner Joe Angotti for his contribution to the piece on cadaver dogs.

I would also like to personally thank Peggy A. Brown for her unending support, input and encouragement.

Further Reading

Dominick J. DiMaio, Vincent J.M. DiMaio, *Forensic Pathology*, Elsevier: New York, 1989.

Vincent J.M. DiMaio, *Gunshot Wounds*, CRC Press: Boca Raton, 1993.

M. Lee Goff, *A Fly for the Prosecution: How Insect Evidence Helps Solve Crimes*, Harvard University Press: Cambridge, 2000.

Randy Hanzlick, *The Medical Cause of Death Manual*, College of American Pathologists, 1994.

Bernard Knight, *Forensic Pathology*, Edward Arnold: London, 1991.

Werner U. Spitz, *Medicolegal Investigation of Death* (3rd Ed.), Charles C. Thomas: Springfield, 1993.

Picture Credits

Allegheny County Coroner's Office: 9, 10, 60, 63, 67, 70, 73 (both images), 85, 89, 95, 98, 105, 110, 111, 116, 124, 133, 135, 144, 161; Richard Burgess: 18, 30, 32, 44, 51, 53, 64, 66, 75, 78, 83, 86, 93, 113, 119, 134; Corbis: 15, 164, 168; Gary Bell/oceanwideimages.com: 91; Getty Images: 33, 34, 47, 54, 123, 136; National Human Genome Research Institute: 141; Rex Features: 131, 167; Science Photo Library: 5, 12, 22, 24, 25, 27, 29, 36, 38, 40, 42, 48, 74, 76 (both images), 80, 82, 94, 100, 106, 109, 115, 118, 127, 128, 132, 138, 143, 147, 150, 153; University of Alabama at Birmingham Department of Pathology PEIR Digital Library: 84, 88, 92; U.S. Department of Commerce Photographic Services: 58.